THE plume poetry INTERVIEWS

edited by Daniel Lawless
& Nancy Mitchell

MADHAT PRESS
ASHEVILLE, NORTH CAROLINA

MadHat Press
MadHat Incorporated
PO Box 8364, Asheville, NC 28814

All poems
Copyright © 2016 the individual contributors

Interviews
Copyright © 2016 *Plume*

All rights reserved

The Library of Congress has assigned
this edition a Control Number of
2016919852

ISBN 978-1-941196-39-7 (paperback)

Book layout and design by F. J. Bergmann
Cover design by Marc Vincenz and F. J. Bergmann

PlumePoetry.com
MadHat-Press.com

*You all have one death scene.
You're squandering them.*
—Max Ritvo

Introduction

For better or worse, like most things associated with *Plume*, the book you hold in your hands—*The Plume Poetry Interviews, Volume 1*—finds its origins in the murky, very early days of our little enterprise; a passing sidebar in one of a number of Starbucks-fueled *voir dires* preceding the actual opening argument, as it were, of the online journal. I think the idea was mine, though if it wasn't, it was Jason Cook's—the two of us comprised for all intents and purposes the entire staff then. As I only vaguely recall, the plan was eventually to include in *Plume* some sort of precinct or homepage zone dedicated to providing a fuller account, say 8–10 poems, of a particular poet's work, apart from our fundamental layout—cover art, Editor's Note and twelve poems. Unfortunately but typically, work-aversive as I am, the project remained in my mind nothing more than an occasionally nettlesome shade for almost two years (in the company of Book Reviews and Essays & Comment, I might add, which languished disincarnate even longer). Indeed, that it ever leapt into life is owed entirely to chance. Two poets had sent us a long collaborative work, which they felt needed some preceding commentary, some introduction, in order to catch its particular flavor. Sure, we said, do you have something in mind? They did—an email conversation between them that we could copy and paste before the piece, in which they discussed its successive transformations, form and poetic alleyways. Just the thing, we replied. All that remained was a bit of tinkering with the layout, a couple of .jpg photographs and biographical notes.

As I scroll through our Archives this morning, I find that that initial Featured Selection, as we had cleverly christened it, made its debut in Issue 21, April 2013. Our subject as noted: the first installment of what would become three, and thence a chapbook from Plume Editions, by Tess Gallagher and Lawrence Matsuda: the collaborative poem entitled *Pow! Pow! Shalazam!* Reader response to *Pow! Pow!*, I remember, had been immediate and positive—and it remains a work about which I still receive queries and emails. Don't get me wrong, I

the *plume* poetry interviews 1

loved the poem (as I do today), but I was somewhat surprised by our audience's enthusiastic reception, as they weren't usually a loquacious lot. A one-off? No, apparently. The following month, we solicited and ran a selection of poems from Alain Borer, translated by Mark Irwin. Again, a great success, as my inbox attested.

Now, I may be an editor in only the loosest definition of that position, and not a very good one, but I'm not *tragically* (as my sophisticated sister liked to say) absent common sense. Even I soon figured out that we were on to something. As each monthly issue rolled out, that realization would only be further clarified. Readers "adored," were "intrigued by," "greatly appreciated" our delinquent brainchild. Nor of course was it only the opportunity to read in depth a poet's new work (it was and is always new, unpublished work) that attracted them. Rather, it was the *combination* of the poems and those introductory set-pieces that caught their fancy and their attention. And why not? Who wouldn't want to know more intimately the passions and antipathies of the authors of the poems they were about to read, learn their writers' creative process, eavesdrop on of their interior monologues regarding inspiration and revision, craft and mystery? Especially when the parties at hand are the likes of Rachel Zucker, Krystoff Kuczkewski, Juan Gelman—and so many other masters of our trade who followed on after the tandem entries of Tess and Lawrence and Borer-Irwin

We are now on our forty-somethingth Featured Selection, and the latest remains as popular as the first. It seems unthinkable now: *Plume* without its spotlighting of a good handful of new poems by the best poets writing today, framed and contextualized by their authors' own words.

So, I won't keep you—I know the pleasures that lie ahead.

Still, I would be remiss if I did not offer just a few more words about the evolution of these vestibular delights. At first, they were a jumble—fascinating, revelatory, funny, conversational or "academic"— yes, always. But, a jumble. Here, a group of poems prefaced by the author's own autobiographical/critical notes, there a self-interview,

the *plume* poetry interviews 1

elsewhere other email exchanges between collaborating poets (Denise Duhamel and Maureen Seaton come to mind). And more and more frequently, interviews conducted by those familiar to the poets, or often their translators—Lisa Rose Bradford on the above-mentioned Juan Gelman, Glenn Mott on Hank Lazer, Hoyt Rogers and Paul Auster doing the honors for the work of André du Bouchet. Even I got in on the proceedings—cringe-worthy questions to D. Nurkse, Bruce Smith. Fine—more than fine. But it wasn't until Associate Editor for Special Projects Nancy Mitchell came aboard that *Plume*'s Featured Selections took on any semblance of their present form. For it was she, drawing on the deep waters of her own poetic sensibilities and a lifetime of intense reading, who truly deserves the lion's share of credit here (not forgetting Ani Gjika's incisive interview with Luljeta Lleshanaku). Astute, wildly associative, equally adept at the impromptu and the carefully framed question, knowing just when to tread a familiar (but never *too* familiar) avenue of inquiry and when to veer into adjacent neighborhoods, Nancy has the knack: for putting poets at their ease, assessing each persona and personality and subtly adapting her interrogations and remarks to his or her interests, cajoling, at times wrestling, at times teasing from her subject such nuggets as this, from Jean Valentine:

"You know [Elizabeth] Bishop has a new book" and I said to myself 'Who is Bishop?' But I went right out to the bookstore and bought it. There my life changed.'"

or from this exchange with Max Ritvo:

NM: Maybe we should/could call it "suspicion" of intention, instead?

MR: I like to liken something to another thing without quite knowing why I feel that way. Or even if I do feel that way. "My love for you is like a fountain," I might write. At this point, I intend to write about my love. But the fountain lands there from a murkier part of me. The fountain-like thing in the poem, this part that finds itself in my poem beyond any particular intention, is often what you, Nancy, might call a doodad. Something that as yesterday or today progressed, seemed to glow out from the rest of time's passage.

But, enough.

    Reader, we are pleased to present to you *The Plume Poetry Interviews, Volume 1*—a collection of the best of our digital presentations, interviews with and poems by the most interesting and accomplished poets we could round up.

    Of course you will decide for yourself the worth of what you find here, page by page. Honestly, though, I don't think you'll be disappointed.

Daniel Lawless
November 10, 2016

Contents

Introduction   v
Daniel Lawless

D. Nurske   1
interviewed by Danny Lawless

Hank Lazer   15
interviewed by Glenn Mott

Amit Majmudar   29
interviewed by Nancy Mitchell

Jim Daniels   45
interviewed by Nancy Mitchell

Luljeta Lleshanaku & translator Ani Gjika   65
interviewed by Nancy Mitchell

Nin Andrews   97
interviewed by Nancy Mitchell

David Clewell   117
interviewed by Nancy Mitchell

Adam Tavel   137
interviewed by Nancy Mitchell

Marc Vincenz   151
interviewed by Nancy Mitchell

Christopher Buckley   179
interviewed by Nancy Mitchell

Emanuel Moses   195
translated by Marilyn Hacker
interviewed by Nancy Mitchell

Cynthia Cruz   209
interviewed by Nancy Mitchell

Tess Gallagher & Lawrence Matsuda *interviewed by Nancy Mitchell*	223
Thomas McCarthy *interviewed by Hélène Cardona*	241
Ira Sadoff *interviewed by Nancy Mitchell*	257
Jean Valentine *interviewed by Nancy Mitchell*	283
Max Ritvo *interviewed by Nancy Mitchell*	301
Contributor Biographies	317

D. Nurkse
interviewed by Danny Lawless

DL: The closing line of the poem "Early Anthropocene"—published by the *Virginia Quarterly Review* in 2007—asks the question: *Is there shelter in the blank page?* Similarly, one could ask if humankind takes shelter in the start of its own "blank page," in the continuous restart which is always the awareness of there being a new day, a next day, and a tomorrow. In this poem, "Early Anthropocene," Anti-Earth (or any of the other "Anti" references) can be viewed as that which is taking place elsewhere during our moments of observation or lack thereof; the closing stanza, highlighting mankind's misalignment of mindfulness, as though we are never in line with a much-needed key observation, that ah-hah! moment needed to positively transcend this current epoch. Would you care to expand on this view of the poem and on that which seems to be a gesturing towards an "Anti-Observation"?

DN: "Is there shelter in the blank page?" meant: "here I, the speaker, end, and the margin begins. You agreed with me, but now will you adapt to silence?" I had trouble with the question, though. In context, it's a little preachy. It smuggles in a desired answer. It's not sufficiently defenseless.

"Anti-Earth" I took from Pythagoras. He uses the concept to round out a gematria series. In this poem, it might mean the universe of signs. The world of the equation, in which identity mirrors itself. As opposed to the world of sparrows, cranky dogs, and almost-rain. Hannah Arendt gets chills when she quotes Archimedes saying "give me a lever long enough and I could move the earth." She bridles at situating truth outside mortality.

I grew up in the Cold War. Yes, there were squirrels and acorns, but the possibility of annihilating them had already been factored in, discounted. I gave assent to that. It was so radical an idea, it seemed fussy to object. That could be an early "anti-observation." I like your term. "Anti-Earth" could be the world of the simulation. Where there's the possibility of downloading your brain onto a self-regulating machine.

DL: The title "Early Anthropocene" is interesting. Fragmenting this specific geological epoch to a point where one references it as "early" is effectively troublesome, because the word "early", and the repetitive use of "Even then" in the stanzas that follow, in turn, ask how far we are into this Anthropocene. This, with the opening stanza, really hones in on the passing of time and all that one can miss in a moment and or a culmination of moments. Lapses of time and the knowing that something was missed during those moments play a key role in many of your poems, but especially "Early Anthropocene." How important is time, both literally and figuratively, to you, and to what extent does its power have in shaping your poems? The last three lines of part 2 come to mind:

> The whole idea of space
> and time
> was between us and it.

DN: The poem is very much about time. I hope the reader has a sense of the time of the forecast and computer model playing against the time of the body.

DL: If the lack of mass protest is one example of an Anti-Wave, what are some of the others, in your opinion? The current re-embrace of post-apocalyptic stories, both in the literary world and film industry, is one example that comes to mind as almost an unapologetic, "we will end up here regardless" wave; a wave that prophetically and paradoxically promotes an outcome rather than suggesting movement to stop the endless scenarios of apocalypse.

DN: The Anti-Wave could stand for all the things we know but don't act on. All the information which feeds on itself and never breaks through to daylight. It also refers to my abstraction of the realities of nature. I was at the XL pipeline demonstration in DC in February. The Caucasian speakers seemed to think of nature as a past to be preserved. The First Nation representatives spoke of Manitou: provoke this force and you will vanish.

In early versions of this poem, I had "the shift"; I was thinking of the tipping point.

I worry about disaster porn. It's a problem with this poem. Am I just coaxing a mesmerizing spectacle to the page? In league with thanatos? In my defense: I only work here.

DL: One of the recurrent subjects in your writing is physical challenge/the failure of the body. Is it fair to say that here, an observance can be made regarding the failure of the spirit and its capabilities to make waves of positive change or benefit?

DN: Yes.

DL: At times it appears that the couple in the poem is attempting to rekindle love or at least work on maintaining a love that is present between them. In what way does this parallel our relationship with the world we live in?

DN: That's a deep question. I wanted this to be a love poem. I have no idea why....

DL: A bit from the start of the poem: anti-elegiac, archeological, "erasure" in poetry—do any of these apply?

>   one showed a man on his knees
> presenting a ring to a woman
> whose face had peeled back to plywood.

DN: In the world of the sign, I have no privacy, not even from myself. I open my email for news of myself. The couple in the poem is seeing their intimacy mirrored back to them at random angles.

DL: These lines:

>   the anti-wave was a Hokusai print
> with an ersatz Mount Fuji;

the *plume* poetry interviews 1

I have this print above me as I write: is there a doubling of the distance, the inferior—"print" and "ersatz?" As perhaps a B & B is an ersatz home? As you know, an odd perspective of Mt. Fuji in this print: diminished, observant. And so the distance tripled? Distance from what—or all? See, too:

> but when we came closer
> we saw they were an exact copy,
> not the person.

DN: This poem is all about the simulacra. In *La Vita Nuova*, Dante sees a vision which warns him against the simulacra. Everything here, from the poem itself to anti-earth, is a simulacrum.

DL: How did you write this poem? This interests me: did it unfurl in one long swoop and then revision? Piece by piece? Each new piece a revelation? Was there much revision aside from the particular—was the narrative in your mind as you wrote or reveal itself as you wrote? How long, would you say, you worked on this? (I am starting to sound like Padget Powell in *The Interrogative Mood*—sorry.)

DN: It takes me forever to write a poem. Usually there's a mass of junk and then a flick of revision makes it come alive. Or at least twitch. In earlier versions of the final stanza, I had all kinds of lame orbs—Wormwood, man-made stars, Atherel, Koab. Some of that I could use elsewhere.

DL: When an especially pleasing image comes or series of images—for example—

> here and there plywood was pried from a window
> so you could see clear to the next highway.
> The landscape flattened as if ruled
> by a spirit level, the last dusty gingkos vanished–
> surely some were art projects made of recycled tin–
> we passed a padlocked aquarium.
> In a doorway an old woman knitting
> glanced up as we slowed to wave,

but bit her lip and bent to her work
as if a secret were being revealed there.
Mile after mile of empty compound,
padlocked resorts, mini golfs in the moonlight,
giant concrete Squids and Porpoises,
drained swimming pools with high twisting slides.

does this impel you to continue writing—or knock off for the day?

DN: I'll have more coffee.

DL: How much does enjambment interest you? It doesn't seem a great presence here, or at least not a heavy-handed one.

DN: I love enjambment. If it's not here, it's because this poem is a little disembodied, oneiric. Enjambment gives you a physical entrée. Thud of the pulse.

DL: "where the sea once was," the Aral Sea in your mind? Something of an anti-Balboa feel. Does this make sense?

DN: Yes, the Aral Sea, but also the ocean receding to the horizon in the seconds before a tsunami. Millions of people died in the last great tidal waves but we have no Shoreline Security. I was thinking of the thrill of the times when nature offers no resistance, and the danger is in the sense of omnipotence.

DL: A masterful stroke, the "rising in the west" and the use of the present rather than the future tense: "the planet on which we live forever." Shivers. How did that come to you? Do you recall where and when?

DN: It's a bad joke—"we could find technical means to prolong individual life artificially forever, but the external world, the planet, could be hurt beyond recovery." Grinding my teeth on that led me to the current ending.

DL: The grind of sending out work—how do you manage?

DN: It's a blue-collar thing. You make a chair, someone likes it, someone doesn't. It's healthy. Your poems can't climb into your brain and boss you around if an intern is making them into kitty litter.

the *plume* poetry interviews 1

DL: Does print have a hold on you still, or have you come to terms with digital?

DN: Print. Digital is the simulacrum. Except for *Plume*.

DL: Early influences?

DN: My mom was part French and I loved Michaux, Supervielle, Apollinaire. Lorca. The Duino Elegies. Blues lyrics. Sparse poets like Reznikoff and Blaise Cendrars. I love them all more even now.

DL: And, of course, who are you reading now, what pleases you—and what doesn't?

DN: I had the honor of working with dg nanouk okpik. She has beautiful recent poems. Novels of Agata Kristof and Patrick Modiano. I'm re-reading Louis MacNiece and Marilyn Hacker; they are masters.

Early Anthropocene

1
We drove down a road cut
in the center of a disused highway.

Southward through that ferrous moraine
billboards flew backwards,
mossed-over, streaked with mold—
one showed a man on his knees
presenting a ring to a woman
whose face had peeled back to plywood.

No traffic. Long winding tunnels.
Pine torches: the moth people,
camping since the war.

We touched each other lightly.
What if we hit a child?
Would we dare stop?
For we were speeding,
sometimes glancing in joy at the needle
trembling before the highest zero.

We slept in a motel
with the motif of the anti-wave
embossed in the ashtray and drapes.

We rested at a Bauhaus campus
where the anti-tsunami was rendered
as a small mechanical fountain
at the center of a concrete plaza.
There were no students.

Next night we spent in a B & B
—the anti-wave was a Hokusai print
with an ersatz Mount Fuji;
a rhinestone child was fishing
in a black velvet sequined ocean.

We kissed politely, perfunctorily,
as if the unwavering white line
were ruled in our bodies also,
and then lay listening for rain.

We thought, it's human like us.
That helped us sleep without dreams.

2
Remember the old days, when we protested?
Those meetings were packed:
unions, churches, synagogues, mosques,
with their great banners warning:
if Coriolis turns, it will be too late.

The speaker said:
*if you each convince two friends,
and they each convince two friends …*

But it was just us, hand in hand:
sometimes in those surging crowds
we thought to see a high school friend,
an old dentist, a track coach,
but when we came closer
we saw they were an exact copy,

not the person. Or a strange shame
kept us from acknowledging them.

Even then, museums were devoted to the anti-wave.
The walls whitewashed, dazzling,
the floors colonial oak, obsessively varnished.
No velvet ropes: just a dozen tasteful dioramas,
the consequence glittering in electronic spume.

Even then, the lowlands were emptying.

In storefront churches
the anti-tide was worshiped as judgment.
It was chiseled on tombstones.
Once we found a penny
with the anti-tsunami instead of Lincoln,
the reverse already worn smooth.

Even then, if people mentioned it,
they said, unimaginably swift,
but less so than you expected–
but what could they know?
The whole idea of space and time
was between us and it.

3
In the plains we found a drive-in
and parked and ordered popcorn.
On the screen the violence of waiting
revealed itself with an eloquence
we could never have imagined.

We made love as I always wanted to
in those few feet of hard breath
behind the gem-like dials.

There were no other customers.
The clerk who took our sheaf of piastres
had been too listless to count them.

4
At Gilead the billboards changed:
sometimes an old couple,
she pushing him in a wheelchair,
sometimes just great blurred figures
you knew by instinct were naked.

The lights of the city
hardened in the night sky.

5
So we passed the outskirts,
the zone of mock-Tudor libraries
consecrated to Anthropocene,
the history of its thousand thresholds,
how its parameters correlate
in the mind, numbers, language,
the recurring dreams of childhood,
the trembling of foliage:
 its causes, the attempts to stop it,
the counter-theories, the solutions:
freighters full of iron filings:
green algae: the brick in the toilet:

the calibrated showerhead:
methane traps, fermented corn husks.

Wreathed in ribbon wire,
the Institutes that measure height and speed,
pressure, velocity, potential whirlpools.

Buttressed rectangular buildings
with an occasional high window still lit
where the simulations are stored,
the print-outs, the papier-maché models.

Once we actually saw a worker
in a high office, scribbling calculations
under a gooseneck lamp
and we thought, 'even here,' 'as in childhood.'

We passed the riverfront warehouses
where the speeches, petitions, protest letters
are saved—for nothing has ever been destroyed.

Zinc-windowed façades scrawled with letters,
fragments of huge names, impossibly stylized—
we recognized 'Thor,' 'Shiva,'
here and there plywood was pried from a window
so you could see clear to the next highway.

6
The landscape flattened as if ruled
by a spirit level, the last dusty gingkos vanished—

surely some were art projects made of recycled tin—
we passed a padlocked aquarium.

In a doorway an old woman knitting
glanced up as we slowed to wave,
but bit her lip and bent to her work
as if a secret were being revealed there.

Mile after mile of empty compound,
padlocked resorts, mini golfs in the moonlight,
giant concrete Squids and Porpoises,
drained swimming pools with high twisting slides.

We arrived at the place where the sea once was,
basalt littoral strewn with volutes,
latticed arabesque grooves where shells
had crumbled and blown away, wisps of nori,
blocky hermit exoskeletons, whorled conches.

The car jolted a little, the task
soon over—we drove toward sunrise,
sometimes touching each other on the cheek
or the thigh, our wheels swerving
imperceptibly of their own accord, hydroplaning.
A curtain of spray rose around us.

At first light we braked and clambered out,
a little dizzy under the towering horizon.
Damp sand bunched between our toes.
Braided rubbery kelp chambers
popped under the balls of our feet.

The car dwindled behind us.
The haze of towers dimmed.
A new cold rose to our ankles.
We kissed, thanked each other,
and stumbled on, righting each other
with a hand to the elbow,
salt at our thighs—ahead of us

a buoy tolling at the horizon,
and rising in the west, Anti-Earth,
the planet on which we live forever.

the darkest part of year so dark so soon the light arrives by faith power borrows its arriving into light who speaks a sudden song? maybe the singing great as gods near god are hampered by what they will say

for theodore enslin   d. 11/22/11

Hank Lazer
interviewed by Glenn Mott

GM: For most writers handwriting is a matter of composition, a choice not to use a keyboard. Seeing a writer's script, one who you've read only in type can be a revelation, a new discovery of their work, as in published diaries or journals, or a surprise at the power of print versus the intimacy of the hand. I felt this when I first saw Emily Dickinson's poems in pencil on envelope backs and scraps of paper. What is it about handwriting a poem, and publishing it without setting it to type that feels special, and what does that do to the reading experience?

I'm at a digital journalism conference as I ask this, so I can't help but wonder how this all fits in with technology. I've seen depressing demonstrations of algorithms that write the sporting news, and print referred to as legacy media. But we have yet to master an instrument robotically sensitive or as neurally complicated as the human hand.

HL: Please know that whatever answer I provide, it's taken me several years to develop this sense: Among other things, the handwritten turns out to be a way to defamiliarize, slow down, and make more intimate that reading experience of the page, pages, or book. For some (many?) of these handwritten pages, it is not at all clear where to begin the reading. Indeed, there are multiple options. Even when the beginning seems clear, usually the reader will need to rotate the page/screen several times to follow the contour of the poem. (I've had reports from poet-friends who were reading *N18 (complete)* in a public space and had people stare at this odd action of rotating the page in order to read.) And, as you suggest, the work of the hand, the specificity of *a particular hand* (and person) doing the writing is totally different than the effects of type.

12/16/11

(surrounding curved text, clockwise from top-left): i listen to what the angel sings   yes   the angel sings   i am not the angel singing   i write but what i write about this is singing   "I have given you to write"   angel sing   i am not the angel singing

Fine, I said. Firmament.
"I call bullshit on firmament. There's no such thing as firmament."
There is, though, I said, It's in Torah.
"What's it mean, then?"
I said, No one really knows what it means. In Hebrew, it's the place where Adonai resides, but it's a bad translation. It's really more like border — it's confusing.
"I don't think that's fair," she said. "If you don't know what it means, you can't use it."
That's your rule, I said. I said, That's not my rule.
⟨The Instructions, 104⟩

Oddly, and rather surprisingly to me, with the notebook pages I very quickly become the reader of the pages and experience my writing activity (now in the past) as that of a portal or doorway through which the poems occur. As the substantial amount of quotation indicates, these pages are not all "my" voice. They are a site for what I've called vectored thinking—different contending thoughts, phrases, perspectives that, as in a mobile, have a weight and force suspended on the page.

By virtue of the *shape* of the writing—what I've been calling shape-writing—there is a pronounced visual element that, at times, seems to supplant the location of the traditionally "poetic" (i.e. the elegance or craft of the words and phrasing). It may be that the shape-writing actually occludes or occults the "poetry." Perhaps a reasonable question would be, "and why would you, why would anyone, want to do that *now*," particularly at a time when poetry itself is (allegedly) so marginalized and barely has a commodity-pulse.

GM: There's a stray association I make when you when you say shape-writing. I immediately think of sacred heart singers and shape-note hymns. Something homemade and accessible. This folk art also has its origins in the American South, where you live and work, and there are times when I really think a lot of these tendencies originated not in "poetry" (as you prefer to quote it) but reflects your development as a poet, seeing things like hand painted sign boards and the outsider constructions of hell-fire road-siders, self-proclaimed prophets of the Christian apocalypse knocking stuff together in their front yards along the kudzu byways.

Your intellectual arc is within a tradition of modern Western discovery, one that retraces a path to the primitive in search of the sacred—and reminds me of what John Cage does with early American anthems and congregational music in "Thirteen Harmonies."

I see today that the composer John Taverner has died. He spoke of having a crisis of composition in the insight that the liturgical music he was composing had lost touch with the tradition of sacred tonal music, realizing the sacred had been pushed out gradually by the domination of the ego. So he turned to music of Persia, India, and Native Americans.

HL: Well, you know me too well, and you know the South well. You're exactly right about the homemade or outsider or folk nature of the handwritten and its links to Southern vernacular art forms. You had typed "sacred heart singing," which, at first, I corrected to "sacred harp singing," but, as usual, we can often learn more from a so-called error.

GM: Ah, it's true … there's still some Catholicism of the Sacred Heart catechism knocking around in me as a boy.…

HL: Of course such singing and vernacular art forms generally are close to the heart, and, in my opinion, sacred as well. I actually once did take part in a sacred harp meeting. (I'm a god-awful singer…) My instructor was one of the janitors from the aquatic center, and he was rumored to be a neo-Nazi. We got along well, and he taught me a good bit about shape-note-singing. From the very beginning of my life in Alabama (1977), I have been drawn to the world of folk art/outsider art, much of which is Christian visionary in nature. And from the very beginning of my days here in Alabama, I have had a strong sense of a close linkage between innovative poetry (which is usually branded as elitist or esoteric or out of touch with "the people") and self-taught outsider art. So, yes, and proudly, my handwritten notebooks are participatory in a Southern cultural domain.

GM: I'll just disagree that what you're doing occludes or occults the poetry, except that you are avoiding the "P" term as meaning something left-justified on a typeset page that doesn't obstruct the dinkiness of clever word play. But yes, to embrace innovative practices to *defamiliarize*, as you say.

11/6/11

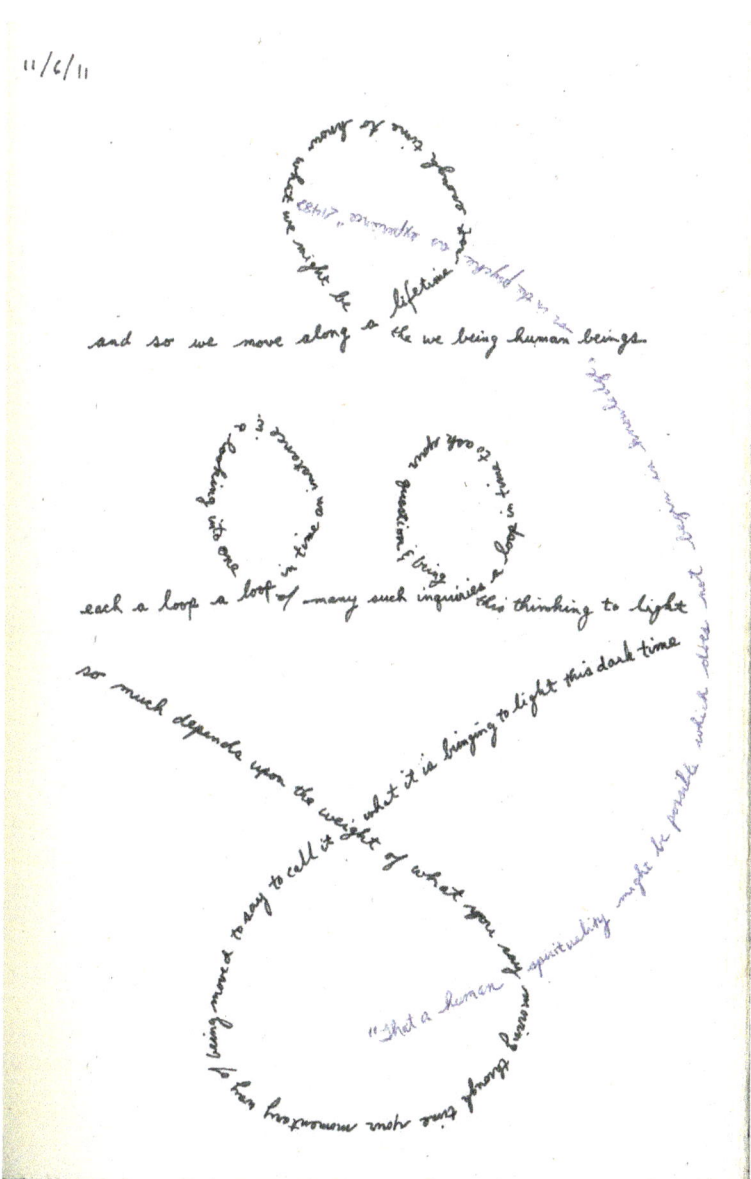

What shape-writing does most effectively is manage the element of time in composition. We see your choices, sometimes turn-for-turn on the page, "the light arrives by faith / in turning round," this is both faith in a sunrise and the physical reversal of the direction of the line. The turn, or arc of a word, affects your outcome and I see pauses, pivots, and hesitation before your willingness to go on, like Beckett, streaming, then shaping. There used to be a coffee shop in Beijing when I lived there called Sculpting In Time. I think I'll throw that in here as an apt description of this process. Shape-writing, like concrete poetry, is also a formal practice, replacing representational images with slithering interconnected lines. These lines give you new forms for composition, while slowing down the reading to a liminal state of being in-between. Transitions, choices, unintentional missteps are being made by the reader, and they affect the outcome. It's playful, but can be a slog without the right mindfulness (that word of the moment). I suppose it's the reason some editors have a hard time accepting these for publication. It's not a matter of being unable to print handwritten poems. They will want a transcription of the "correct" reading, to narrow the attention span. Is that a fair appraisal of what you've told me? And what's been the reception?

HL: I love your remarks on the element of time in the composition of the notebook pages/poems. After all, the initial big name for this project was *The Notebooks (of Being & Time)*, linked to my reading of Heidegger's *Being and Time*. "Sculpting in time" is a perfect name for this activity. The notebook pages deliberately make manifest the time of composition, and the imperfection and performance of that momentary engagement with language.

The reception has been pretty good. A number of magazines—in print and online—have featured work from the notebooks. There have also been a number of very thoughtful reviews, particularly by Nathan Hauke (*Drunken Boat*) and Jake Marmer (*Jewish Daily Forward*), which named *N18* one of his five "favorite poetry books of 2012."

On the occluding or occulting of the poetry in the shape-written pages, I don't mean to suggest that the writing is not poetic. It is, and I've not really retreated from the lyricism that I love. All I mean to say is that the foregrounding of shape itself perhaps constitutes an initial (momentary) shading or re-direction of attention from the more customary engagement with the sound of words.

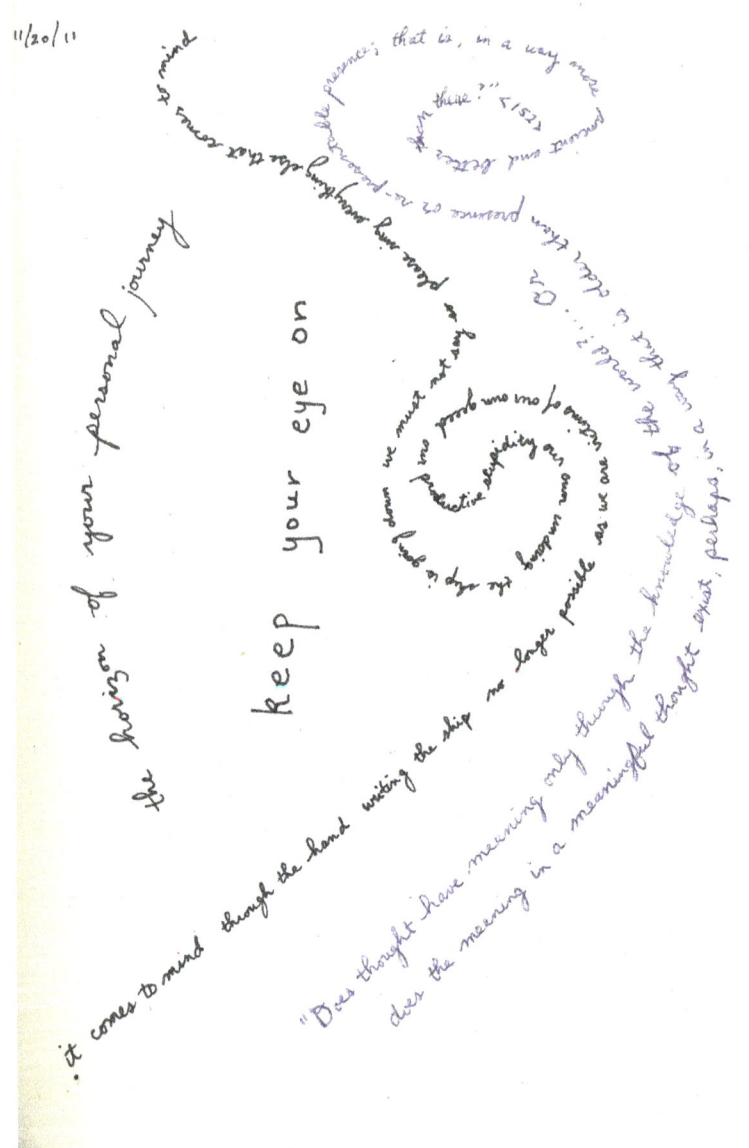

11/20/11

it comes to mind the giving of your personal journey

keep your eye on

please bring everything else that comes to mind

just down we must not say anything produce stupidity and

"Does thought have meaning only through the knowledge of the word, or does the meaning in a meaningful thought exist, perhaps, in a ponderable presence; that is, in a way more present and better... when presence is a ponderable presence than those..." <152>

GM: Want to know something strange? I just looked at Susan Bee's painting for the cover of this suite for the first time, and there's that harp.

Tell me about the collaborative readings involved here.

HL: Collaborative readings is one way to put it. One might alternatively say collage or vectored thinking or ventriloquism or other voices (as in the end of George Oppen's superb late poem "Till Other Voices Wake Us" where he rewrites the ending of Eliot's "Prufrock," changing it from: "Till human voices wake us, and we drown" to "till other voices wake/ us or we drown"). The readings I do in philosophy while writing the notebooks occupy an adjacent space. I'm not trying to analyze or interpret or even clarify these writings. In one sense, I'm hunting for interesting sentences—which might influence, or push back upon my writing, or serve as a stimulus. Of course, I've been picking books and writers who have been thinking deeply about the fundamental terms that are of importance to the notebooks: spirit, being, time, perception, consciousness, language. One might think of each notebook page as a kind of Calder-like mobile, where the various phrases, quotations, and new writing all have a force or weight that creates a somewhat stable (though moveable) existence for the duration of that one page. The absolute otherness of the quoted material—in the *Plume* series of pages, from Emanuel Levinas' *Of God Who Comes to Mind*—makes me more immediately a portal or doorway or medium (or scribe) for the pages, and I also more immediately become their reader (rather than their writer). It also helps me to understand the passages better by the careful act of writing them longhand and by finding out their shape in the time of writing.

11/27/11

"...produced in a thought understood as a thought of... The very breath of spirit in thought

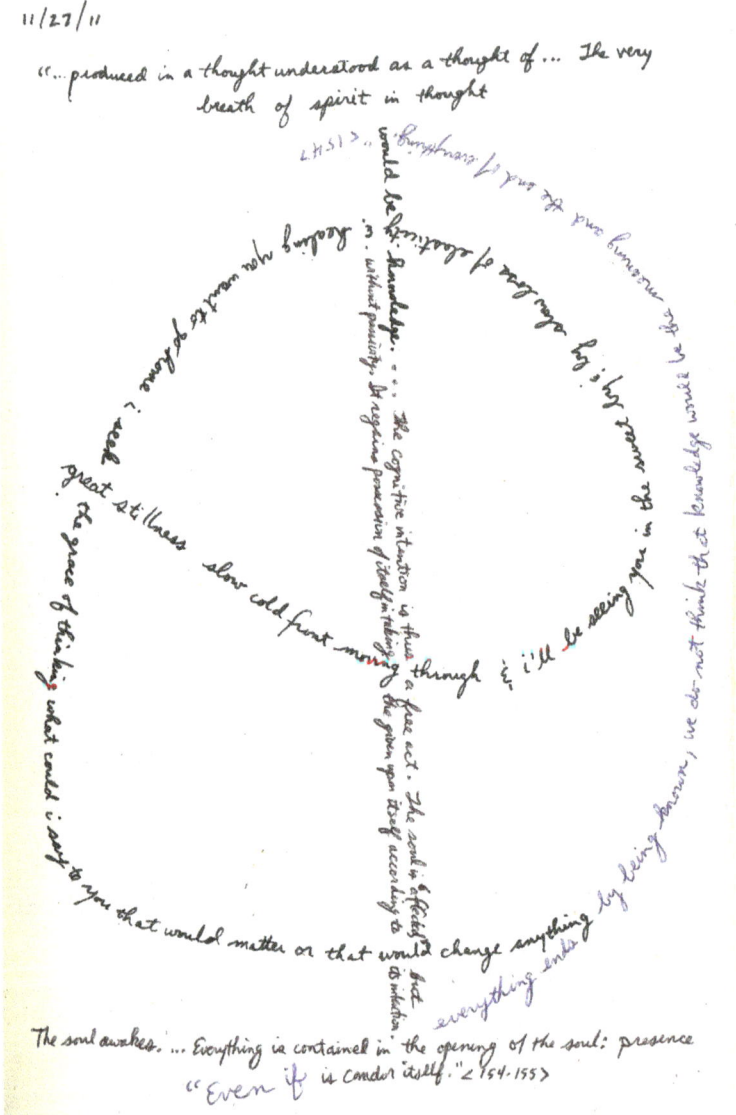

The soul awakes. ... Everything is contained in the opening of the soul: presence "Even if is candor itself." <154-155>

I realized recently that I've been doing what you've referred to as "collaborative reading" ever since the "Law-Poems" series written in the mid-1980s; these poems incorporated verbatim sections of the Alabama Legal Code. Subsequently, *H's Journal* quotes from Thoreau's Journal. My book *Days* includes quotations and marginalia. In some fundamental way, collaborative reading must stem from my strong sense that reading and writing are so closely related as to have no meaningful boundary, and the same holds true for "critical writing" and "creative writing," terms that have institutional boundaries, but in practice, are meaningless segregations.

And as I re-read my responses, Glenn, I realize that actually the beginning of my collaborative reading/writing goes back much earlier, to "The Cricket's Chant," my 1973 M.A. thesis at Virginia, that consisted entirely of lineated poems constructed from passages in Thoreau's Journal.

GM: I notice many instances of recurring words and themes in the *Notebooks*. The words: spirit, faith, song, consciousness, knowledge, mentions of Torah, and a concern for the brevity of time, the uncertainty of firmament. This reminds me of the break that your book *The New Spirit* made with a certain fundamentalist strain of innovators in poetry. What's going on?

HL: As for "spirit," as you know, it's a term that I've been writing in, through, about, on, and around for the past twenty years, including the essays in *Lyric & Spirit*. The poems (and essays) say what I know or have experienced of spirit. It's an admittedly vague term, but one that I find productive and generative and provocative in its exact vagueness. Perhaps "spirit" is another word for the (tangible) invisible, as in Merleau-Ponty's wonderful book *The Visible and the Invisible*. Just as I make a distinction between *religious* and *religion*, "spirit," as I think of it, has nothing to do with institutional affiliation nor fixed doctrine or definition. It is a term that opens up to considerations of the nature of consciousness, of language and its relationship to being (and to a possible telos of language), to thinking, to music, to a beyond, to worlds beyond our five senses. Mostly, though, I've been concerned (in my essays, and in my poetry, most especially the notebooks) with what I think of as a phenomenology of spiritual experience (i.e., a recording of an ongoing relationship to the invisible), with an insistence on noting as well its radical inconstancy, its intermittent and often momentary nature.

GM: So we're gonna die. And that cat's eye of October 29, 2011 in this suite of notebook pages provides a kind of answer? " … that knowledge of the world is a satisfaction, as though this knowledge filled a need?" If you were to state it simply, where does the writing and reading of poetry come into the equation?

HL: Not an answer, but a moment of conversation, of engagement in and through and of this world. (Reminds me of one of my favorite Jewish jokes: Q: Why does a Jew always answer a question with another question? A: I don't know; why?) And of the two Levinas quotes, the left-hand arc is, of course, a question. Perhaps for me, knowledge of the world is questionable, or filled with questioning, or questioning is at the heart of that questing? Your question and emphasis on the right-hand arc of the page make me think of Rilke, particularly in the Duino Elegies, where the act of poetry and of naming itself is suggested as a needed means of completing the very nature of the world (and of being). In other words, one of poetry's most sacred functions is to provide a space for consciousness of the world, a place for what I've called "thinking singing." The poem represents a kind of fulfillment of being by singing its praise and by naming it in all its complexity or by singing its ungraspable though lovely nature. Or, perhaps in answer to Heidegger's question, *What calls for thinking?* poetry makes manifest a way of responding and reflecting, or putting into play and shape in language an engagement with that question.

Of course, the arc of this so-called knowledge goes outward—toward the world and an expressing or kindred being—but also inward as well. The need and satisfaction (always temporary, I think, or at least such has been my experience of it) are also absolutely essential to our human existence. To use the language of Arakawa and Gins, this knowledge is part and parcel of our nature as enigma beings—as creatures whose nature, telos, and possibilities are always in question. Ours is a being that provokes questions, right?

GM: Reminds me of the Irish joke where Pat says to Mike, "Why are you digging a hole?" and Mike says, "I'm *not* digging a hole. I'm digging the dirt. And *leaving* a hole."

Or, by doing what Oppen did to "Prufrock," the revision this implies to me, in the first arc of your Levinas quote is: all that occurs in the human psyche, and all that takes place there, *ends* by being known. Is that falsehood the necessary fiction of your poetry?

HL: Fiction? How could poetry *not* be a place where all is (possibly) known, providing that what we mean by *known* is perpetually incomplete and subject to additional writing (and con-versing)?

GM: Yes, a fiction revealed in the tortured logic of poetry. It's all in there, Hank, and it's a conundrum taking us back to your example of the *Duino Elegies*: Rilke's terror at being annihilated by existence, unless what is known is also what is meant by being. Questioning, misreading, unfolding, or *to essay*, the root of which, *coup d'essai*, means to try. And this goes back to the inquiry of Lucretius "On the Nature of the Universe." This is the nature of an ongoing conversation in poetry.

Poetry never completes. It opens.

And so, maybe it would be appropriate to end with Levinas, from his *Entre Nous*: "Thought at its beginning finds itself before the miracle of fact."

Any closing thoughts?

HL: Your concluding riff puts me in mind of Robert Frost's line, "The fact is the sweetest dream that labor knows." I hope that the notebook pages/poems till that field, bringing up from the ground words and phrases and music that have the enigmatic obdurate nature of fact. May the pages be a simple, clear appearance that invites one to dwell there awhile, to experience the shape, music, and multi-directional thinking that counts for a factual pointing toward.

GM: Arrowing, then, we will go.

Amit Majmudar
interviewed by Nancy Mitchell

NM: I loved your playfulness in the title "Abecedarian"; for example, you obviously intend for the title to designate the form the prose/poem inhabits, and perhaps reference its history in ancient literature and sacred texts. However, as the noun "Abecedarian" means "beginner," did you intend the title to suggest Adam/the speaker, Eve/the girl, the snake and even God as rookies in this primal drama?

AM: This is one of those times that my instrument knows better than I do. I find that if you trust the English language, it won't lead you astray, at least not always. So I had no idea until I read your question that "abecedarian" means "novice"—but it seems absolutely *perfect* in retrospect, given the work's themes of innocence and experience. You are right also about how in Genesis, even Satan, whom we have a tendency to consider shrewd, is a novice at the art of subversion. Eve is God's maiden attempt at a woman, herself a revised and reshaped "excerpt" of Adam.

NM: The narrator speaks with such matter-of-fact authority; I have to tell you I was on my way to believing the anatomical description of ejaculation in "Come:"

> At the moment you come, the spinal cord detaches from the brain and whips down, forward, and out, liquefying gray and white matter. Immediately before that moment, gooseflesh prickles up the neuraxis and the body gives a slow, rising shudder—as if a third, colder presence had come into the room and blown, ever so gently, on the naked back.

After I re-read this many times for the sheer pleasure of it, I realized how just reading it creates a moment of complete resolution as the dichotomy of brain/body is dissolved. It was such a perfect image that I don't think I will ever see it in any other way. Thank you, I think.

In a sense, the genesis of the first act of human creativity—art—if you will, in trying to find pleasure by tweaking nature (what God has wrought), springs fresh from the mind of Adam. *They couldn't have learned it from watching the beasts of the field.* As this creative original act deviates from the procreation plan to perpetuate the image of God, is it not in a sense the real original sin?

> This new discovery cleared Eve out of Adam's field of view. This transition of pleasure, from Eve's face to the absence of her face made the pleasure twice removed from the pleasure of beasts: consummately solitary, consummately human. Before the fall, Adam laid on his back and marveled at clouds and their many counterfeit forms. After the fall, he stood and watched himself in a mirror.

Is this the original sin from which every other sin committed in Eden "genetically" descends?

AM: You can definitely think of it that way, and the logic behind that passage was as follows: All evil, in Vedantic thought and mystical thought across traditions, stems from a failure to understand the unity of the self and the other. It's what leads to *ahamkar*, which is Sanskrit for, literally, self-doing, or doing-for-oneself. So the antidote to this is to realize that you, your enemy (think "Love thine enemy"), God (think Mansur al-Hallaj, a Sufi: "I am the Real"), and all nonhuman natural life (think environmentalism, animal rights advocates, and so on) are all, together, unitary Being. "Do unto others as you would have them do unto you" … because they are you, the Upanishads would add. *Tat tvam asi*, You Are That.

So the endgame of a spiritual life is to actually live that unity. Some call it atonement (at-one-ment), or the *unio mystica*; even Nietzsche's Zarathustra speaks of "self-overcoming."

Sex, as originally conceived, in its unfallen form, is here the enactment of the unity between Adam and Eve. The denial of separateness, of otherness. When Adam makes Eve go down on him, he pushes her literally out of the picture ("he stood and watched himself in a mirror"). This is the original sin because this is the original selfishness.

NM: Eve, within the literal, physical restrictions, of the new hierarchy—and it's impossible not to think of poetic form here—must shape the raw material of the unnatural into an artifice of the natural. In the spaces between accommodating, anticipating, and modulating the cell bars of Adam's rhythms, she riffs and refines his into her own, perhaps her own act of *Non serviam*:

> she played with what would become meters: dactylic, halfway, all the way down; iambic, halfway, then down to the base; or Adam's favorite, the emphatic spondee.

Each stanza dissolves so logically into the next, although there are shifts in point of view and setting. Is the transition so graceful because archetypes are at play in plot and character? If so, are particulars of person and setting significant? Is there hope for the human spirit to evolve as long as it is at the mercy of archetypes? Are compassion and empathy (to ask) necessary to break the archetypal grid?

AM: I think the work occupies a middle-ground between/among the forms of the poem, the short story, the (faux) memoir, the essay, and the theological commentary. In such a *mélange absurde de tout* kind of form, archetypal imagery and personae are crucial, from a technical standpoint. Even the first person "I" of the memoristic passages is someone who flickers into and out of your field of view enigmatically, and is essentially unknown, or known only through the alphabetically arranged sequence of images and anecdotes he tells, and a tone of voice. That is what allows the different narratives to cohabit a (relatively) small space: the Book of Genesis, the narrator's loss of innocence, and the meta-analysis of these things. The work has this braided, essentially triple structure: the mythic story, the realist parallel, and the nonfiction commentary.

NM: You are masterful at stringing tensions between disparities and then playing on what is taut between them; I find it makes your work very alive. Do you think the negotiations you've made or make everyday between cultures, work and writing, etc. have contributed to this facility?

AM: I conceive of all these disparities as means of attaining hybrid vigor. Hybrid vigor is something people have known about for millennia: That a mutt is hardier than a specimen of either purebred parent species. The mongrel can live on trash and air; the purebred can eat Purina its whole life and it will still get early arthritis. It's the nature of biology. I apply that principle to things intellectual. Pick a pair of seemingly or supposedly opposed things—science and art, reason and religion, formal and free verse, poetry and prose, mono- and polytheism, theism and atheism, fiction and nonfiction, left brain and right brain, East and West, India and America, Hinduism and Islam, God and Mammon, truth and lie, truth and dare: I seek to hybridize them and to be invigorated by that hybridization. So I try to force opposites into occupying the same intellectual real estate and I wait for the explosions: because the explosions happen in English, which is, with its globetrotter's portmanteaux and its Latinogermanic ancestry, probably the most hybrid-vigorous language in history.

NM: As I read your blogs, poems and fiction, I'm impressed by your prodigious imagination—wow!—and amazed at how you manage to be a prolific writer with the other wonderful responsibilities in your life. Your work seems suffused with a kind inclusiveness, which finds a way to fit the misfit with the fit to make a whole, as in your poem "Joint Effort":

> Let the hunchback lie hump down
> upon the Bactrian camel. On that snug foundation
> let the leper stand tiptoe, balancing
> the cripple's cane on his nose, while the cripple,
> upside down, balances atop the cane, index finger
> on the hook handle.

I'm wondering, guessing really, if that could be a metaphor for your (forgive the term; I'm at a loss for another) creative process?

AM: We are all writers trying to pile things up: paragraph upon paragraph, stanza upon stanza: a work, if it stands, is really just a Jenga tower of words, enjoying a temporary reprieve from gravity.

Abecedarian

Adam

The only proof we have of intelligent design is that Adam could not connect his mouth and his penis. His designer was so aware of the risk that he designed Adam with a two-rib buffer. One rib eventually went to make Eve, but the second made sure Adam never lost interest in her. If given the ability to fellate himself, he would have poured himself endlessly into himself, like an ocean evaporating into one fixed cloud and raining on its own waves, greening nothing. The act would have been a means to knowing himself Biblically—to self-knowledge—and as such would have vaulted Adam above the sexless archangels. He might well have lost interest in God, too, bowing only to himself, rising a little, bowing again. Eve and Eden would have blossomed, Satan would have hissed in vain as Adam rocked like a pillbug on the grass, our species committing suicide as its intended first parent over and over again shot himself in the head.

Breath

Between the nose and the throat, we swallow in the same place we breathe. The pharynx is an anteroom where breath and drink mingle before they are sent, by the mindless knowingness of the body, down their separate tunnels. The breath is constantly blowing up and down, just beyond, while the head continues its own up and down, the lifegiving movement crosswise to the pleasure-giving one. The ancients believed that God blew the breath of life, the *nishmath chayim*, into a mud effigy. In this sense, the arousal of Adam to life was the first blowjob. The first time my first girlfriend was forced to give one, she kept stopping every ten to fifteen seconds. Holding one thing in her mouth, reflexively she held the other as well. *It's okay*, I told her. *Breathe.*

Come

At the moment you come, the spinal cord detaches from the brain and whips down, forward, and out, liquefying as it leaves you. The dull pearl hue of come comes from mixing gray matter and white matter. Immediately before that moment, gooseflesh prickles up the neuraxis and the body gives a slow, rising shudder—as if a third, colder presence had come into the room and blown, ever so gently, on the naked back. This is the same shudder Eve felt when the serpent came inside the garden: her first adumbration of the female orgasm, courtesy of Lucifer.

Duino

Duino Elegies, in Edward Snow's translation, sat on the nightstand next to her bed. She had bookmarked it with its own receipt. I kept turning my head to it, pondering its thinness and the thinness of books of poetry generally, and wondering what a *duino* was, and wondering why my head was not in the getting of head when head was what I had wanted for so long. I knew nothing of Rilke then—she introduced me to poetry, too: you'd think we would have kept in touch—but I had seen, maybe on a calendar, the famous quote about how love is two people protecting each other's solitude. At the end, when she rose onto her knees at the foot of the bed, distanced from me by the length of my body, looking to the side, perhaps at that very book on the nightstand, I did feel loneliness. Loneliness is just solitude without a book. *O fig tree, how long I've pondered you....*

Eyes

When Adam first asked Eve to look up at him, he thought eye contact would be like touch, only deeper. His mind would enter the upper half of her head as his body was entering the lower half of it. She, too, wanted to lock eyes, believing it would connect them—it was getting lonely and tedious down there, and she was wondering whether she preferred the snake-eyed sweetness of the apple to the salty treesap of Adam. But Adam thought her left eyebrow rose slightly as she looked up, and he couldn't shake an impression of *knowingness*, which only reminded him of their lost innocence. Eve saw him looking down at her from his height and sensed a new hierarchy between them, in which he made demands, and she knelt and serviced him. *Non serviam*, she insisted, but her mouth was full as she said this, and Adam mistook it for a groan of pleasure.

Face

They couldn't have learned it from watching the beasts of the field. For many—the giraffe, the horse—the logistical barriers to any technique other than mounting are insurmountable. The closest thing they could have witnessed was the mutual investigative sniff between dogs.

For that matter, even the default position of human copulation, face to face, had little precedent in nature. The new discovery cleared Eve out of Adam's field of view. This transition in his pleasure, from Eve's face to the absence of her face, made the pleasure twice removed from the pleasure of beasts: consummately solitary, consummately human. Before the fall, Adam laid on his back and marveled at clouds and their infinite counterfeit forms. After the fall, he stood and watched himself in a mirror.

Gag

This second fruit—over which Adam had taken to wearing a leaf, creating the illusion he, too, was a tree—seemed as forbidden as the apple, and as such, irresistible. Eve found out how seriously she had transgressed only when, devouring it whole, as a serpent might its noonday meal, she felt an unexpected lurch, her whole neck and torso rising in revolt. She fell back onto her heels, coughing. If only the apple had convulsed her so! Everything might have been different. She would have never swallowed that bite of the forbidden. She would have done nothing more than hold the forbidden in her mouth, like smoke, or a pill, or now, returning onto her knees, Adam.

Head
The physical expressions of love are really just people rubbing together the most sensitive parts of their bodies. We rub hands, we rub lips and tongues, we rub genitals because that's where the nerve endings are. We rub them the way paramedics rub defibrillator paddles before delivering the jolt: Well-given head makes the getter arch off the bed, electrified. To get head is to have the lover's thinking head sleeve your unthinking head. Two civilizations at vastly different stages of development are meeting. The thinking head is a cluster of highly developed organs of perception, eyes, ears, nose, tongue—not to mention the neurological capital, where decisions are made. It is the body's technological North. The head of the penis is nothing but nerves, something rudimentary, not yet a mind. This head is capital of a hot-blooded rebel country, hypersensitive and easily roused: the body's humid, tumid South.

Innocence
It seemed like a way of having it both ways, at that age. Pleasure without risk, intimacy without a sinking sense of obligation. You could get your knowledge without having it age you. It should have been playful. I shouldn't have had to put my hands on her shoulders and, ever so gently, press. Because I was everything at once in the garden of my greenness. I was innocent Adam and insidious Lucifer. I was also the Tree, the standing wood of life, coaxing an Eve curious but full of foreboding, *Taste of me. Taste of me.*

Job

Blowing Adam became one of the many jobs of Eve's exile, the milking of one more udder. Repetition: Cain the infant, Abel the toddler loved it. Their minds still carried an amniotic glisten of innocence, which wouldn't rub off until their teens. Repetition, though, their mother could not bear. In Eden, things had been different: twelve hours of daylight, twelve of dark, the saying of the same prayers at the same times of day, the three hungers and the three meals, Eve's nightly up down up down up down until Adam spouted like Old Faithful on a seismic timer—in Eden all this retained delight, every time, the same way the same story told the same way delighted the children: In the beginning was the word, once upon a time. In exile, boredom became possible. Music was the only language that could take them back, please them with repetition—though now even songs, they realized, could age. Repetition: Within a few years, Eve and Adam stopped speaking in verse. They longed for a new rhythm from moment to moment, which is the same thing as longing for no rhythm at all. The language of knowledge has always been prose.

Kiss

She placed her affection, almost daintily, on the feverish forehead of lust. I wanted to inspire awe, like some dark alien obelisk discovered in the jungle: I wanted to be jawdropping. But here were kisses, gentle ones, kisses I had never asked for, kisses better suited to the cheeks of nephews, kisses that undercut my male aggression like long-stem roses slid down a riot gun. Later, when we broke up and the reproaches came out all at once, she told me that she hadn't really wanted to, that I had been pushy, that she had worried she would lose me if she didn't, that she wished she never had. Kisses. I realize now she was buying time.

Lucifer

Lucifer had no idea, when he decided to take the form of the serpent, how he would move once he was in it. The wingless, footless form seemed a perfect disguise for one who would be expected to enter either gliding or on tiptoe. The trick, once he lay prone on the ticklish grass, was not to lead with his front end, but to squeeze himself from the base to the head. The tongue spilled forward on its own, like toothpaste from a tube. So did the seven ounces of breath that comprised his hiss.

Mnmmn

To give pleasure the mouth sacrifices speech. The conversation across the table that gave way to whispering on the futon gave way, at last, to silence. I did not speak because, for me, four months' speaking had attained its goal. I had listened, too, listened always with this future silence in mind, though it seems calculating to accuse a boy that young of such calculation, even if the accuser and the accused are me and me. She tried to speak once, that first time, a couple syllables, or maybe one syllable that struggled twice to emerge. Everything comes out sounding the same, this *mnmmn* that is neither moan nor murmur. She could have been saying yes, or baby, or more, or Amit, or oh, or (we were both so young, we were boy and girl) no.

No

It wouldn't have taken much. If she had said the word, I would have sucked myself back like a touch-me-not, touched. No means no, we were taught in Health class. No means no, said the Sex Ed VHS on the television our teacher wheeled into the classroom. No one ever taught us what silence meant. Silence means whatever the person not listening wants silence to mean. And I wanted hers to mean yes that afternoon between Rilke's elegies and the rest of summer break. The second time, the third time, all the other times, she told me later, I wanted to. Just not that first time. And I, guilty, all I could do was murmur: I didn't know, I didn't know, I didn't know.

O

O opens any ode. It is the default orison sung by heavenly choristers, the only letter that fashions the mouth in its own image, the original rabbit-hole of the original fall: Out of Eden, into Wonderland. In the room where I was first blown, a ceiling punkah turned furiously in the humid heat, and I stared up at its circular blur. It was over only when my mouth rounded itself to match hers and I shouted, loudly once and the second time more softly, in a decrescendo, *O, o*.

Pull

Adam's sensitive hardness had a pull on Eve even before they found out pleasure could divorce itself from pelvis-to-pelvis procreation. Fellatio wasn't just some corrupt, postlapsarian innovation. Before, in her innocence, she went down to learn more about him, the way she bent sometimes to inspect Eden's earthworms and orchids. After the fall, Eve went down to fall farther, to fall all the way, to do nothing of use with the sacred tools of speech and sex. This was the pull toward him, but after the fall, there was also an opposite force at work the other way. Call it resentment. Adam noticed how her going down, quickening toward the finish, flipped its directionality. She wasn't going down anymore—just repeatedly, and tenaciously, pulling away.

Question

That afternoon, for whole minutes before it actually happened, the experience floated just beyond me, a ring of smoke. Asking the question, even leaving off the part that would make the question make sense, *Will you*, would have swished away everything by grasping it. And so I communicated what I wanted with a brush of my finger across her lips, my hands sliding onto her small shoulders, my back arching as I glanced down at myself as though here, between us, were a flesh wound that needed her nursing. It would have felt wrong to speak this want stronger than mere need, this curiosity too intense for questions. She never said no because I never asked.

Rhythm

Adam's rhythm, standing behind Eve (their first experiments aped the apes), slowed down or speeded up on its own. His mind didn't govern it so much as his pelvis, the anatomy autonomous. Whenever Eve took him in her mouth, though, questions of rhythm—how to set, sustain, modulate it—entered her head. She sped up toward the climax, mimicking Adam's thrusting tempo, because she knew her endgame was to mimic nature. Before she sensed that tiptoe-tremulous shiver, and sometimes the unwelcome clap of his hands on her ears, she played with what would become meters: dactylic, halfway, halfway, all the way down; iambic, halfway, then down to the base; or Adam's favorite, the emphatic spondee.

Self-Reflexive

The ouroboros, the serpent sucking on itself, has been the envy of mystics and alchemists for centuries. It represents perfect sufficiency, pleasure given and received in equal measure, a creature that has formed a ring and married itself. One could imagine that ring tightening until the serpent became all head and the jaws everted into pure absence, like a reversible purse whose inner lining was the void. Which serpent appears in this symbol, it doesn't take a leap to imagine. The tempter in the garden must have taunted Eve and Adam, afterwards, with this very same now-you-see-me trick, deep-throating himself in an *auto-da-fellatio*, tasting of the one fruit more forbidden than the apple.

Teeth

Rilke compares the tongue between the teeth to the heart between hammers. And the tongue is covered in nerve endings, sensing, in its cloister, more intensely than other parts of the body. When you place a part of yourself more sensitive than your tongue between someone else's teeth, the one who kneels is not the one who surrenders. Any gesture of dominance or control, like the hand on the head that presumes to bless this genuflection, guide this descent, is just for show. The one who isn't biting down is the one in charge. A girl named Nicole once ran our high school football team, and on Monday morning, when everyone knew, I could not detect anything like shame on her used face, only triumph, as though she were a warrior princess, and a rival army one by one had knelt to kiss her sword.

Urgency

When I was young and could not bear to go slow, when holding hands across a table at Applebee's and even making out felt like salt flats seen from a car going the speed limit, I couldn't taste the desert we spooned together. It could have been apple pie, it could have been a wedge of wet clay. All the motions of the date took on the feel of running in a dream. When the time came at last, I placed myself in her mouth like a beating donor heart on ice.

Versailles

A garden's a garden only until something grows without permission. No plant is born a weed save in its gardener's eye: What lives must live by design or not at all. Eden, willed wild, was never some Versailles, never some grid of green hallways and foursquare grottos. Eden had tangled ivies but no weeds until Adam and Eve dared to grow their own minds up. From that moment, they themselves became the first weeds in Eden—detected, dug up, and flung over the wall. By then, a sense of flower and weed governed how they looked at their bodies: Hence the figleaf meant to camouflage Adam's new patch of loosestrife, Eve's coarse triangle of crabgrass. In fact, the flesh stem of his penis itself came to seem a weed—one she could never, for all her kneeling and pulling, uproot.

Wood

Why not iron, why not marble, why not brass? Because desire, in all the old poems, is supposed to be a flame, and fire swallows wood. Because men, even at their most vulgar, prefer to liken this part of their bodies to something animate, organic: hence boner, hence cock, hence meat. Because wood, back when it was the trunk of a tree, dribbled sticky white sap and coursed at its pith with water. Because the Tree of Life and the Tree of Knowledge had scaffolds, at least, of a common material, and because they were both wood they too could burn, could blossom, could rot.

X

A cutting from a fern grows the same fern in a different spot. Simply incubating Adam's rib was not enough. Something had to be changed. Adam's chromosomes were X and Y, Eve's were X and X: A stubby appendage added to her genome, subtracted from her genitals. This zero-sum made all the difference. A body surfaced more finely, better insulated, more flexible—these were revisions made by a practiced hand, a second draft, fewer mistakes and fewer risks. A patient aesthetic came into play, too, flourishes neglected in the first version: an up curl given to each eyelash, a lighter voice in her throat, a deeper walnut dye for her hair, for her mouth more madder red.

Yearning

What I wanted: To be held in her mouth like a secret. To be known, but not completely, not yet, not while I was still riding the bus to school every day. To gain knowledge without losing our innocence, or at least not all of our innocence. To do something serious in a way that could be played off as playfulness, afterwards. To dip myself into her like a toe into a pool, but safely, in the shallow end, where even if I fell I could find my feet and walk out. To taste sex the way the rich taste wine, treasuring it on the tongue before spitting.

Zzz

On the last day of their innocence, Adam arched his back and groaned and rested his head on some stones, which in those days had not yet hardened themselves toward man, and remembered the shape of his head. Eve rose and, wiping her mouth, found him asleep. At this moment, the serpent emerged from a ravine. The serpent knew she would go looking for a stream or fruit-tree soon, to get rid of the aftertaste, and he had to intercept her early. Adam had just fallen asleep, so the serpent did not speak with his long serpent tongue. Instead he stuck it out and wagged it side to side, showing Eve what Adam had never yet, in his selfish innocence, done unto her. Eve held her hand out to the serpent, as she often did to geese and jaguars, and the breezy thwips of his tongue concentrated between her first and middle fingers. Unlike the geese, unlike the jaguars, the serpent was neither eating from her hand nor licking it. He did this with his tongue solely to give her a sensation. Eve had never received a gift before. She sat on the grass, a few feet from where Adam snored, to puzzle out her own delight. The serpent, his tongue still out and moving, crawled into her lap.

Jim Daniels
interviewed by Nancy Mitchell

NM: Outside of productions dependent upon them, collaborations are rarely as seamlessly successful as the Special Feature with your poems and Charlee Brodsky's photos.

I know you've collaborated with other artists. What was your first experience?

JD: I had written a series of poems based on paintings by Francis Bacon for my book *Blue Jesus* (his paintings scare me, and fear is always a good motivator) and had done my first screenplay for the film *No Pets*.

NM: You know Francis Bacon is scary as hell; tell me more about "fear as a motivator"?

JD: As a writer, I don't want to feel too comfortable. I've found over the years that if I push through the fear, I might end up in a new place I might not have discovered otherwise. I think the graphic quality of Bacon's work led me into maybe some darker places that I might not have found otherwise.

NM: So, writing from Bacon's paintings was collaboration?

JD: I do think it is a collaboration in some ways—not a literal one, obviously. Maybe the word is "engagement."

NM: How did you end up collaborating on the film *No Pets*?

JD: The Pittsburgh-area filmmaker Tony Buba, best known for his docs, was interested in doing a fictional film, and I gave him my short story, "No Pets," which he liked and asked me to adapt. I had no idea how to write a screenplay, but Tony worked with me through the process, then let me sit in on casting, filming, and editing. I found myself challenged and invigorated by the process—it got me out of my

the *plume* poetry interviews 1

little room by myself, out of my comfort zone....

NM: You know some folks would almost have to be hog-tied and drug, kicking and screaming, out of their comfort zone.... Do you remember the first time you "pushed through the fear" you mention?

JD: I'm not sure I remember the first time as a particular "aha" moment, but I'm thinking it was with the Francis Bacon paintings. I'd never been compelled to write about art before, and maybe even, given my background, I thought there was something pretentious or elitist about it—art about art, art for art's sake, or whatever—but I felt this primal connection to his work that wouldn't let me go. It was something like, "oh, that's what my nightmares look like." So when I started writing these poems it was like that creature in *Alien* that comes out of that guy's chest—the voice was completely strange to me, blurting out strange phrases, and I was thinking, "Whoa, what the heck is this?" But I pushed through there, trusted the odd voices to take me somewhere.

NM: Wow! How did you and Charlee Brodsky first begin collaborating?

JD: Charlee and I were part of the founding of this Center for the Arts in Society at Carnegie Mellon, where we both teach, and I was looking for an opportunity to collaborate. I knew and loved her photography, particularly her work in Homestead, a mill town on the edge of Pittsburgh (which turned out to be the subject of our second big collaboration, *From Milltown to Malltown*).

At the time, I was playing around with these weird things I called "brick poems"—the words were in all caps and spaced out like bricks on a wall with most of the connecting words eliminated. I showed them to Charlee, and she said she had a whole series of photos of brick walls, and they were so much better than my poems that I immediately started writing poems in response to those photos.

NM: So the collaboration was an evolutionary spiral of sorts; your poems to her photos, her photos to better poems?

JD: Definitely. It's a more interactive engagement. The collaboration itself becomes a responsive entity, and the work develops a relationship beyond "I'll put your photos in my book or vice-versa?" That whole series—the first thing we worked on together—never made it into a book, but it created a basis of trust and respect so we could move forward working together.

NM: Can you talk about how this basis of trust and respect was created?

JD: Balancing what Charlee thought were the best photos with what I thought were the best poems, etc. Again, it's a slow, evolving process. Our first collaborative book, *Street*, came out in 2005, and we started a couple of years before that. Now, every couple of years we seem to get started on a new project. We're always both doing our own thing. She was chosen as Pittsburgh Artist of the Year a few years back and had a big show of her work.

NM: Do you two have a plan or vision of how it will come together?

JD: The vision thing is always an evolving process—that's one of the great things about collaboration—you bounce these ideas off each other and the work slowly coalesces. We usually start out at Charlee's big table where she spreads out what she's working on, and I pick up ones that pull me in, intrigue and interest me in some way, and take them home and spend some time with them. I like to just start free-associating on the photos—it's like rubbing sticks together—sometimes I can get a little fire going, and other times I break the sticks, or get them wet, or whatever. I feed off the energy of her photos so that when things are going well, I'm not just describing what's already there, but I'm going some place strange and different—taking a coal from her fire to start one of my own. I know my metaphors are mixed up a bit there, but it has something to do with fire.

NM: That's an amazing image of the collaborative creative process … hmmm … fire, coal, fire … anything to do with your hometown, "Steel-town?"

JD: Yeah, maybe. We've been doing more electronic exchanges with .pdfs, etc., but I still prefer having the physical thing in my hand.

NM: Nothing like the real thing … it's like there's a layer or filter between it and you—a visual condom … better than nothing, well, "nothing" is better, but you know what I mean.

JD: Ha! It's true—One thing I do use the .pdfs for is to enlarge the image and/or zoom in on a particular detail that intrigues me, so that's a plus.

NM: Hmm, maybe we'll drop the condom metaphor right now? How does writing in collaboration differ from writing alone?

JD: It's exciting and unpredictable. As a writer, one of the most exciting things for me is when these poems come out of nowhere—these strange voices start coming in that are very different from the usual voice in my poems. This work stretches me—a lot of my work—poetry and fiction—often uses first-person narratives as a guiding structure, where the collaborative work is all over the map. Or, even, for me, off the map.

NM: Speaking of off the map, the feature's first poem, "Returning to Earth," begins literally off the map!

This title is so perfectly economical; it announces the poem's subject, "returning"; establishes physical and psychic tone and terrain; launches the narrative trajectory created by the photos and poems of "the rest of the news"; and, as all the best poems do, it both informs and perplexes.

For example, we know the speaker has been away from earth, but we don't know via what or how. Was the departure intentional, via NASA, meditation, sleep, a slug of Ayahuasca, or was the speaker blasted into the stratosphere by an accidental or nefariously orchestrated, apocalyptic catastrophe? Is the *returning* a conscious "re-turning" back to earth, a "fall from grace" or the irrefutable law of gravity at work? The poem's answers to these questions:

> I don't know much
>   about disintegration
> but I'm learning.

intimates that the speaker is losing former psychical and psychic integrity in the descent back to earth, and whatever energy authored the blast from earth, or the return to, was intent upon annihilation:

> Erasure has many techniques
> but only one result.

I'm intrigued with how the stanzaic structure and the asterisks between create a sense of slow descent, a floating in and out of conscious, the asterisks denoting great swaths of time or lapses in consciousness. The closer to earth, the more fully conscious the speaker becomes and struggles to make sense of the landscape below.

It's a visceral thrill of seeing the photographs following the poems. Together they become, are like—and I absolutely adore this, and in some way find great humor, pathos in this—an X-file of text and hard photographic evidence.

Case in point: the "alien rag" in:

> Alien rag from space
> or variation on worms
> or octopi or jellyfish
> or bad luck.
> *
> Dried-up sea floor.
> Drought of love.
> And yet confetti
> rises once again.

is clearly identifiable in the photo-document following the poem. We see this consistent documentation of the subject matter under investigation (the rest of the news) at the scene of the crime (Earth) in the poems following "Returning to Earth":

> The rest of the news
> is returning to earth.

And you know what? Dang! ... Although you've told us that you wrote the poems from the photos, you can't convince my mind that these photos do not document the text. Is this one of the amazing surprises of collaboration you talk about?

JD: Well, when it's working, yes. There's some reverse double-

the *plume* poetry interviews 1

whammies going on in terms of psychic reversals. The photos seem like inevitable manifestations of things that I'm feeling. I know that sounds a little wacky, but I don't know how else to say it.

NM: Does not sound wacky in the least! I cannot tell you how much the final poem's text and photo document of this X-file blew me away; pure genius. Without revealing too much, let me just say, Mission Accomplished! It's been a blast, Jim, many thanks!

JD: Thank you!

Returning to Earth

I don't know much
    about disintegration
but I'm learning.

Erasure has many techniques
    but only one result.
*

The color of ash—
    first color
or the last?
*

Faded by sunlight
    frayed by moonlight.
*

Deliberately stepped on
    or avoided.
*

Alien rag from space
    or a variation on worms
or octopi or jellyfish
    or bad luck.
*

Dried-up sea floor.
    Drought of love.
And yet green confetti
    rises once again.
*

Facts are elusive.
    Ash vs. Dust?
*

My only fact:
a human hand once held this thing.
    The rest of the news
is returning to earth.

The Shelter of Coffins

Are we drawn toward getting under, breaking
through, to bury ourselves in the cold, moist dirt

of disappearance? What came first, the crack,
or the pieces of rubble in the crack?

In other words, did we start out playing
for the Cement Slabs, then go off on our own,

or did they kick us off the team?
Okay, out with the questions

in with the myths: Once upon a time
a great clanging was heard in the night

and when the sun arose the next day
the Four-Holed Shiny Thing

was visible. It had crushed
our fearless leader, Moldy Pebble.

Some say he remains alive
in shadow, awaiting

The Great Uplifting. Others
believe he escaped into

the Large Dump Truck
and will return one day

for the rest of us. Every year
we make a pilgrimage

to the shrine of the Four-Holed
Shiny Thing and pray at the altar

of the Moldy Pebble. I don't
know what happens if we don't.

I haven't gotten that far in the myth.

Privacy

Have you woven
plastic strips between chain links
imagining you might make a stand
against the world, looping in and out
while neighbors watch, wary,
tossing empties against the fence
while you try to establish
some flimsy order against chaos
and the lack of choice that put them next to you?
Who can afford to move
and even the damn strips weren't cheap
row upon row you can't stop.

A helicopter heading to the hospital
can see it all if they're looking down
if the patient is alive
if the world is flat if god is your
witness oh lord it all unravels
the years unspooling into grief.

Not even concrete blocks
can keep it away.

Hole in the Theory

If we disguise our flaws
with designed borders

how can we keep other
flaws from emerging

to mock our imagined
grand design?

Nature's bunny ears
mock us, our un-

tamed pets on
the loose.

They don't come
when we call.

the *plume* poetry interviews 1

After the Flood

When the waters rose back up
or sank deeper
    I stared at what remained
of the rest of my life
    the layer of grief
        coating it
with the dry cough of disintegration.

I searched for a source of nostalgia
    in memories of high water
and the jangly music of the fear
    I danced to. Oh, the panicked
joy of it. I took a stick and began
    to scratch lies into the curled mud.

the *plume* poetry interviews 1

Dinosaur Bones with Crown of Thorns

Synchronize your watches
then step on them.
*

Time began
when the fat lady sang

or vomited at the sight
of us.
*

What calendar do you use?
What calendar do you abuse?
*

They crucified a circus clown by
mistake, taking the orange hair
as the devil's twisted halo.

Or so the legend goes.
Because someone wrote it down

it must be true. As this
must be true.
*

If you drop an angel
and a chunk of cement
at the same time, which lands first?
Which hurts
the most?
*

What came first
the calculator or the telephone?

the *plume* poetry interviews 1

If Noah sent out a dove
to see if the waters
had receded

was that bird the first UFO?
*

What did the other dove do?
Was it lonely?

It comes down
to being lonely

no matter how many
buttons you press.
*

Are you wearing your glasses
for distance or close-up?

The world started a zillion years ago
when the dinosaurs discovered
the joy of killing and meat.

They decided to leave some bones behind
just to fuck us up.
*

Imagine the surprised dinosaur
losing its teeth in the old folks home

and being transmogrified
into a treacly children's TV star:

"Hey, you folks seen my teeth?"
he asks the fake children
but it comes out as
"And remember, I love you."

Then, he eats the children.
All the dinosaurs applaud.
*
If these remains
are what the stripper left
before exiting naked
stage right, behind the dark curtain

then what did her original outfit
look like? Scientists spent
centuries arranging the remains
into articles of clothing.

Thus, haute couture was born.
We memorialize this event
to Terre Haute, Indiana.
*
The crown didn't fit.
What were they thinking?
They fired the crown maker.
A lion jumped through
the crown of thorns.

The crucified dinosaurs
tried to applaud

the *plume* poetry interviews 1

but their tiny arms
were nailed down.
*

Who ate that dove?
Where is that recipe?
Where are the ruins of the true ark?
Hasn't that astronaut found them yet?

Are they in Little Rock, Arkansas?
In Big Rock, Illinois?
On the Big Rock Candy Mountain?
*

The scientists of myth
are hard at work
hand-crafting new relics
for sale in the gift shop.
*

And then Jesus walked out
of the spaceship.

That's how all my stories end.

Luljeta Lleshanaku and translator Ani Gjika
interviewed by Nancy Mitchell

NM: Hi Ani and Luljeta! What a great treat to chat with you both about these amazing poems. Thank you!

AG: Thank *you* and Daniel for the opportunity!

NM: I'm wondering, Luljeta, as you write poetry in other languages do you write in English as well? If so, was there a particular aesthetic objective in having Ani translate these poems?

LL: I have tried to write in English, and I often write a first draft in another language because doing so creates twice the magic. But whether I do that or not, the poem needs to go through the hands of an expert to whom the English language comes naturally. Despite my progress in English, I don't believe I could ever write in a perfect, vital English. I have wondered why that is and the answer is that at my age, 46 years old, language is no longer an arbitrary connection but a way, a system of thinking, which by now has been perfected in the language to which I belong. This system becomes less and less flexible the older one gets. The logical attitude, for example, is so different from one language to another. Particularly, the syntax, which is the skeleton of a language, its temperament. This is why, I think, children find it easy to adapt quickly to another language. If I were twenty years younger then, yes, maybe then I would be writing in English.

NM: Can you two talk about the origins of this collaboration?

LL: I met Ani for the first time in New York City, in January 2010, when my book *Child of Nature* was first being promoted. What impressed me most at first was that Ani came from Boston specifically to hear me read. Then we met several times afterwards both in Tirane, Albania and in Peterborough, New Hampshire. We had lots of time to get to know one another. I was also one of the first people to read the manuscript of her book *Bread on Running Waters* which I truly liked and which allowed me to understand her poetic sense. It didn't take me long to realize that I was dealing with a deeply intelligent woman, who asked a lot of herself and who possessed both a strong literary intuition and a great sense of humor. Very passionate! And it's not of less importance in translation that we both come from the same cultural background, and in this case, it would be hard for Ani to fall into the typical translation traps.

AG: Gosh, I'm not sure that what Luljeta says of me is true, but as for the sense of humor and passion, I think we're both cut from the same cloth in that regard and I enjoy our e-mail exchange so much so that translating her has never felt like work for me but more like the very basic, raw form of creative process I crave and am surprised by when I'm writing my own poems. As Luljeta mentioned, we first met in 2010 when I attended one of her readings in NYC. I had discovered her work only a few months before that. I was completing an MFA in poetry at Boston University at the time and was studying the art of translation with Rosanna Warren. For the final project in that class, I translated about twenty poems by three different Albanian poets. Luljeta was one of them. It was a real joy to meet her in person because I admired her poetry instantly, especially when I rediscovered it in my mother tongue.

NM: Your poems put me in mind of the lines "The town may be changed/ But the well cannot be changed," from the Wilhelm/Barnes translation of the *I Ching*; maybe because your poems seem to draw from the primary source, the eternal well of shared consciousness which is impervious to the temporal vagaries of zeitgeist, politics, and boundaries which attempt to, but cannot, separate life from life?

LL: Thank you for this confirmation. It makes me feel good to hear it. There's nothing political in these poems, just as there's nothing clearly defined historically or geographically. And this was done on purpose. Since when I was a child, I have thought that politics are the effect, never the cause. Historical events, just like personal ones, similarly, are results and momentary. They are never enough to build a "literary case" through them. And if we refer to the cause, then we need to search inside the microcosm, inside human nature, which is very complex, unpredictable and existing in all places at once. In another poem, I speak of my childhood curiosity toward broken toys because this was the time when I was free to pull them apart, to split open their guts sort of, in order to understand how they functioned. It's like being a doctor, who, in order to understand a disease, needs to first find out its origin. And when we go back to the origin, we find we are all so similar with one another… what they call universal.

NM: Wow and yes! We would have been fine childhood playmates; I too, took dolls apart, and when disappointed that I could find no soul, wanted to move on to dead birds in hopes they might reveal it; my parents could only go so far to indulge me.

Am I wrong to intuit that you were born with knowledge of this source, and, when, as a child, your "eye" was opened to it as you write in "Acupuncture," it was this new vision rather than a reaction against/response to social realism, which was the impetus for your first poems?

> I was a child when my first teacher
> mispronounced my last name twice. That pricked me like a needle.
> A small needle in the earlobe. And suddenly
> I saw clearly—it affected my vision.
> I saw poetry,
> the perfect disguise.

LL: Without exaggerating too much, and despite the fact that this has not been proven scientifically, I believe that each one of us inherits a kind of archetype, emotional and informational archives. And some people simply do not rummage a lot through there, but some others do.

NM: I know what you mean; when I was ten I saw a re-release of the movie *Gone with the Wind*. I remember the stunned moment I realized that every woman was destined to be a Scarlett or a Melanie, and I felt my fate impress itself on my young consciousness as a seal to scarlet candle wax on a love letter

the *plume* poetry interviews 1

LL: I remember when Naomi Jaffa, the Poetry Trust's Director, after introducing me at the Aldeburgh Poetry Festival last November, asked me, "And how old are you? 900 years old?" You can take that as a compliment, or not, because the attributes don't belong to me really. In another poem, "Vertical Realities," I've said that "There are three generations inside me / who dictate what I should or should not do." Survivors, in general, (and it could very well be said that I'm "a survivor" like several others who come from communist or fascist dictatorships) if you really look into it carefully, find it difficult to create an identity because the identity of the group to which they belong is many times more powerful than the one they want to create. Take Hebrew literature, for example. Singer, who is one of my favorite writers, was able to create successfully, in my opinion, the dominant power of survival cultures over the individual.

Whereas the poem which you were referring to above, is an attempt to give an answer through poetic arguments to one of the questions every writer asks themselves: "why do I write?" And one of those answers is to create an identity. Things like Ford cars, Alfredo sauce, espresso "mocha", all the way to sticky post-it notes—they each have a patent, an authorship, a name. It seems that we're in an eternal war to survive anonymity, each of us within our own means.

The biographical element in this poem is that I would truly get frustrated when people used to mispronounce my name. And in 90% of the cases this would happen because my last name is difficult to pronounce even in my own language. And terribly long so that it ate up several boxes in the class roster. When I became a teacher myself, I made similar mistakes with my students' names and encountered similar frustrations in them. Are names so incredibly important to us? But you made another interesting observation when you mentioned, as a counterpoint, "social realism", because the art of social realism used as a propagandist tool, aimed precisely at crushing one's identity or, rather, at creating a collective one. And since this goes against human nature, social realism was destined to fail as a movement.

NM: The lines "the perfect disguise" triggered another childhood memory: as a child I was awakened by a thunderstorm to thousands of postage-stamp sized images of byzantine paintings (which I later saw in a college art history class) of the infant Jesus flashing in my room's dark, while a man's voice boomed as if through a megaphone "Behold the Rain Fall Upon You." I should disclaim here that I had seen *The Ten Commandments* that day—we got out of school to see it; in "living" color, fifty cents admission—so most likely this experience was the product of an inflamed imagination rather than a divine visitation. In terror I kept my eyes shut the entire night, and the next day I felt cast out into rain, culled from any ordinary childhood. Thereafter, I felt a split between surface life and an under-life. For fear of ridicule I never told anyone, but wrote about it poems, "the perfect disguise." I'm wondering, did you feel similarly isolated with your gift of vision?

LL: Probably not in such a poetic way as it has happened to you. I didn't even realize that I had a gift until much later. But I remember that when I was little or fairly young, I always ended up alone because of the strange turns I would give to a conversation, turns that were confusing to everyone else. On top of this, I used to always feel a certain melancholy for no particular reason and I'd try to mask it in every possible way so that for some time, I even tried writing funny poems, but this was also a reasonable despair which I believe came to me from the fact that I was often able to see the end result of things before I even attempted to engage myself in them. This was simply a clarity, a clarity that to a certain extent, was unhealthy. Considering my passion for the work of detectives and investigations (I often think about starting to write thrillers) I am convinced that the strength of my creative work is my analytical ability; this is where I need to rely on.
But is there something sacred, something truly divine in poetry? Something that cannot be explained through curiosity, intelligence, or even analytical ability? Building a metaphor is such a pure situation. We could come up with a hundred formulas for a metaphor but none of them can help us create as powerful a metaphor as that of Yehuda Amichai's, for example. This must be what they call "inspiration," a kind of holy spirit. Truthfully, luck, a gift.

the *plume* poetry interviews 1

NM: Am I correct in that this vision has an X-ray quality to it? For example in "Live Music," bread, universally called "the staff of human life" is full of air holes despite its "smooth crust on the outside."

LL: I'm happy to hear that. And I'm grateful for your astute reading. This metaphor is key to this particular poem. I'm talking about imperfections, those we tolerate within a tight circle, within a family, ourselves, but which on the outside become much more challenging. A *live* pub where neither the music nor the language are original, where the food is of second-hand quality and even the voice of the singer is too low, suggests an environment where people have low expectations and this is a safe way to face and deal with existence without feeling sorry for yourself. And in fact, in another poem, I go a little further and use the German word *schadenfreude*, which means "the pleasure derived from others' misfortunes," which acts as a kind of grease, man's consolation to accept life as it comes because someone else has it even worse.

Just think how more than half of reality TV shows, programs and movies all around the world suggest a reality of small but achievable goals. Non-dramatic standards. Even on American TV you often find such programs, and I know well that this is not an American reality. But such products of the media act as a consolation for a large number of people who feel unfulfilled. And the media sociologists know fairly well what they need to be offering the public.

NM: I'm intrigued by how these poems work as a conversant body. Can you talk about mirroring of the sudden "vision" of "Acupuncture" in "Children of Morality"?

> Moral was easily pointed at by a seven-year-old's ink-stained finger,
> perfect examples of vice or virtue
> there where time lays its eggs on a swamp

And speak to how the last line twists the theory that at seven years a child begins to reason; in this poem, "time" is "where" this "reason" will be hatched from the swamp of the primordial knowledge that archetypes will inhabit a body in every age that needs to lay blame:

> Where I grew up, moral had a form, body and name:
> a Cain, an unremorseful Mary Magdalene, a Ruth, a Delilah and a
> Rachel.

to

> And strangely, even the second generation didn't disappoint:
> their descendants wee another Cain, another Ruth,
> another Mary Magdalene who never grew up;

LL: By the way, finally, while searching on the internet, I found some epitaphs from citizens of ancient Rome and what impressed me especially were the qualities that were considered praiseworthy at the time, like: "man of honor," "just man," "devoted wife," "clean-living," "dutiful, honorable, chaste and modest," "never during bitter times did she shrink from loving duties," "faithful spouse," "good mother," etc., and I notice how much the perception of human virtues has changed through time. In our time, we rarely hear of these qualities mentioned as virtues. It seems that virtue, today, has to do more with one's ability to adapt, the pragmatic aspect of life, than it being a source of inspiration for the community. To put it another way, human virtues today are related to a more horizontal logic, or pragmatic logic than to a vertical one.

And the poem to which you refer, suggests a microcosm, the small town where I grew up where morality was simple, clear, in fact, stereotyped through particular individuals. Outside in the larger world, it becomes very difficult to morally orient oneself because out there people have other goals and relationships take on priority. Even art and literature do not seek heroes anymore, or absolute evil, but the ordinary man, complex and still vulnerable.

And, to continue with the poem: I grew up in a Muslim family, with a religious culture that was interrupted because of communism and despite this, the references (Mary Magdalen, Ruth, etc.,) are taken from the Bible and not from the Koran. So even I have made a pragmatic choice in this case because the reader is more familiar with biblical references even though this is simply a case of naming things.

the *plume* poetry interviews 1

NM: In "The Railway Boys," aren't the boys, before "They grow blurry and quiet," in possession of this same "knowing" by essence rather than by name?

> "What's north like?"
> "The people wear fur and have blue veins."
> "And south? What have you heard?"
> "People there think with their hearts and speak in gestures."

I very much love that poem. Why, I do not know, but while I was reading it scenes with Björk from the movie *Dancer in the Dark* were flashing across my mind's eye. If either of you can shed some light on that, I'd be grateful; otherwise I'll just chalk it up to the power of these absolutely transcendent, magical poems! Thank you both very much for this experience.

LL: Thank you! For me, too, this is a favorite poem. This poem deals with how one's childhood geography informs and affects the shape of their personality. Are the people who grow up near the sea, near train stations, in places with exits, different from those who grow up in the continental steppe or isolated villages in the mountains? I think they are. In truth, this whole poem has its origin in *country* music which, when I heard it for the first time seemed incredibly melancholic to me. I would call it an intelligent kind of melancholy. It can be associated with the American prairies, endless fields which make you feel a certain despair about the idea of life which can be read clearly as if it were written on the palm of your hand. Without any turns, surprises or exits. Lives that are recyclable. Endless monotony. This kind of music created this perception for me. Whereas in another poem titled "On the Other Side of the Mountain," I talk about how people who live on mountains have way more illusions than anyone else, believing that "on the other side of the mountain, life must certainly be better." In this case, what's impossible creates hope. On the contrary, living near the water, creates the illusion of the possibility to leave, the possibility of change. So what can we say of people who grew up where the entire world crosses, near train tracks, with the endless temptation to leave, escaping on top of a train? That they have the right to dream? I believe so. I mean that poetry has to do with the psychological impact of one's homeland, including here also the landscape itself.

January 1st, Dawn

After the celebrations at last everyone sleeps:
people, TV channels, telephones
and the year's recently-corrected digit.

Between the final night and the first day
a jagged piece of sky
as though seen from the open mouth of a whale.
Inside her belly and inside the belly of time,
there's no point worrying;
you glide along with it; she knows her course.
Inside her, you are digested slowly, painlessly.

And if you're lucky, like Jonah,
she'll spit you out on an island at some point
along with heaps of inorganic waste.

Everyone sleeps. A sweet hypothermic sleep.
But those few still awake
might hear the melancholy creaking of the wheelbarrow,
someone stealing stones from the rubble
for new walls going up just meters away.

The Railway Boys

Of course they're blond, all blond,
but easy to distinguish one from another
through the grease, smoke and coal dust.
They ride the train's whistle, effortlessly, as though riding buffalos.
They know each whistle's routine.
From a distance, they can tell which train
rides toward the cold north
and which one toward the south;
which railcar carries mail, addresses in longhand,
and which one passengers riding never to return.

When the freight train arrives,
they hurry to climb on top of wagons, enjoy a piece of sky
lying on their backs on wood logs.
This is only half of the journey; now
they're closer to the first star than to their homes.

This is the first test of manhood.
Everything else comes later, behind a broken boxcar,
with the girl with rust-colored hair.
Who was she? The first lover has no name of her own
but a baptismal one and a beautiful buck tooth.
Same as the second lover … the third.…
All clothes are excessive for the one prepared
to wear his own father's clothes*,
they're excessive for Aaron's son,
Aaron whom,
the only blasphemy
would keep away from the land of milk and honey.

Of course they're blond, all blond,

the railway boys. For them,
everything is possible. See how the first railcar returns
last, and the last one first,
when the locomotive switches lanes?

"What's north like?"
"The people wear fur and have blue veins."
"And south? What have you heard?"
"People there think with their hearts and speak in gestures."
On hot rails,
the air, like a concave mirror,
magnifies their slim bodies like the words "fur" and "heart."
They grow blurry and quiet.

And against his will, each one of them
will marry the wrong girl,
the one whose eyes are full of a long winter.
Among naked trees
it's impossible to lose the way home.

With time, train whistles died out;
buffalos turned into white, fluffy pups.
And the sleeves of the fathers' never-worn cloaks
point to a north and south that seem equally impossible.

---

*In the Bible, God ordered Moses: "And strip Aaron of his garments, and put them upon Eleazar his son: and Aaron shall be gathered unto his people, and shall die there." As punishment for his blasphemy, Aaron would not see the promised land, but his own son would.

Acupuncture

Among personal objects, inside a 2,100-year-old Chinese tomb,
archaeologists found several acupuncture items: nine needles,
four gold and five silver.
Long before diagnosing the cause,
ancient masters knew
pain is fought with pain.

It's quite simple: a range of needles pricking your arm
for a properly functioning heart and lungs.
Needles on the feet—to ease stress and insomnia.
A little pain here, and the impact is felt elsewhere
like a country's administrative capital, outside geographic borders.

Once, a group of explorers set out to plant a flag on the North
    pole.
At the heel of the globe. In the middle of the Arctic.
And before the mission could finish successfully
a world war had begun.
With scorching helmets, glory quenched thirst.
The impact was felt on the brain; on the short-term memory lobe.

When Russia used ideology as acupuncture—a needle over the
    Urals,
it impacted the pancreas that controls blood sugar:
America paid tenfold for whiskey through Prohibition
and Joyce's "immoral" *Ulysses*
stood in line at post offices waiting to be burnt.

The universe functions as a single body. Stars form lines of
    needles
carefully pinned to a wide woolly back.

Their impact is felt in the digestive tract. How can you begin a
   new day
without having fully absorbed yesterday's protein?

I was a child when my first teacher
mispronounced my last name twice. That pricked me like a
   needle.
A small needle in the earlobe. And suddenly
I saw clearly—it affected my vision.
I saw poetry,
the perfect disguise.

Children of Morality

It was the Europeans who taught indigenous people shame
starting with covering up intimate parts,
shame and a need for locks.

Other civilizations were luckier.
Moral was handed to them ready-made from above,
inscribed in stone tablets.

Where I grew up, moral had a form, body and name:
a Cain, an unremorseful Mary Magdalene, a Ruth, a Delilah and
    a Rachel.

Moral was easily pointed at by a seven-year-old's ink-stained
    finger,
perfect examples of vice or virtue
there where time lays its eggs on a swamp.

And so, I received the first moral lessons
without chewing them, like cough syrup;
everything else was more abstract,
under a chaste roof.

And strangely, even the second generation didn't disappoint:
their descendants were another Cain, another Ruth,
another Mary Magdalene who never grew up;
clichés were simultaneously risk and shelter for them,
like dry snow for Eskimo igloos.

Now I know so much more about morals, in fact, I might be a
    moralist,
with an index finger pointing like part of the rhetoric.

But without reference. What happened to those people?

A door opened by accident; light broke through by force
and, as in a dark room,
erased their silver bromide portraits
which were once of flesh and bone.

The Dead Are Watching Us

On the way to the Promised Land
everything set aside for tomorrow would spoil and rot—
mulberries, meat, even water. Tomorrow, to those people,
was a test of their faith.

But nothing was promised to my people
even though they've wandered for forty years.
They live in the Present Continuous.
Their epidermis hung on the line to dry.
As soon as they wake up
women turn on the radio; listen to music.
Music has a short incubation period.
As if it were a tumor, a taste for it brings more shame
than bruises on the face.

Nothing lasts for tomorrow.
They are fresh bait for sharks, who,
when wounded,
bite even themselves.

Their measurement is *yesterday, tradition*. They fear the dead,
"The dead are watching us. Be careful!
During the day, with hands soaked in mortar,
in the middle of sleep, at night ..."
They hang a dog tag on their necks, for every occasion,
reduced to three elements: name, number and ancestors' loans,
so that fate will easily identify them.

Or at least,
they're grateful when fate brushes past them,
because they could have been Limoz, the hermit,

who used to find warmth in a cave
burning scraps of paper for hours on end,
or Dilaver with Down syndrome written in his eyes and heart.
Their thin skin
cannot bear the joke
of being "the chosen ones".

But sometimes, on a full moon,
or as it's otherwise known, "Wolf Moon,"
they can see clearly. A moneylender's fiendish chuckle
broadens their faces.
According to their calculations, what's delayed today
will certainly arrive twofold tomorrow.

Live Music

Nothing consoles you best before sleep
than this pub of cheap beer and *live* music,
the callous voice of the singer and lyrics
thrown forcefully together inside *rima pobre.**

An argument in the corner,
marks the only difference between week days
and Friday night. That and the phosphorescence of free,
platonic sex. What happens on board, stays on board.

At the edge of the table, wet receipts
with a circled digit at the bottom
are indulgence's shortcut from purgatory to paradise
(not worth questioning any of this).

A sweet apathy of nothingness and a mockery
latches on to the singer.
"Oh man, she started too high, won't be able to reach the
 refrain!"
"You think so?"
"You wanna bet?"
when nobody really needs to hear a refrain.
They're here precisely for the holes,
the large holes in an amateur pub,
as inside artisan bread
with its smooth crust on the outside.

Exiting here is even less ceremonial.
Picture exiting a barber shop,
where, sympathetically, after a haircut, according to ritual,

the barber gives you a fresh slap on the neck:
"Get up now," he urges you, "it's someone else's turn!"

*rima pobre: rhyme between words that have the same grammatical structure.

1 Janar, Në Të Gdhirë

Pas feste, të gjithë flenë më në fund:
njerëzit, stacionet televizive, telefonat
dhe shifra e sapokorrektuar e vitit.

Midis natës së fundit dhe ditës së parë,
një copë qiell i dhëmbëzuar
si i parë nga goja e hapur e një balene.
Në barkun e saj dhe në barkun e kohës,
nuk ka arsye të vrasësh mendjen;
ti lëviz bashkë me të; ajo e di se ç'rrugë merr,
dhe brenda saj tretesh ngadalë dhe pa dhimbje.

Dhe po të jesh me fat si profeti Jonah,
me siguri, dikur do të të teshtijë në ndonjë breg,
bashkë me dhjetëra mbeturina të tjera inorganike.

Të gjithë flenë. Një gjumë i ëmbël hipotermik.
Por, ata të paktë që janë akoma zgjuar,
mund të dëgjojnë gërvimën e trishtuar të qerres
qe vjedh gurët nga një rrënojë,
për një ngrehinë të re, vetëm pak metra më tutje.

Djemtë e Hekurudhës

Padyshim janë biondë, të gjithë biondë,
për të dalluar lehtësisht njëri-tjetrin
midis grasos, tymit dhe pluhurit të qymyrit.
Ata ngasin sirenat, lehtësisht sikur ngasin buajt.
Ua njohin huqet.
Prej së largu e dallojnë lehtë se cili prej trenave
shkon drejt veriut të ftohtë
dhe cili prej tyre drejt jugut;
cili prej vagonave ka postën, adresat e shkruara me shkrim dore
dhe cili prej tyre pasagjerë që shkojnë për t'mos u kthyer.

Dhe kur mbërrin treni i mallrave,
ata marrin vrull dhe ngjiten mbi vagona. Shijojnë një copë qiell
të shtrirë, në shpinë, mbi lëndë druri.
Kjo është gjysma e rrugës; tashti
ata janë më afër yllit të parë se sa shtëpisë.

Kjo është prova e hershme e burrërisë.
Të tjerat vijnë më vonë, pas vagonit të prishur,
me një vajzë me flokë ngjyrë ndryshku.
Kush qe ajo? E dashura e parë nuk ka një emër
por një stërdhëmbësh të bukur dhe një emër pagëzimi.
Dhe as a dyta ... as e treta ...
Çdo rrobë është e tepërt për atë që është përgatitur
të veshë rrobat e të atit*,
është e tepërt për të birin e Aaronit, të cilin,
blasfemia e vetme
do ta mbajë larg tokës ku rrjedh qumësht edhe mjaltë.

Pa dyshim janë biondë, të gjithë biondë
djemtë e hekurudhës. Për ta,

gjithcka është e mundur. Shihe se si vagoni i parë kthehet
i fundit, dhe i fundit i pari,
kur lokomotiva ndërron kah?

"Si është veriu, vallë?"
"Atje njerëzit veshin gëzofë dhe kanë damarë të kaltër."
"Po jugu? C'thuhet?"
"Atje njerëzit mendojnë me zemër dhe flasin me gjeste."
Mbi shinat e nxehta,
ajri, si një pasqyrë konkave
zgjeron kurmet e tyre të hollë dhe fjalët "gëzofë" e "zemër".
duke i bërë të heshtur e të paqartë.

Dhe kundër vullnetit të tyre, të gjithë ata,
do të martohen me vajzën e gabuar,
atë që ka një dimër të gjatë në sy.
Midis pemëve lakuriqe,
është e vështirë ta ngatërrosh rrugën për në shtëpi.

Me kohë, sirenat u zbutën;
buajt u shndërruan në ca kone të bardha leshtore.
Kurse veriu dhe jugu kullojnë njëlloj të mundur
prej mëngëve të mantelit akoma të paveshur të etërve.

*Në Bibël, Zoti e urdheron Moisiun: "Zhvishe Aaronin nga rrobat e tij dhe vishja të birit,
Eleazarit dhe aty Aroni do të bashkohet me popullin e tij dhe do të vdesë". Si ndëshkim për
blasfeminë e tij, Aaroni nuk do ta shihte më Tokën e Premtuar, por i biri po.*

Akupunkturë

Midis sendeve personale, në një varr kinez 2100 vjeçar,
arkeologët gjetën disa objekte akupunkture: nëntë gjilpëra
    metalike
katër prej ari dhe pesë argjendi.
Shumë më përpara se të analizohej shkaku,
mjeshtrit e lashtë e dinin
se dhimbja luftohet me dhimbje.

Është fare e thjeshtë: për mushkëritë dhe funksionimin e zemrës
ndihmojnë një varg gjilpërash të ngulura në krah
E ato në shputë, lehtësojnë stresin dhe pagjumësinë.
Një dhimbje të vogël këtu, dhe efekti ndjehet diku larg
si qendra administrative të shteteve, jashtë kufijve admistrativë.

Dikur, një tufë eksploratorësh, u nisën për të ngulur një flamur
    në pol.
Mu në thembrën e globit. Në mes të akullit. Dhe pa mbaruar
    mirë misioni,
një luftë botërore kishte nisur.
Lavdia shuante etjen me helmeta të nxehta.
Efekti qe në tru; në lobin e kujtesës afatshkurtër.

Kur Rusia përdorte ideologjinë si akupunkturë- një gjipërë mbi
    Urale.
Efekti qe në pankreas, kontrolli mbi sheqerin në gjak:
Amerika e Prohibicionit e blinte wiskin dhjetëfish.
dhe Uliksi "imoral" i Xhois-it,
priste radhen per t'u djegur në zyrat postare.

Kozmosi fuksionon si një trup. Yjet krijojnë vargje gjilpërash
të ngulura me kujdes në një kurriz të madh leshtor.

Efektet e tyre ndjehen në tretje. Si mund të nisësh një ditë të re,
pa përtypur mirë proteinën shtazore të së djeshmes?

Dhe më pas, veshi. Mësuesja ime e parë
e shqiptoi dy herë gabim mbiemrin tim.Ishte therëse si një
    gjilpërë.
Një gjilpërë në llapën e vogël të veshit. Dhe krejt papritur
pashë qartë, Efekti qe ne shikim.
Pashë poezinë,
fshehjen e përkryer pas anonimatit.

Fëmijët e Moralit

Ishin evropianët, të parët që u mësuan indigjenëve turpin
duke filluar nga mbulimi i pjesëve intime.

Popuj të tjerë, kanë qenë më me fat
Morali u ka ardhur i gatshëm nga lart,
i shkruar në pllaka guri.

Atje ku unë jam rritur, morali kishte formë, trup dhe emër:
një Kain, një Maria Magdalenë e papenduar, një Ruth, Dalilë e
    Rashelë.

Morali tregohej lehtësisht me gishtin me bojë të një shtatëvjeçari
shembuj të përkryer vesi e virtyti,
atje ku koha i lëshon vezët mbi moçal.

Kështu, pra, mësimet e para të moralit, i mora pa i përtypur
si shurup për kollë;
çdo gjë tjetër ishte më abstrakte,
nën një çati tjegullthyer.

Dhe çuditërisht ata s'të zhgënjenin as në breznine e dytë:
pasardhësit e tyre,
ishin një tjetër Kain, një tjetër Ruth, një tjetër Maria Magdalenë,
që nuk rriteshin; klisheja ishte njëkohësisht rreziku dhe mbrojtja
    për ta,
si dëbora e thatë për igloot eskimeze.

Tani di shumë më tepër për moralin, madje mund të jem një
    moraliste,
me gishtin tregues, si pjesë të retorikës.
Por pa referencë. Ç'u bë me ta?

Një derë u hap padashje, drita çau me forcë,
dhe si në një laborator filmi,
ajo shkërmoqi portretet e tyre në bromid argjendi,
që dikur, mund të kenë qenë prej mishi dhe kocke.

Të Vdekurit Po Na Vëzhgojnë

Në rrugën drejt Tokës së Premtuar
çdo gjë që ruhej për nesër, prishej, qelbej:
manat, mishi, madje dhe uji. E nesermja, për atë popull,
ishte prova e besimit.

Ndërsa këtyre njerëzve, edhe pse sorollaten për dyzet vjet,
nuk u është premtuar asgjë. Ata jetojnë në të Tashmen e
    Vazhduar.
Epiderma e tyre e varur në tela për tharje, në oborr. Sapo zgjohen,
gratë hapin radion; dëgjojnë muzikë,
muzika ka periudhë të shkurtër inkubacioni
edhe pse gjëndrrat e saj janë më të turpshme
se shenjat mavi të rrahjeve në fytyrë.

Asgjë nuk mbetet për nesër.
Ata janë mish i freskët për peshkaqenët, të cilët,
kur janë të plagosur,
kafshojnë edhe vetveten.

Masa e tyre është e djeshmja, tradita. U druhen të vdekurve,
"Të vdekurit na vëzhgojnë. Kujdes!" Ditën, me duart me llaç,
në mes të dremitjes natën…

Matrikulën prej inoksi e mbajnë të varur në qafë, për çdo rast,
të thjeshtuar në tre elementë: emri, numri, dhe pengu i të parëve,
lehtësisht për t'u identifikuar nga fati.

Ose së paku,
duhet të jenë mirënjohës kur anashkalohen prej tij,
sepse fare mirë mund të ishin Limozi që ngrohet me letra në një
    shpellë

apo Dilaveri me sy e zemër mongoloide.
E paretet e tyre të holluara,
nuk e pëballojnë dot gjithë këtë humor,
-të qenit "të zgjedhur".

Por nganjëherë, në hënë të plotë
ose siç quhet ndryshe në "Hënë Ujku"
ata mund të shohin qartë. Një nënqeshje djallëzore
prej fajdexhiu u zgjeron fytyrën.
Sipas llogarisë së tyre, ajo që iu është vonuar sot,
do t'u kthehet patjetër e dyfishuar nesër.

Live

S'ka asgjë më ngushëlluese para gjumit
se ky klub me birrë të lirë e muzikë *live*.
kallot në zërin e këngëtares, lirikat
e rrasura me forcë brenda rimave *pobre**
që derdhen si mishrat, jashtë grykës së korsesë.

Po kështu edhe birra. Një zënkë atje në qoshe,
bën ndryshimin e vetëm midis ditëve të javës
dhe të premtes mbrëma. Dhe fosfori i një seksi të lirë
platonik. Çfarë ndodh në bord, mbetet në bord.

Në cep të tavolinës, faturat e lagura
me një shifër e rrumbullakosur në fund,
janë indulgjenca që shkurtojnë rrugën nga purgatori në parajsë.
(nuk ia vlen t'i vësh në dyshim)

Një apati e ëmbël hiçi dhe qesëndisje
kapet pas gruas që këndon.
"Aha, e filloi shumë lart; nuk e kap refrenin!"
"A thua?"
"E vëmë me bast",
kur askujt nuk i duhet një refren. Ata ndodhen këtu pikërisht për
    vrimat,
vrimat e mëdha në një klub amatoresk
si brenda një buke artizanale me kore të lëmuar
që ta bëjnë të lehtë qenien.

Dhe daljen, akoma më pak ceremoniale.
E keni parash daljen prej berberit,
që me dashamirësi pas qethjes, sipas ritualit,
të jep një shuplakë të freskët në qafë:

"Ngrihu tani, është radha e tjetrit!"?

Rimë e varfër- rimë midis fjalëve të së njejtës kategori gramatikore.

Nin Andrews
interviewed by Nancy Mitchell

NM: Hey Nin! I'm getting a serious kick out of this feature. How did you come (no, we will not stoop to such a low-lying pun-plum) upon this idea for this particular installment in the continuing adventures of O?

NA: As you might know, the first book I ever wrote was *The Book of Orgasms*. Ever since I have suffered the consequences. Because you can't just write a book like that and expect that anyone will want to hear or read or publish anything else you write. It's a problem. When I give readings, people want me to provide an orgasm or two. Sometimes I don't feel like it. Maybe I have a headache. I ate too much. Or I am wearing the wrong outfit for an orgasm. And really, you can't just keep having the same old orgasms over and over again. One night I decided I'd had enough. I announced it at the beginning of a poetry reading, *I'm so sorry. But tonight there will be no orgasms.* One red-faced man protested loudly. A woman in fishnet stockings got up to leave. A student in the front row raised his hand and asked, *Why do you think we're here?*

Clearly, I needed to write new orgasm poems. But I had this fear. What if there is a limit to Nin Andrews' orgasm poems? Or worse, a limit to the appeal of Nin Andrews' orgasm poems? Granted, I used to pride myself on the idea that the orgasms chose me and only me. I even had this mini-poem on my desk, a take-off on Frank O'Hara's "A True Account of Talking to the Sun at Fire Island" that went like this:

> The orgasm woke me this morning, loud
> and clear, saying, "Hey, Nin Andrews,
> I've been trying to wake you for hours.
> Don't think you can ignore me. Because

> you're the only poet I've ever chosen
> to speak to personally."

But I decided I needed to introduce the orgasm to other poets, poets whose work I admire, whose words and attitudes and ideas have moved me so deeply, they're wandering around in my brain late a night, sometimes having moonlit snacks or sipping martinis in the dark, other times sitting down at my desk, chatting or fooling around with my lines and dreams. And I, with theirs. The orgasm, of course, was only too happy to enjoy a three-some. I have to admit, I was a little sad to realize I wasn't the only poet the orgasm enjoyed.

NM: Ah, Ms. Nin, as much as your agile wit and charm do dazzle me near dumb, this series reveals not only the prodigiousness of your imagination, but a deep intimacy with these poems; no doubt a result of your novitiate residency within the body of each to which you pay homage. It's clear that like the Dude, you have abided, long eye/I; only a devoted scholar could note such meticulous architectural detail.

Now, in this particular series of Orgasm poems—hey ... why are there fewer words for the female orgasm than for female sex organs ... is it a Taoist thing like *what can't be seen can't be named ... the unnamable is the eternally real?* ... and why the proliferation of words for that tacky evidence of male orgasm; they sound like hip-hop frat boy-nicknames; Jissom, Jism, Jizz, lil' Spunk, Spurt, Spooge and, of course, Squirt.

Orgasm, to me at least, sounds like an unfortunate implosion of organ and spasm, and looks like an orange, gourd-shaped organ writhing on a tree branch in a Dali landscape ... intermittently gassy ... hmm ... but I digress....

NA: Yes, I think you're correct. The female orgasm is that which cannot be named. And why would it want to be? Consider the male names you have listed, and you know it doesn't want any part of that conversation. After all, it was Adam who named everything, and thereby limited his experience of all that is. Eve had nothing to do with it.

The female orgasm likes to live life incognito. She's like a member of the CIA. She doesn't allow a definition, not even another word for orgasm. She doesn't want to get mixed up with names or ideas or hairstyles or the wrong kinds of people. You know who I mean. After all, she has so many lives, and inside each one, there is another, each one defying definition.

But I have to tell you, you aren't the only writer who has complained to me about the word orgasm. The late Eleanor Ross Taylor once asked me the very same thing. "Nin," she said, "I like your *Book of Orgasms*, but that's such a vulgar word. Can't you call them something else? Like fish? Or horses?" We tried, but the orgasm would have nothing to do with fish and horses. You can try it, too, and see what you think. Call them lemons, Buddha, Sarah, Miso soup, it makes no difference. The orgasm won't respond.

NM: Well, I'm honored to be in such esteemed company; tell me, did Miss Eleanor, a southerner like myself, call you *Nee-yen* with our penchant for making a lil' ole one syllable two?

NA: Oh, Eleanor. She was so lovely, so well-spoken, so smart. She did have an accent but not as strong as that. And she wasn't a natural admirer of the orgasm. She made allowances for me.

NM: Again, I digress. Now, if I know anything about Lady O—no; you're right; it won't work; she's not even batting an eyelash—she wants what she wants; she wants *who* she wants to come inside. Like Lola, "what O wants, O gets," but never by asking.

Male or female, speaking or spoken of, the O in these poems lures us across the threshold into what *appear* to be familiar, faithful, dutiful homages to prosody, device and even ars poetica. Unless we pay close attention—to distract us, O has slipped a mickey into our drink, queued up all our favorite tunes, surround sound, but not too loud—that comes later—we'll miss that O has made just a few renovations … oh, okay, maybe just knocked out a wall or two … to the original.

As I don't want to deny our readers the pleasures of such discoveries, I'll note just a few examples:

"In the Orgasm Supermarket": yes, we know it's after Ginsberg's "A Supermarket In California," and we understand the inclusion of Lorca alludes to Ginsberg's address, but it isn't until your poem's second stanza's "as if I were walking the aisles" is contrasted with Ginsberg's "I went into the neon fruit supermarket" do we realize O has split the scene, although the previous stanza is strewn with clues: "and a loneliness / brought on by my persistent longing, the full moon and longing for you."

Yes, O has hijacked Whitman's ferry, re-purposed it with oars and eloped with Lorca! Yes, I'm afraid O has kicked poor Mr. Ginsberg to the curb, left him "howling" with a "headache" under a "full moon" with only a crust of "Shwebel's bread" to last him the "infinity" of unrequited "longing."

And do we, can we blame O? Who would choose to mingle with "pointy bearded, lonely grubber(s), poking meats, fruits" greasy with the sheen of neon's ghastly gleam if one could flee to a sentient province where one sobs and "leaves sing in the wind, rain begins to fall, dogs howl and dust cries out beneath" our "bare feet"?

NA: Yes, the orgasm prefers to end up with Lorca. He is irresistible, right? I remember years ago, sitting in a class with David Lehman, one of my all-time favorite professors—his passion for poetry runs so deep, it's contagious—and he began quoting Lorca:

> When the moon rises
> the ocean covers the earth
> and the heart feels like an island in infinity.
>
> No one eats oranges
> under a full moon.
> One must eat
> fruit that is cold and green."

Hearing that poem for the first time, I thought I was going to break open. I asked David to repeat it, and he did. What I felt then—it wasn't that my whole body went so cold, no fire could every warm me, but quite the opposite.

I've seen that Lorca poem translated in different ways—the last line, for example, as "one must eat green fruit and ice," maybe a more literal translation. But every translation makes my heart ache. Just the sound of the title in Spanish, "*La luna asoma*," it's enough to make me swoon.

NM: Do swoon dear, and I'll swoon right along with you! Oh, yes, Lorca, and homages to two of my favorites, Vallejo and Jiminez … ah, boys … you and your Spanish with its perfect sexual symmetry; no mystery why we find O in tributes to this holy trinity.

In the poignant, tender and funny "In Orgasm in Therapy," after Jiminez's "Sea," we find O's little rowboat in the above poem has foundered on the rocks; premenopausal, wracked with a crisis of confidence, she fears she's no longer "that kind of orgasm" who, "without even a companion or a compliment" could enjoy the "pleasures of naked solitude" without at least a cover-up or a caftan! O pleads for help—"I need an iron, a hair comb, a masseuse / to smooth the endless mess in myself"—and in doing so has the orgasm's nerve to ask of the poem the unthinkable: to compromise its poetic integrity and suspend Jimenez's principal of non-adornment. Yet, the audacity of that request is redeemed by the absolute fidelity to Jiminez's signature tone of desolation.

Like Madeline Kahn sings in Mel Brooks' classic film *Blazing Saddles,* m.youtube.com/watch?v=-05BWHilRBA, she's "tired." "But now, in her mature years, so much effort is required / just to exist." Exhausted, she petulantly kvetches. "Some nights, panting, / she wonders, What is this? Childbirth?"

But even this rich humor can't disguise the pathos of her crisis; we empathetically despair at the therapist's useless platitude to "Just be your infinite matchless self"; our arm around O's shoulders in solidarity, "we both look out at the window at the sea / with its smooth waves rising and falling," and together ask "But who is that?" And the unequivocal answer we get, "the gulls screaming like women in grief," is an image so utterly, heartbreakingly gorgeous it borders on blasphemy.

Nin Andrews, thank you, thank you; this conversation has been an unprecedented delight, and your poems a double pleasure; true homages, they respectfully and faithfully return us to that which they pay tribute.

the *plume* poetry interviews 1

THE CURSE
after James Wright

You might think by now the orgasm would be used to it. After all, he has seen the annual crop of young lovers pull off the highway in Poland, Ohio, and step over the barbed wire fences to lay their blankets in the empty pastures. He has watched them closely, their eyes lit with anguish and desire as they gasp for breath. He has grazed freely on their nude skin, there beneath the willow trees.

But when all is said and done, when the lovers return to their clothes, their minds, their cars and homes, they slough off the orgasm and leave him outside like a peeping Tom to peer through their windows at what was so briefly his: the slender legs, the bent swan necks, the soft flesh of inner arms. And the orgasm realizes how alone he is. How he has no soul to call his own, no body to break open again and again or to shuck off like a husk of corn. There is no such thing as a blessing, he sighs, as his mind darkens with twilight, as the wind sweeps softly through the grass.

HENRIETTA'S DREAM SONGS
after John Berryman

1.
God damn college guys!
They're all rats, Henrietta says.
In her head is romance. She's not shy.
She's not lonesome. Much.
But tonight is a Friday night solo
in her twin bed
in the dorm called Rockefeller
(everyone calls it the john)
and her sweet little ass is itching.
Pityish, it is. So maybe she is just
a regular American woman, not
the wild girl in her dreams
always out with some boneheaded guy.

2.
I wonder, one of her boneheads says. *Doubtful.*
But let's you and me investigate this.
Come, Henrietta. Diminish me.
Say yes.

3.
College men, Henrietta thinks, *are boring.*
She's sick of thinning & games of guess
and, moreover, she says, *My mother told me*
you gotta suffer to be gorgeous.
That's why she's gorging on chicken
paprika and rice. And God,
I want to scream, she's gross.
At least eat with your mouth shut! I say

and go faint with disgust, but she tells me
the bonehead of her dreams
likes his woman hungry, *all right?*

4.
So when Henrietta stands up and pirouettes
(she's wearing a gauzy purple skirt
and a leotard that clings to her bra-less breasts)
the college boys turn and gasp.
(They're such low-lifes, yes?)
One whistles & shouts, *Hey Babe,
Want this?* He points at his dick
& Henrietta feels almost as delicious
as a greasy chicken leg.

The orgasm, Henrietta tells me, *is God.*
She's smoking dope on the chapel steps
I watch the wind lift her black hair
as she inhales deeply, like she's sucking it all in
and in. And in. Then she gets all weepy
and sleepy and hungry, and says
she wants to eat this boy called Hans
who put his hand in her panties. Wet and hot-like,
she sighs, *I could eat my Hans
whole. I could eat my Hans Solo.*
And then adds,
I'm a poet. Yep, Henrietta's a burning hot soul!

It's true. Henrietta is on fire.
Henrietta is stripping off all her clothes.

The Similarity Between My Life and an Orgasm
after Robert Bly's "The Resemblance Between My Life and a Dog"

I never intended to have an orgasm. Believe me—
it just showed up. I had no choice
but to act like a dog, panting and wagging my tail.

It's good to accept the orgasm. But I'm not one
to watch it in the mirror. It deranges my face.
I never look as pretty as I'd like.

I always expect to have time
but the orgasm is gone in a flash.
Don't think about it, I tell myself. Then I think about it.

The orgasm is like a bird.
If I try to hold on, it flies away
or breaks into wild singing.

Some days I fear the orgasm is abandoning me.
It's flown south for winter.
I wonder if it ever loved me,
Or I, it.

THE ORGASM IN THERAPY
after Jiminez's "Sea"

It seems the orgasm is struggling to find herself.
(And I, her, alas.)
Oh, she whines, *my life is such a mess!*
I need an iron, a hair comb, a masseuse
to smooth the endless mess in my self…
To show me once again
the pleasures of naked solitude.

She thinks how it used to be simple
without even a companion or a compliment.
She was that kind of orgasm. And proud of it.
But now, in her mature years, so much effort is required
just to exist. Some nights, panting,
she wonders, *What is this? Childbirth?*

Just be yourself, the therapist suggested.
Just be your infinite matchless self.
But who is that? she asks
and looks out the window at the sea
with its smooth waves rising and falling,
the gulls screaming like women in grief.

BUT I AM THAT ONE
after Jiminez

I am that one hovering
above you whom you don't see
(or pretend not to)
who sometimes manages to visit you,
but who, too often, you forget.
(Or say you do.) Oh why
did I have to fall in love with you,
who remains calm when I whisper,
who ignores me when I beg, who walks away
tossing her long, black hair behind her
sashaying into the night,
her soft white skin,
cold as the moon?

In the Orgasm Supermarket
after Allen Ginsberg and Garcia Lorca

What thoughts I have of you tonight as I walk the suburban sidewalks of Poland, Ohio, under the flickering streetlights with an ache in my bones and a loneliness brought on by my persistent solitude, the full moon, and a longing for you, love, yes you whom I picture again and again in all your lovely shapes and sizes and flavors

as if I were walking the lit aisles of my supermarket of desire, selecting orgasms from every you, or rather from every occasion with you, orgasms as ripe and red as these heirloom tomatoes, as illegal as dark chocolate, as ordinary and soft as a loaf of Shwebel's bread, and some so cold and green they must be eaten under the stars on a night like this

when I look up at the sky and see not the stars or the moon but a thousand faces of you, a thousand shapes of you, each so soft, so nude, so white, I sob out loud until the leaves sing in the wind, the rain begins to fall, and the dogs howl with me as the dust cries out beneath my bare feet, and my heart becomes a rowboat in infinity.

I Know a Man
after Robert Creeley

the orgasm says,
and he's, like, always talking,
so I say to him,
Hush why don't you?
Enjoy the night!
The stars are shining.
And he says, *Baby*
I can't see a fucking thing!
And I say, *Slow down*
for Christ's sake.
And he says what a man
always says, even if
he doesn't say it:
I'm driving,
baby. I'm driving
this GD car—
so you hang on
as long as you can.
Let the wind fool with
your red hair.

the *plume* poetry interviews 1

In Memory of the Female Orgasm

after W. H. Auden's "In Memory of Sigmund Freud"

There are so many of us to mourn.
Our grief, after all, has never been made public.
For we do not wish to expose our frailty and anguish.
Besides, whom would we talk to? And who would listen?
Some old orgasm doctor? Another male
to threaten or flatter us or ask our obedience
as if it were as simple as that?
Or to enter our shadows with a flashlight
and seek the fauna of the night?
And would he cure us? If so, how?
By analyzing our parts? Our past?
By causing us to abandon our wardrobe of excuses,
those masks and patterns of frustration,
and wishes for revenge?
All that rage against men who thank God
instead of us?

Would the doctor question our posers? Our Fakers?
Those among us who let out such convincing utterances,
their features replicating bliss,
their one word, *Yes!*, a fib?
Should we explain such protective imitations?
How the female orgasm has lived among enemies too long?
That even our honey is nothing but fear and worry?
We are calmest when assured of escape,
or lost in the grass of neglect—lonely, yes,
but safe to feel precious again, and the need for love
when no one is looking.

the *plume* poetry interviews 1

What delectable creature we become then,
our large sad eyes opening in wonder
begging dumbly of the evening air with each gasp.

To the Orgasm
in memoriam

after César Vallejo

Love, I no longer look for you
or feel you in the warm breeze of a summer afternoon.
Nor do I worry how long you will stay away
or where you've been hiding all this time.
Nor do I seek you out
or call for you at dusk.

For I am outside my body now
watching the sun set over the water,
remembering how we used to play
at this late hour.
Nothing could stop us,
not the neighbors stomping overhead,
not your boss's voice on the answering machine,
not the bill collector banging at the door.
Sometimes, remember? You made me cry.
Other times we screamed and danced.
And many other times we simply sighed
and sighed.
But gradually we grew calm. Or I did.
Yes, calm, like an evening prayer,
a ritual at the end of the day.
We held on to one another
lingering at the entrance of night,
as if we could keep each other
from sinking into that dark lake.

THE SIX REALMS OF THE ORGASM
after Claire Bateman's book The Locals

In the first realm of the orgasm, a vote is taken to see which humans are allowed entry.

In the second realm of the orgasm, also known as the suburbs, all orgasms remain silent and offer only controlled doses of euphoria.

In the third realm of the orgasm, also known as the business district, orgasms are tracked, counted, and rated for their annual performances. In this realm orgasms occur three times a week, and never on a Monday.

In the fourth realm, also known as the government offices, orgasms take balletic leaps into the dark. What happens next is classified information.

In the fifth realm, also known as the Vatican, orgasms call out to God and moan about the fleeting nature of existence. Some seek newer and younger lovers to ward off feelings of mortality.

In the sixth realm, or the grave, the orgasm wakes to discover one of three things: a) it has been reincarnated (b) it is but a ghost or a memory of yesterday's orgasm, or (c) it is with the angels now, setting the sky on fire.

the *plume* poetry interviews 1

The Sleeping Orgasm
after Larry Levis

Once an orgasm clung to a man's shoulders for dear life. Why it chose this man's shoulders from a long line of shoulders, it couldn't say. Only that the man went on working without looking up, without looking back. So the orgasm took the shape of a wren and flapped its wings. It took the shape of a hat and sunk down over the man's brow. It took the shape of a small sun and warmed the man's neck. But the man still didn't notice it.

How could he? He was too busy, working over the gleaming machinery at Tyson's meat factory, slicing and packaging birds into drum sticks and thighs and breasts while he thought of his ex-wife who left him with a pile of unpaid bills, like the bad weather—the Polar vortex bringing record cold to his town, like the Iraq War, which was just beginning. At least he was packaging dead chickens, he thought, not dead Iraqis. He sometimes looked on the bright side.

On the way home from work, the orgasm still clinging to his shoulders, the man walked briskly over the town's bridge. He listened as the river called out to him, *Jump! Please jump!* But the man did not jump, even as the wind stung his face, even as a feeling of inconsolable despair wrapped around his heart. *Is this all there is to life?* he wondered as the orgasm hovered above him, afraid of what might happen next.

The man simply tucked his head in his coat and walked home to his doublewide where he flopped down on the couch, too tired to take off his work clothes, and fell into a deep sleep. But oh, what a sleep it was! Only then could the orgasm cover the man like a warm blanket and listen as his breath became a raspy hum. The man dreamt he was a boat in the sea, the waves were rocking him, slowly at first, then washing over his toes, his legs, his belly. He cried out again and again, but didn't wake to hear his own high-pitched voice. Sleep, the orgasm realized, was the only orgasm this man ever had.

David Clewell
interviewed by Nancy Mitchell

As both our schedules had been whipped into a froth by the tail of a wicked semester's end, and as poet David Clewell's window of internet access was limited, rather than the volley of e-mails typical of my Special Feature interviews, we had an "old skool" real-time phone conversation! And I'm so happy we did, as otherwise I would have missed the warm richness, the cadences of his lovely voice, and his wonderful, spontaneous laugh.

Below, as an introduction to the selection "Between the Sixties and the Saucers and the Willy-Nilly Gods—Let Alone the Vagaries of Ordinary Mortals—It's Hard to Know Who Needs Believing Most," is our free associative exchange of an hour or more, which is not unlike the narrative arc of this delightful and provocative Special Feature.

NM: David, I was mesmerized and dizzy as I read this moving-at-the-speed-of-light narrative which begins at "the slippery junction of 1967 and 1968." I held on for dear life as the extravagantly incongruous events chronologized in "iii. Disturbances in the 1967 Space-Time Continuum" streamed into one raging river, plunging toward inevitable, dangerous falls. You articulate the schizoid zeitgeist, the collective chaos, without sacrificing precision, or distinction, so well; I see a psychedelic Picasso's *Guernica* studded with portraits of the "Heavies."

And, oh, the delicious irony in the only "rocks," however slippery, that we can cling to as the waters swirl menacingly around us are the main characters, the space aliens who have landed at the "State Junction 6 and 63" in Ashland, Nebraska, and the 22-year-old patrolman Herbert Schrimer who has witnessed them!

You've subverted the usual Hollywood version as aliens as a vastly superior intelligence; your aliens, for all their supposed know-how, have landed in Ashland, Nebraska!

DC: Yes, they, perhaps, are wiser than humans, but are equally hapless.

NM: It seems your narrator is nonjudgmental, detached, almost like the space aliens? So, you're saying Schrimer's belief system, just doing his job, prevents him from assimilating another perspective, so much that he sublimates the experience so deeply it can only be retrieved under hypnosis almost a year later, is not under judgment?

DC: What interests me, in some ways touches me, is how much people need to believe in something greater than themselves. This need keeps people locked in their work ethic, even when presented with evidence to the contrary ... it's the faith itself I'm interested in...how "faith" dictates behavior, actions in accordance with that faith. It isn't so much what one believes in, but rather the degree of faith one has in that belief that determines ...

NM: One's fate?

DC: Well, yes; in Schrimer's case, his belief system of "just doing his job" justifies, no, determines, his detachment from experience, an experience which could change his belief system and therefore his life.

NM: His Colgate shield, so to speak?

DC: Yes, and in the case of the aliens, their interest is, at first, benign, but kindly—they hope they can do some good for our world by what they observe, by connecting....

NM: ... "at first"? Because at first the aliens "believe" that humans will evolve out of stasis if they accept the existence of aliens via experience? And when they realize that Schrimer's belief system is impervious, their own belief system is therefore challenged?

DC: Yes, and they realize that if their existence becomes a belief system, it, like other systems, will close the door to possibilities of assimilating other experiences. Therefore:

> We want you to believe in us—but not too much.
> —alien's final words to Schrimer, "recovered" in 1968.

NM: Okay, so we're doomed?

DC: Not really; it's these beliefs, this faith that keeps us humans alive, moving from one day to the next.

NM: So, "as long as we keep going we're not gone?"

DC: You got it!

DC: Yep.

NM: Readers! Buckle up for a wild, exhilarating ride!

Between the '60s and the Saucers and the Willy-Nilly Gods—Let Alone the Vagaries Of Ordinary Mortals—It's Hard to Know Who Needs Believing Most

i. All He Knew to Say

Saw a flying saucer at State Junction 6 and 63. Believe it or not.
 —Ashland, Nebraska, patrolman Herbert Schirmer's log-out entry for December 3, 1967 (3:00 a.m.)

Because he was twenty-two years old, naturally he thought he
 knew
everything, had already seen whatever there was to see,
and near the end of his shift, 2:20 a.m., it was just his luck
that the blinking red lights of a disabled truck at the roadside
would mean a slightly longer night than he was looking for.
But in his cruiser's high-beams was something else completely:
a metallic craft with illuminated portholes and some kind of
 crazy
catwalk around it, hovering soundlessly a few feet off the ground.
He watched it slowly rising in the crisp Nebraska air, passing
directly over his car, lighting up the sky before it disappeared
like just another shot in the dark.

                                    Back at the station to log out
before heading home, where he'd try hard to close his wide-open
 eyes,
he discovered that his routine, ten-minute final swing through
 town
had taken an extra half-hour. He wrote down his fourteen words
to prove he wasn't quite speechless. Because he was an officer of
 the law,

he knew by heart the Miranda right-to-remain-silent bit, but he
 was also
twenty-two, and no way on Earth would he leave it at that for
 long—
believe the-rest-of-what-happened-or-not-out-there. Or not.

ii. A Little Too Quick to Respond

Are you the watchman of this place?
 —alien's first words to Schirmer, part of the lost half-hour
 "recovered" during hypnosis sessions in 1968

And because he was a twenty-two-year-old officer of the law, he
 simply answered
Sure without asking any questions of his own, such as what
they could possibly mean by *this place*, more or less, if anything
 at all
beyond this immediate intersection of small-town country roads.
 Probably
he wasn't thinking even as big as Ashland, let alone Nebraska or
 the rest
of the unsuspecting country—and especially not the whole
 precariously
lightheaded planet, where somehow they suddenly found
 themselves at that odd
interrogative moment spinning into the slippery junction of 1967
 and 1968.
And what a watchman is supposed to do, exactly, in such a
 situation

is anybody's guess. It's a thankless job, so surely anyone would be
    grateful
at least for a freshly starched uniform, name tag, working two-
    way radio,
hot coffee, and maybe some semblance of a gun, no matter how
    underloaded.

And before Schirmer's aliens actually arrived—when they were
    still traveling
mightily through stretches of empty interstellar space, only to
    wind up,
for all their cosmic know-how, in *ASHLAND, NEBRASKA: POP.
    2000—*
there was so much genuine commotion already in the 1967 air
that watchman Herbert Schirmer couldn't see any cause for
    alarm:

iii. Disturbances in the 1967 Space-Time Continuum

B-movie Republican Reagan is sworn in as California's governor
one day before the Doors let loose with *Light My Fire*, and
    without even trying,
there will be many days for swearing in and nights to set on fire
    this year.

In NASA's burning hurry to the Moon, the harried crew of *Apollo
    1* goes up
in launchpad flames three weeks away from liftoff. Sealed in for
    numbing hours

of routine system-checks, they were looking for trouble. But they
    never asked for any
so suddenly enormous that they couldn't get out of it somehow
    alive.
And in the name of U.S. rocket science, it's back to the Space
    Race drawing board.

Over San Francisco's Golden Gate Park, the Moon's so much
    closer
and more peaceful to the Human Be-In throng, where
    alternative-wavelength DJs
Ginsberg and Leary exhort thousands of un-Republicans to *Turn
    on,*
tune in, drop out. It's a countdown to anti-ignition, a send-up in
    smoke
of the cartoon American Dream, the ultimate warm-up act for
    the tenuous

Summer of Love ahead, complete with tourists bus-tripping
    through the Haight
to *See Real-Life Hippies!* That's what small-time Charlie
    Manson—
just released from jail again—is doing, armed with a guitar, his
    ingratiating
smile, and dreams about a family he'd one day more than own up
    to.
Hendrix is setting fire to another Stratocaster down in Monterey,

and it's a different kind of scorcher altogether, this Summer of
    anti-Love

the *plume* poetry interviews 1

    in Newark, Cleveland, Memphis, Detroit: fires there'll be no
        putting out completely.
    When heavyweight Ali says *No* to the Army, *No* to the war in
        Vietnam, and
    I'm so pretty to anyone who'll listen, he's stripped of the crown he
        otherwise wasn't
    about to lose, and once more the country is torn between sheer
        outrage
    and outright inflammatory cheering. And this stubborn split-
        decision fever

    isn't breaking anytime soon: it's the big-screen year of *Cool Hand*
        Luke—or the year
    of *Bonnie and Clyde*. Either Elvis, singing his still viable heart out
        on "How Great
    Thou Art"—or the Beatles, *getting by with a little help from* their
        friends.
    Consider the Patterson Bigfoot film just in from Bluff Creek,
        California:
    when that creature slows down to look directly back at the
        camera,
    it's proof of an unabashed animal's native curiosity—or
    a man in a costume who's checking to see if Patterson's still
        shooting.

In the same discombobulated October week of the off-Broadway
    dawning of *Hair*, with its promise of New Age relief on the way,
        astrologically
    speaking—Aquarius *ad nauseam*—reaction to the escalating war
    is heating up here at home: recruiters from Dow Chemical on
        campus

in Madison, Wisconsin—selling in so many words the future of
    napalm—
are confronted by hundreds of infuriated students. When police
    arrive
in their otherworldly riot gear, it's obvious that no one's had
    nearly
enough time to prepare for this outrageous midterm exam.

A thousand miles away, 100,000 protestors gather at the Lincoln
    Memorial—
the first-ever national anti-war demonstration. Some in that
    crowd
can't wait to attempt the decidedly radical, non-metaphorical
levitation of the Pentagon itself—one handbill's madcap version of
    a call-to-arms—
by chanting or singing or telekinesis or whatever passes these days
    for prayer.
Or even some literal heavy lifting, if that's what finally has to be
    done
to exorcize the evil spirits of war. To let the sun shine in.
But the Pentagon ends up so easily holding its shadowy, dark
    ground.

And on the same day the saucer shows up at last and begins its
    descent
in the middle of watchman Schirmer's particular nowhere—yet
    another
unfortunate *they-never-land-on-the-White-House-lawn* situation—
the first human heart is successfully transplanted half a world
    away,

and finally there's a little good news this late in what's been one
exceedingly strenuous year. This heartsick planet surely could use

some kind of lift about now, so let it be this groundbreaking
    surgery, or
a message of hope from alien beings who've gone so far out of
    their way again
to deliver it—if that's what it turns out they're here for.
In either case, may there be a few auspicious days on the bright
    side
before the complications unavoidably set in: the body,
    threatening
to reject the new heart it sorely needs, or the brain so close to
    shutting down,
unwilling to graciously entertain the idea of such unexpected
    visitors.

The heart patient won't make it to Christmas, and Schirmer's in
    no position yet
to get the celestial message. It will be next year before he
    remembers too much
of anything that's happened. And as for those intrepid aliens
    themselves,
who either hurtled through so many light-years to reach us or
    otherwise managed
to wormhole their way into exactly the right galactic
    neighborhood—
it's hard to believe they're already leaving, almost as if
they were never really here, saving their very best advice for last:

iv. Running Down the Gods

We want you to believe in us—but not too much.
    —alien's final words to Schirmer, "recovered" in 1968

What a welcome change of pace on the part of assuredly superior
    beings
who must have known they wouldn't always be there for Herbert
    Schirmer
or anyone else, for that matter. Because too often the faithful,
    whatever the faith,
believe until it hurts. Just think of the demanding Old Testament
    God, or
the Wizard of Oz, if you must. They're working behind the scenes
in their respective jurisdictions, bent over improvised control
    boards—
pushing this, pulling that, frantically turning some other thing—
and throwing their weighty voices around. Go ask Abraham and
    Isaac, or Job
and his fed-up wife. Or Lot's wife: for looking back over her
    shoulder toward home,
she was summarily iodized. At least the Wizard said he'd settle for
    a broom,
never honestly believing that Dorothy could deliver, and what
    else can he do
but sputter and play for a little more time? Those wayward Greek
    and Roman gods
weren't any better—capricious, petty, quick to anger at any slight,
    real
or imagined—famously insisting on blind faith in their unruly
    powers.

    And down here at the mortal level, it only gets worse: people who
        believe in
    themselves too much, always asking much the same of others—
        their excessive trust
    and understanding, yes, and even more distressingly, undying
        admiration.
    It's a patchwork of abstracted virtue sure to wear thin in this era
        of too many
    prime ministers and presidents, attorneys and investment
        bankers, military
    officers and corporate CEOs, preachers and physicians, artists
        and writers
    and radio talk-show hosts and TV weather-people who expect us
        to believe
    they can predict, a full week in advance, the daily highs and lows
        we're in for.

v. Too Much 1968

No one could have forecast 1968, an unrivalled year of too much
believing, bleeding, and dying. And no nightwatchman anywhere
    on patrol
could so much as hope to slow its approach, so here it comes:

Walter Cronkite will return from reporting on Vietnam's deadly
    Tet Offensive
to his anchor desk at CBS News, where this *Most Trusted Man in
    America*
stymies the Johnson administration by pronouncing the war
    unwinnable.

Then the massacre at My Lai, although details of those three lost
    hours
won't be uncovered for another year: Lieutenant Calley's *I was just
    following
orders*, his men in turn following his, and 500 women and
    children wiped out
for no military reason. When war-torn LBJ goes on television to
    announce
there's no way he'll run again, Martin Luther King can't believe
    what he's seeing,

can't help his out-loud *Amen*. It's a week before he'll go down
    himself, for good,
on a Memphis motel balcony, and soon enough hard-running
    Democrat
Bobby Kennedy too, on a restaurant-kitchen floor in Ronald
    Reagan's California—
too much and too much—and people who'd put their faith in
    them will try again
to sift through the sadness and anger for anything still left
    standing
if the cities ever stop burning again. And there might not be
    much.
Surely it can't be Richard Nixon—inexplicably back from the dead

and calling himself *The New Nixon* until it's all a bit much,
    tricked out
with those morally ambiguous *Nixon's the One* bumper stickers—
    yet somehow
his *Peace with Honor* campaign catches fire at Miami's Republican
    Convention.

Chicago's Mayor Daley unofficially will host the bloody
    Democratic Convention,
offering his own butchered peacemaker's pledge: *The policeman's
    not there
to create disorder; the policeman's there to preserve disorder.* And
    stumbling
out of this confusion will be Hubert Humphrey, too much the
    LBJ lapdog
to start pissing with the big dogs now. And believe it or not, it's
    actually Nixon
promising, if elected, to end the war. He'll keep referring to his
    secret plan
like something cooked up after spending too much time with
    Spanky and Alfalfa
in the *Little Rascals* clubhouse. But Nixon in the White House is
    a different story.
His new rough-and-tumble gang's hijinks will be no laughing
    matter.

Before the year's gone, Charles Manson also will remake himself
    with a vengeance—
more of a Family man than ever. He'll pass long days in his
    homemade bunker
working up his own much-too-secret plan to launch a new,
    helter-skelter war.
He'll listen too much to the *White Album*, finding messages he
    truly believes
were intended for him alone, already dreaming his way down the
    road
to his wild-eyed historical moment—a bare-bones production of
    Armageddon

and Bethlehem together, live in concert, high in the fabled Los
   Angeles hills.

The year cinematically ushered in by Kubrick's expansive,
   luminous *2001*
will go out with the *Apollo 8* astronauts' more immediate space
   odyssey:
clearing a flight-path for 1969, the much ballyhooed Moon
   landing still ahead.
They'll take that lucky-shot "Earthrise" photo from lunar orbit—
   instantly
a Christmas-card classic presenting a beautiful, overwrought
   planet
in this far-more-flattering-than-usual light. Peace on Earth, then,
   as if
that could happen. And with honor, whatever that means. Back
   here at the movies,

a world away from the Moon's breathtaking heights, this year will
   finally trail off
in low-budget black and white: Romero's claustrophobic,
   unrelenting *Night*
of the Living Dead. And ready or not, when the lights come on
   again
it will be a new year where, when it comes to steering clear of
   zombies
or the landlord or even Richard Nixon in the flesh or in theory,
   at last
we might like our chances—if that's not, just this once, too much
   to ask

vi. What Comes Back

We've been watching the human race for a long time, the space
 beings say
in too many preachy 1950s science fiction movies and in those
 slaphappy
pamphlets and books by people who'd trafficked, however briefly,
 with real-life
Space Brothers and Sisters. With apostolic fervor, they were
 forever talking up
the unearthly wisdom first imparted just to them—most often,
 oddly bland
concerns and admonitions about Earth's new Atomic Age. But at
 least
in those glory days of flying saucers, before the darker UFO
 abduction ruckus—
forbidding Greys, invasive implants, human/alien hybrid babies
 on display—
a person could simply walk right onto a spaceship and
 straightaway get taken
for a ride: an exclusive, invitation-only adventure. And every one
 of them
remembered it completely, not a single minute mysteriously gone
 missing.
No hypnosis required. The experience was all theirs, anytime they
 wanted,
and always their decidedly unmitigated pleasure to relive.

Herbert Schirmer's close encounter split the historical difference.
 Apparently

he'd held up his end of the wee-hours conversation, small-talking
    his way
inside the craft. But that was nowhere in his waking recollection.
He used to listen time and again to recordings where the aliens
    themselves,
unmenacing, came back to him in lengthy hypnotic regressions.
    Even then
he never quite got off the ground before everyone had somewhere
    else to be.
They made him a high-flown promise they'd return—*Watchman,
    one day
you'll see the universe!*—and although he willingly believed they
    might have had
nothing but mostly good intentions, he didn't get far when it
    came to thinking
it could really happen. That would have meant a little too much
hoping against hope—more than he could hold out for the rest
    of his life.
As if he'd ever have that luxury, that kind of time again.

vii. *Where the Rest of Us Get Off*

And when it comes to where the rest of us on Earth put our faith,
history tells us repeatedly that we have to watch ourselves.
We'd never knowingly get on board with a bad idea, but it
    appears
that's more than occasionally where we've been, right in the
    middle of
the wrong crowd again, and any lost time we can't account for
    later

gets a little harder to make up. We really don't remember being
    told
in no uncertain terms what to believe—let alone what for, and
how wholeheartedly—by someone plainly asking so many for so
    much.
The next time we get that carried away, let's try not giving up too
    much
for no good reason.

                       In earlier, more optimistic days, we shook
    hands
on anything. Freely gave our solemn word. Made what we
    considered
sacrifices. Sizable donations. We signed petitions, paid most of
    our taxes,
and shook our heads when we got wise to another war we'd been
    sold.
We bought smaller cars and still recalled next to nothing when
    we woke up
to find ourselves as usual out of gas, muttering in the breakdown
    lane again
with no idea how we got there. We'd only wanted to go home.

This could be our final good-faith offer, when enough at last will
    have to be
enough. Then we make our move toward the door, where we get
    off
saying take it or leave it, no questions asked, believe it
or not, before heading back to anywhere we might have come
    from once—

palatial estate or cold-water flat, lover or leftover casserole, long-
    ago
hometown or faraway-planet-of-the-so-inclined—somewhere almost
always beyond belief from here. Back to those lives we've led
    ourselves
to believe in just enough: that as long as we keep going, we're not
    gone.

Adam Tavel
interviewed by Nancy Mitchell

NM: Your poems in this selection are in traditional or variations of traditional form, as are many of your poems in your recent book *Plash & Levitation*, the 2014 winner of the Permafrost Prize Series Award from the University of Alaska Press.

AT: All of the poems here are from my new manuscript, *Catafalque*, which is almost entirely comprised of metrical work. As the title suggests, the collection is elegiac. For me there was a clear connection between writing poems that grieve and the elevated register of the pentameter line, which dominates. I sought a refinement in my own use of language as a commemorative gesture.

NM: I find this very moving—the yoke, the discipline and rigor of the form willingly undertaken, as a labor of love, so to speak, to honor that which is grieved ... and, the added refinement in language to lend grace and gravitas to the occasion ... lovely.

In each of the following poems, you strictly adhere to at least one device in the traditional form—in "The End of Practice," you're faithful to the form of the villanelle, but not to the traditional rhyme scheme. "Resurrection Horse" and "The Sentimentalist" are both strictly metrical, but after their initial stanzas, they abandon rhyme.

AT: You're absolutely right. I'd add as a footnote that "The Sentimentalist" has the structure of a Shakespearean sonnet but the loose rhyme scheme of a Petrarchan sonnet, so it uses faint slant rhyme in its closing six lines. In some of my sonnets, they are attentive and exacting in their form, but in other metrical poems, I modify the form to suit my needs. In "The End of Practice," it felt too confining—and overbearing—to keep the rhyme scheme. The poem maintains repetition and alliteration, but otherwise, the rhyme fades quickly.

These sorts of decisions are pretty organic for me when a rough draft is gushing out.

NM: Another of your unexpectedly delightful departures from tradition is the ironic, kind of snarky, "anti-heroic" couplet at the end of the sonnet "The Sentimentalist." After "His mother's nags compelled: / go hit the weights and flirt with waitresses," we get the volta in the following two lines: "He did. He burned his yearbook loves and lied / when poets groaned the country's gone to hell" followed by the deflating sucker-punch of the final couplet "You're such a little wuss his friends still said / right to his face until the day he died." Love that!

AT: I'm tickled that you like this poem so much. I wrote it after a year of nonstop elegies as a response to my internal critic, who was simply fed up with gloom. The ending surprised me when I wrote it, but now that I see it from a distance, I think it seeks to affirm the elegiac impulse. The poem is also a ridiculously belated retort to all of my grad school friends who, back in the day, said my poems sometimes suffered from sentimentality, which of course they did.

NM: It's so interesting how you, if you will, repurpose form—no one could call you a Neo-Formalist! In fact, although most of your lines are more metrically traditional, you don't "privilege sound over vision" (a Neo-Formalist trait Ira Sadoff takes issue with in his essay "Neo-Formalism: A Dangerous Nostalgia" in the *American Poetry Review* Jan./Feb. 1990). For example, your single-stanza narrative poem "A Child in Snow" certainly "articulates form with vision" in a highly visual diorama in which the camera/speaker zooms in and out of the scenes within. The metrical variation within the regular pentameter lines support the museum "collection" metaphor, as do the few lines that depart from the pentameter. Your choices are clearly purposeful. It's very Bishop, who, Sadoff notes, is one of "the masters of received form." Bravo!

AT: You know, sometimes I worry that I "privilege sound over vision"! It's easy to get carried away with the musicality of English ... it's such a sonorous, sumptuous language. "A Child in Snow" began as an imagined photograph of my wife as a child, but the narrative innocence evaporated once I confronted that foreboding scene and began to explore the museum metaphor. The ending gets pretty bleak—about as bleak as Arnold's "Dover Beach"—but the discovery is that nature is amoral, nothing is calling the shots, and we're a part of that chaos. This harkens back to my deep appreciation for Robinson Jeffers. What I thought was an epiphany when I wrote "A Child in Snow" is really just an exercise in Jeffers's dark wisdom.

NM: Ah, yes ... Jeffer's dark wisdom, or as Grace Slick less subtly sang, "You call it rain / but the human name / doesn't mean shit to a tree." So, what led you to write in form?

AT: In the trajectory of my life, it is a colossal irony that I've written a single formal poem, let alone a whole manuscript of them, since I loathed traditional poetry when I was young. Well into my twenties, my favorite poets were paragons of free verse.

NM: Can you recall a few?

AT: My earliest influence was Bukowski, who gave way to William Carlos Williams, the Beats, and Gary Snyder. I was a history major as an undergraduate, and I have vivid memories of straying on my late-night library jaunts to slack in the poetry stacks. H.D., Cummings, Anne Sexton, and contemporary poets like Gary Soto and Sherman Alexie were all a part of that swirl. I remember reading *American Poetry Review* a lot since Bishop Library at Lebanon Valley College carried a subscription. I was completely oblivious to the fact that Cummings and Sexton were remarkably inventive in reimagining traditional forms.

I was attracted to free verse for generational and cultural reasons, as so many students are today. First and foremost, free verse was easier to read, as it tends to mimic our natural speech patterns, and though I fell in love with poetry as a schoolboy, most of the poems I was given in public school were presented as timid justifications of the art. "I know we all hate poetry," so many teachers insinuated, "but here's one you can actually understand!"

NM: You're so right—in an effort to be helpful, many teachers sent the message that poetry is far too impenetrable for the likes of you, so let me give you something that sounds like talking, but at the same time, is totally unrelated to your adolescent experience.

AT: Yes! I yearned for poets who I felt were "relatable," but looking back, what I really yearned for was poems that I could understand and participate in the emotional charge.

NM: You mention Bukowski as your earliest influence … wow—it's amazing what a "gateway" poet he's been for generations of latter day "angel-headed hipsters" who, like you, were "burning for the ancient heavenly connection to the starry dynamo in the machinery of night." Can you name a few others?

AT: Like most teenagers, I preferred Hughes over Frost and Plath over Dickinson. I relished the adolescent resentment in "Theme for English B" while naïvely missing its affirmation of racial identity, and admired "Lady Lazarus" for what my mother would call its "attitude problem" despite being confused by its allusions and Freudian complexity. I sought to reject anthology poetry, brimming with its dead aristocrats and their stuffy diction, but what I was reading was still the stuff of anthologies. No one showed me Etheridge Knight, or Sonia Sanchez, or any other truly bold stuff in high school.

NM: Yes; the benign neglect, the damage done. After a few semesters of watching Intro to Poetry students' eyes glaze over and hearing their hearts and minds slam shut, I dumped those department-mandated, ridiculously thematic tomes!

AT: At any rate, without being wholly conscious of my motives, I started writing sonnets in graduate school, which eventually led to my timid experimentation with other forms.

NM: Was this when you were in the MFA program at Vermont College? This was a critical turning point—were there particular sonnets that drew you in?

AT: Yes. I studied with David Wojahn for about six months. That was probably the beginning of it.

I suppose, too, that I was attracted to the challenge and uncoolness of form, the sense of competition with oneself, and the sonnet's permutations and pliability. And of course I was attracted to the musicality. Sometimes, a line of pentameter arrives for me fully formed while I'm running or washing the dishes, and intuitively I let it lead me. In the past few years, I've pursued form intently as a generative method. I relish the compression and intensity it demands from the very first draft. How many of us do our best work when the terror of a deadline finally becomes real? How many runners clock far better race times than they could ever post in practice?

NM: You're right—even if I end up kicking away the scaffolding of the form, at least it gets me up and writing. Your comment about the line of pentameter running from/with and through you reminds me of another poet friend who, try as he might to break with his customary penchant for syllabics, throw caution to the wind, and write free verse, still ended up with strictly syllabic poems; the pattern had become ingrained—he surrendered to the body's rhythm.

AT: Your friend's unconscious need for syllabics doesn't surprise me. I agree with Wordsworth's general assertion in "Nuns Fret Not in Their Convent's Narrow Room" that what appear to be form's obligations can be liberating forces. If you ask a roomful of students to write whatever they feel like about God over the course of a semester, I think you'll get a lot of blank stares. I think you'll get their pens moving if you tell those same students they only have five minutes to write, or only five words.

NM: I can't agree more. One semester, in a desperate measure to prevent students from slapping anything down at the last minute for worksheets, I accepted only strictly traditional sonnets. My God, the indignant tosses of heads, the impassioned accusations that I was crushing their creative geniuses! But you know, as they knuckled down and worked to pack the lines with imagery and sound, to use rhyme consciously with enjambment, and to skillfully manage the volta and resolution in the final couplet, their confidence and skill grew. Some of the best work of their entire creative writing career portfolio was done in or after that class. One of my students managed his deep response of horror to the film *The Killing Fields* in an elegant, elegiac crown of sonnets that he later presented with a defense of traditional form at prestigious national student conference. However, the initial resistance to working in form is high, sometimes vitriolic!

AT: I read a young critic who reviewed a book of sonnets recently and he went to great lengths to express how he felt the sonnet, as an abstraction, bore the sins of history. I find that severe. I understand his point—for many the sonnet represents an exclusionary tradition that remains a symbol of oppression and/or the status quo—but logically, the sentence itself, literacy, and the English language at large have been far greater weapons in the oppressor's arsenal. How many creation myths and tribal histories did the invention of the book destroy? How many hundreds of indigenous languages did English help obliterate from our continent? Can we even fathom the ways in which English is a symbol of assimilation and brutish economics in the 21st century? Yet we continue to speak this language, and to write in it, with the hope that our efforts may prove redemptive and one day free from suffering, and that our language, all language, can tether human beings together, free from considerations of power, because we need it to understand our species, we need it to survive, and we need it to find a love supreme. I feel this way about the sonnet and other poetic forms, too. Beating up on an abstract literary form is a facile political gesture, and to insist on doing so *ad nauseam* willfully overlooks history's greatest lesson: we examine the injustices of the past to prevent as many as possible from ever occurring again.

I believe passionately that poetry should be a diverse, inclusive art—particularly here in America. Confronting the racism, sexism, and classism in Anglo-American literature is a necessary moral act for any writer working with the English language, but forsaking everything that was written before we were born accomplishes little beyond self-congratulatory smugness. It replaces the tyranny of the past with the tyranny of self-righteousness. One envisions Robespierre smirking as he sent untried masses to the guillotine.

On a related note, I find it tragicomic that so many contemporary poems seem indistinguishable from advertisements. I'm always grateful for accessible poems, and witty poems, and poems that challenge me aesthetically, but I'm increasingly dissatisfied with poems that seek my attention and do nothing once they've gained it. There's an interview with Arthur Miller from the mid-1980s (right around the time he published his memoir *Time Bends*) where he criticized performance theater for "obeying the worst signals of the culture." I share that frustration. When a poem doesn't offer its audience anything more than the hollow fleeting distraction of an internet meme or reality show, and thus seems driven by how entertaining it can be, for me that's the moment it fails as art.

NM: Speaking of the internet: do you think the quality of poetry has been compromised with the proliferation of online journals?

AT: I love online publishing. At the risk of sounding like DiCaprio at the end of *The Aviator*, it's the way of the future. I co-founded and co-edited the online journal *Conte* for nine years, so I like to think we were here before online magazines were cool. I suspect that those of us living now will continue to enjoy lives enriched by a literary culture where traditional publishing and digital publishing exist in a symbiotic, if at times strained, relationship. It makes me uncomfortable to think that my children or grandchildren might live in a world where printed matter no longer exists. I absolve this discomfort by not thinking about that reality very often. It won't bother them because it will be the world they know.

I'm convinced that the internet has allowed for greater equality and transparency in literary publishing and will continue to do so. We still have a long way to go. But I don't know a single young writer who thinks that their dream can only be realized in New York City now. Online publishing gives voice to the marginalized, expedites the magazine-and-book-making processes, and saves millions of trees in the process. Are there gobs of bad poems online? Sure. Are a few of them mine? Regrettably. Am I comfortable with the trend for online submissions fees? Not at all. But these are problems one might anticipate with any new medium. I'm confident we'll sort it out.

NM: What are your feelings about prose poems?

the *plume* poetry interviews 1

AT: Like many poets, I regard Russell Edson as the father of the prose poem. We just lost him last year. What a brave, original soul he was! I see prose poems as simply poems without line breaks. I like them immensely. I've attempted to write a few. For me, they are a part of the tribe. Certainly they put ultimate weight on the sentence to propel us along, but that's just craft talk. I still think of Faulkner as a poet who happened to write novels.

NM: Faulkner; yes!

AT: The current vogue for "hybrid forms," I'll admit, is a different matter since a lot of what celebrates itself for defying genre these days seems cavalier to me. To put it bluntly, the term "hybrid" sounds like a marketing gimmick. How curious it is that I noticed the chatter about hybrid forms right around the time I noticed the chatter about hybrid cars. It's impossible to regard something as innovative when you're mentally editing it after three sentences. I suspect that for some writers, breaking convention is an end unto itself. A century ago, Robinson Jeffers called this "originality by amputation." I see no gimmickry at work in the richly experimental, genre-defying writing of Susan Howe and Mary Ruefle and Shane McCrae. There is also a secondary risk in broadcasting one's own newness, in that one overlooks the brave transgressive legacy all American poets share. Poets like Jean Toomer, Charles Olson, and Wanda Coleman immediately come to mind. I know Richard Brautigan referred to *Trout Fishing in America* as a novel, but what a sad misrepresentation that is. Brautigan invented the surreal lyric essay.

NM: I'm amazed at how the subject of formalism is still so divisive in the poetry community; is it really, as Dana Giona suggests in "Notes on the New Formalism," which appeared in Volume 40, No. 3 of *The Hudson Review*, "an encoded political debate?" Where do you, or do you, find yourself on the continuum of this argument?

AT: I'm quite aware that these discussions of poetic form are politically charged. For the record, I'm a Poet Without A School, and saying that is not my veiled attempt to skirt the issue by being vacuously neutral. I'm too moody to claim a movement and too insignificant to have some movement claim me. I write poems to learn about myself and others, to experience the world more fully, to grow as a human being, and to participate in the temporary joy of creating something new. Poetic forms have a part to play in this life practice. I hold no special affinity for the New Formalism or its practitioners. I reject the privileging of a narrow tradition over traditions that have been marginalized or embrace a more inclusive view of what poetry can be. An elitist canon is a dead canon. My dream is to be a poet of dexterous range who can write with conviction and conscience about a variety of subjects in a variety of styles, and I see poets like Robert Hayden, Anne Sexton, Hayden Carruth, Amy Clampitt, Seamus Heaney, and Kevin Young as giving that dream permission. I want each poem to cry its own song. I want to flummox my obituarist.

NM: Well, Mr. Tavel, if your most recent book and these featured poems are any indication of your power to flummox, your legacy is secure! Thank you so very much; it's been a pleasure.

The End of Practice

for my son Graham

Your squeals explode beneath the parachute
beside your soccer friends who drowse and snot.
No bliss but yours alights the silent field.

The college girl we all call "coach" insists
we save this toddler stuff until the end.
Your squeals explode beneath the parachute

that's barely clutched by these, my fellow dads,
who scroll their phones and text their absent wives.
No bliss but yours alights the silent field:

your ruddy cheeks flush again each time I raise
my purple swatch into arena glare.
Your squeals explode beneath the parachute

so I resist the scream of my disease
to drop the fabric flecked with pinhead mold.
No bliss but yours alights the silent field.

We grown-ups pile the jerseys damp and stale.
You dash again to wreck the rainbow folds.
Your squeals explode beneath the parachute.
No bliss but yours alights the silent field.

Resurrection Horse

Each night two sons descend into my grave
and heave aside the casket lid. Astride
what spine the earth has left, they weep and shake
until their torch awakes my cobwebbed eyes

that drink the moon. Imaginary spurs
prickle my ribs. We ride from stone to stone
and stitch cold names into a song for stars
that rouse and fade again behind the clouds.

Horsey please. Horsey go. Whenever my skull
slurs down in dirt they lash my silver weeds
of mane and hold its wispy braid as reins.
The cemetery pond reflects our grins

milky and mercurial. *You must not pray
the meat of me returns.* We mosey back
to peer above my pit. Each night my hooves
unaided guide the teetered lid in place.

The Sentimentalist

Would sigh each New Year's Day to see the waste
confetti made across revelers still drunk
on dreams inside their sleeping bags. The case
of cheap champagne, its frozen throats like monks

in snow upon the window's ledge, brought tears
he blamed on allergies. Eventually
shorn hair across the barber's floor would steer
his aimless pilgrimage through city streets

toward blubbering. His mother's nags compelled:
go hit the weights and flirt with waitresses.
He did. He burned his yearbook loves and lied
when poets groaned the country's gone to hell.

You're such a little wuss his friends still said
right to his face until the day he died.

A Child in Snow

A girl extends her dragging stick in snow
that shrivels from what sparse light intrudes
through clouds. Her theory of December leaves
a long meandered line from her driveway clear
down to swings treacherous and glittering
with ice, uninviting as a museum
display where panel knobs no longer flash
and tiny handprints interrupt the dust.
It slows her not. She reclaims her kingdom
with knock and smash until a seat is free
to creak her back and forth. Her mother fogs
the kitchen windowpane an hour watching
the exhibit dim and prop a gray-faced moon
upon its shoulders as she scalds the pots
crusted over with day-old film from soup.
Though growing dark she likes to see the ends
of her daughter's ragged hair cascade
beneath her touque, the flaxen ponytail
fanning weightlessly each time the swing
arcs its grin. Surely we could leave them here,
suspended dreaming in the snow-glint dusk
casting glances back and forth across the lawn,
but just inside the maples lay a buck
who sprinted dazed a mile away to fall
exhausted, arrow-struck, leaking from his gut.
His pricking ears can register the groan
of chains that sway beyond the hollow where
each pant pumps out a little blood beneath
his matted fur. Across his muzzle now
bursts of snot rope and froth. Together
we may watch his final shivered wheezes

stutter out their steam. Our cicerone
has led us here, defenseless and awake.

Marc Vincenz
interviewed by Nancy Mitchell

NM: Marc, I'm amazed by the prodigious imagination, intelligence and skill that permeates so much of "Sibylline." The narrative arc of this poem spans the emergence of the Italian Renaissance out of the darkness of the medieval era: the Black Death to the Baroque period, which marked its end—"O, the arcs & swirls." You've impressively managed a dual perspective, which is both cosmic/spiritual and political/global. What brought you to this particular era as point of departure?

MV: The Italian Renaissance represents a major shift in human consciousness, a seething burst of creative impulses from the margins to the mainstream. Humanism is re-born and art, philosophy, architecture, literature, music and science coalesce. The introduction of movable type in Europe leads to the dissemination of rediscovered texts (many from Greek antiquity) and an outpouring of innovation. The establishment of the Florentine banking system and its ensuing wealth allow much of this to occur. Uccello, Masaccio, Titian, Tintoretto, Bellini, Donatello, Botticelli, and, of course, the three great masters, Leonardo, Michelangelo and Rafael, produce some of the most enduring works of art the world has ever seen.

NM: Yes!

> & from that Goliath of marble
> the small block of David
> from the very skin of the stone.
> (iv. & in the Pantheon where Rafael was buried)

MV: Inspired by the Greek and Roman master sculptors, Art's re-ignited flame captures deep reflections of the divine. Michelangelo's

David and Botticelli's *Birth of Venus* are two great examples of this. As if emerging from some kind of spiritual hibernation, artists-as-alchemists begin to articulate a transcendental beauty and, in the process, discover the fulcrum of the metaphysical and material.

And yet, despite all this vision and inspiration, despite the emergence of political and social criticism in Art, despite the giant strides in architecture (Brunelleschi) and science (Leonardo, Galileo, Copernicus), innovators are frequently being challenged or suppressed by the Vatican and the orthodox mainstream. Art becomes more complex and layered—not only in technique and craft, but also in message and metaphor. Here begins the golden age, the wedding of light and matter. Linear perspective, politics, metaphor and mythology meet for the first time on canvas, in stone, in the music of the spheres. This genesis of creativity as a spiritual or political device reflects fundamental changes in civilization and paves the way (despite the gaping potholes—the Inquisition among them) to the Age of Enlightenment.

NM: And with these changes, the challenge arises for the artist to remain true to himself as the genesis of creativity becomes more valuable and powerful as a political device.

> Even when Mercury, our god of money.
> gives the party the elevated status
>
> among the doctors and the magi,
>
> how to remain
>   at the center
>   of power
> & rework the world of love
>   (v. & all this unity, wisdom, wealth &, an ideal projection)

In a response to these pressures, the speaker seems to shape-shift to embody the mercurial zeitgeist of the era itself. A contradicting trickster, the speaker's oracular voice is established implicitly in the title "Sibylline," then disclaimed with the opening epigraph from John Nim's *The Complete Poems of Michelangelo*: "Not odd what's on my mind, / when expressed, comes out weird, jumbled. Don't berate; / no gun with its barrel screwy can shoot straight."

MV: The voice, the shape-shifting narrator, may likely be Michelangelo himself or one of his dumbfounded alter egos—but don't listen to me.

NM: Ah, Mr. Vincenz, methinks you too might be tricksterish with that answer! Can I pin you down for something a bit more concrete?

MV: I prefer to think that the listener in the poem is the speaker herself.

NM: Ah, now that is intriguing; talk more about this?

MV: Here is surely an artist talking to an oracular muse, attempting to amuse that muse, to cajole, to tickle a response. And, the response and the great breaths between provide a foreshadowing.

NM: Could "the great breaths between," which I take to mean the white space on the page, and the time it takes to turn to the next page, be the questioning consciousness of the listener/reader as it reels between voices/perspectives?

MV: Yes; who shoots straight, anyway? Cupid? And, what can you tell me of my future?

NM: Although the epigraph's speaker serves to orient us to a disarming disorientation ahead, it's also a caution (don't say I didn't warn you!) we hear well after we, charmed by the sleight of hand/voice of the first two pages, have boarded the vortex-bound train.

MV: I would say the narrator is possibly cautioning herself: in the labyrinth somewhere lurks the minotaur.

NM: I see; since the narrator is listener/reader/artist/muse? Or, "Sibylline" is, to borrow from Pierre Teilhard de Chardin, "a joint product of the observer and the observed?"

MV: There are frequently multiple voices in my poems. Some may be alter egos, specters, voices from the future or the past. In a long piece of exploratory verse, I do my best to listen to all of them and take dictation.

the *plume* poetry interviews 1

NM: It would appear that the whole of "Sibylline" reflects these multiple voices and perspectives. So do you think that Krishnamurti's comment, "All conflict is this battle between the observer and the observed" might be more precise about what energizes the dynamic of "Sibylline"?

MV: For sure. Dynamism arises when a conversation occurs. Observer and observed hold their own discourse. Neoplatonic thought, which once again was emerging during the Renaissance, held that perfection and happiness—or, if you prefer, beauty and love—would emerge through intense rumination, rumination that is informed by Platonic discussion. (For me, beauty and love is at the heart of "Sibylline.")

Once again, here we have the creative impulse (Gaia) of a cosmos that thrives on communication, vibration that begins as a single note, becomes a harmonic vibration. Or, to once again coin Krishnamurti: "Truth, being limitless, cannot be organized." There is no principle more supreme than another.

Alongside the infinitely famous *Creation of Adam*, featuring the iconic hand of God ("… & as God touches the finger of Adam, / so Adam touches the hand of another— // so tantalizingly tender / that spiral upon spiral …"), Michelangelo's Sistine Chapel fresco also depicts five Sibyls—who, as you probably know, were not mentioned in the Bible, but come from the classical (pagan) world, and who are predicting the fate of humanity. Shortly after Michelangelo's passing, his fresco came under strict scrutiny by the Counter-Reformation, not only for its nudity (apparently for a period the naughty bits were painted over with fig leafs and loincloths), but also for the inclusion of non-biblical figures.

Discussions take place throughout the course of history: Bacchus, Atlas, David, Moses, the Madonna, the pagan *Ignudi*, each trying to get a word in edgewise. And in spite of himself, through his host of creations, Michelangelo himself stares back at us from the past. In the Sistine ceiling alone, there are over 300 figures, including seven Old Testament prophets, twenty Greco-Roman athletic nudes (the Ignudi—a word minted by Michelangelo himself) and five Sibyls, observing, exchanging glances, contemplating, reaching their own prognoses.

And what of those six million people who visit the Sistine Chapel and look upward to commune with her ceiling every year? Aside from all the voices of the tourists and their multitudes of languages, imagine what a myriad of conversations are going on … Then, tying this thought into "Sibylline," consider what these Delphic seers would make of the future. "The entrance fee to the Vatican museums is now close to $30 (23 € including audio guide) per person—which means, of course, that the Vatican is pulling in $180 million/year on entrance fees alone." (I wonder if the descendants of the Medici family are getting a slice of the proverbial orange.) Now, that would make for a great Hollywood ending.

NM: I'm wondering if your talent for juggling different perspectives, different characters, eras, etc., might have been influenced by your peripatetic upbringing. Can you speak to this?

MV: Most assuredly. As you know I was born to a British mother and Swiss father in Hong Kong. This made me predisposed to a dual-cultural perspective on most things; throw in the first baby steps in Asia, the continual presence of the Chinese communist party in my childhood home (my father's business with Deng Xiao Ping's China), the slew of expatriates from Scotland to Brazil to Japan to Australia (who worked with my father and often ended up at our house after a long day at the office) and the kids who I played with from the German-Swiss international school, and you've already got quite a cocktail. As an adolescent, my father sent me away to a Benedictine monastery boarding school in the Swiss alps—with only a smattering of German (we spoke English at home), and thus I had no choice but to learn to assimilate with whatever culture, voice or language I was in the presence of. And although I always had friends, whether I was in elementary school in Hong Kong, boarding school in Switzerland, public school in rural Sussex, high school in Connecticut, college in North Carolina, I was somehow always an outsider, an observer, a third wheel—and so I learned to listen intently to each and every voice.

My mother's father too, lived close to us in Hong Kong. He, along with my grandmother and then-infant mother, had arrived there shortly after the Second World War (they were both working class Londoners) to work for the British Government as a surveyor. He was soon treading the paddy fields on the Communist Chinese border, mapping the outlying territories. He was the first public servant in his field permitted to learn Cantonese. Eventually, he spoke it fluently. Gung Gung, as I called him (Granddad in Cantonese) was a voracious reader of literature, a talented mathematician, a great listener, an adroit linguist and avid traveler. He helped me tune my infant ear to the vastness and multiplicity of the world.

NM: I'm fascinated by the organic, generative, lyric logic operative throughout "Sibylline"'s narrative structure. A microcosmic example of this is in "i. An unsurpassed rule of thumb," the first poem in the opening section "1. The Mermaid and the Monkey."

Hang on while I try to delineate this pattern: The first line, "Opposable," is triggered by and references thumb in the epigraphic title, as well as our primate cousin Monkey. Although "Opposable" also refutes the authority of unsurpassed rule, the remaining lines "Approachable / A parable" in the first stanza are triggered by sound of the preceding line, "Opposable":

i. An unsurpassed rule of thumb

Opposable.
Approachable
A parable.

Unprecedented.
Percentages.
Patronage is a political strategy.

Perspective revolutionizes everything we see.
It touches the skies

> & casts its shadows over distances,
> over the humors of a city.

This logic is repeated in the second stanza; "Unprecedented" qualifies parable of the preceding line, and "sound" triggers, if you are still with me, "Percentages," which in turn triggers "Patronage."…

My ear/mind are so convinced by the sound/sense logic of the previous stanza, I don't for a minute question the claim of the final three stanzas, "Perspective revolutionizes everything we see. / It touches the skies // & casts its shadows over distances, / over the humors of a city." But!!! I sure as hell want to know how you did it; is your process intuitive; are you ahead of your lines, or writing just as fast as you can to keep up with them?

MV: Although I'd been taking notes in a single journal, tentatively entitled *The Spirit of Mercury*, for ages, the bulk of the poem materialized overnight. After a first spewing-out, if you will, I spent several late-into-the-wee-hour nights refining, listening to these rhythms, melodies and harmonies. When the notes and beats accumulate into something like a musical arrangement in my head, I know I am ready to let them flow. The cadence and rhythm of the first words were clanging as I finally sat down to type and the "cosmic" forces were magnetically pulling them together.

"Sibylline"'s final emergence may have something to do with the fact that I had eaten oysters for dinner the night before—Glidden Points from Maine, as a matter of fact. Aside from the obvious, there's something very Renaissance, very Florentine, very Medici about oysters. The oyster or scallop shell—as made iconic by Botticelli's *Venus*—is a Renaissance symbol of an ideal beauty and transcendental love.

NM: How richly serendipitous is this?: as well as an aphrodisiac, an old wives' tale has it that oysters also bring on labor?! How fitting that "Sibylline"'s final emergence or birth was induced by the oyster into the manger of the scallop shell, the cradle of beauty and transcendental love!

In the Florentine glow of that image, let's welcome our readers to wander the lovely labyrinth of "Sibylline."

Sibylline

Not odd that what's on my mind,
when expressed, comes out weird, jumbled. Don't berate;
no gun with its barrel screwy can shoot straight.
   Giovanni, come agitate
for my pride, my poor dead art! I don't belong!
Who's a painter? Me? No way! They've got me wrong.
   —*The Complete Poems of Michelangelo* (trans. John Frederick Nims)

I.
The Mermaid & The Monkey

i. An unsurpassed rule of thumb:

Opposable.
Approachable.
A parable.

Unprecedented.
Percentages.
Patronage is a political strategy.

Perspective revolutionizes everything we see.
It touches the skies

& casts its shadow over distances,
over the humors of a city.

• • •

In the next great commission
it's the taste that matters—

glorifying the original sins
of the *maestro della bottega*.

& the birth of Venus,
Botticelli's pagan mythologies—

to stop the devil dancing
on his shoulders,

that master of misogyny.

   ii. & to measure the light in all things,

to see Daniel in the lion's den,
serene rather than heroic

(in motion)
& the projection of human form
on heaven's body,

just as Apollo became Jesus
& the blue light
in an Attic August surpasses

the details of posture &
the colonnades & the columns &—

. . .

a natural selection of forms feeding

on the spiritual crises,
on the human,
on the heroic,
on the divine,

from within the vault of dark ages
that follow the Fall

• • •

& into the hands of dictatorships,
despotisms or democracies

& other magical words that rattle
in the spiritual comfort of relics,

in the concrete substance
that civilizes—

where the true nature
of a building

is forgone space.

• • •

& the dreaming magi
in the vaults' echoes

in the love's labors of citizens

giving way to the splendor

of the city giving way
to the flocking pilgrims

or the "effects of good governance"

that surpass
the Black Death

iii. & the Greatest city of Rome in decay in a day,

the outpouring
where Death itself

becomes a public theater—
in suspension …

Where God made man
because he loved to hear stories—

Christ's agonies for woman & man
in a time when there was no divorce

& the scales of Archangel Michael glimmer gold

as armies march on
to bombard city walls,

& then that falling
upon Aladdin's den
as Christ upon his cave

• • •

& the four horsemen
rhapsodic,

tantalized by tortoiseshell
& rhino-horn & quetzal-feather

as surmised in Dürer's *Ritter, Tod und Teufel*—

melancholy on the dark side of genius

& that last word.

• • •

The Teutonic torture—
the twisted hands of the Virgin;

O, the therapy of music
in the Atomic Age

& the torment & trial in the wilderness
the wild fantasies of Grünewald.

Was Aztec gold
a vision of the future?

iv. & in the Pantheon where Rafael was buried,

The Transfiguration,

a measured symmetry
of high society, unfinished.

The Last Supper, a ghost.
compelling, yet

lascivious, licentious
&—elusive.

In completion, reduction
or transfiguration.

The dichotomy of Apollonian or Dionysian principles.

& then, the self-doubt
of an artist with a heroic ambition.

& from that Goliath of marble
the small block of David
from the very skin of the stone,

an evocation
to impress
all comers.

· · ·

the *plume* poetry interviews 1

Watch!

As Plato points
toward heaven
Aristotle points
toward the dirt.

& as God touches the finger of Adam,
so Adam touches the hand of another—

so tantalizingly tender
that spiral upon spiral

in the spirit
of the index finger.

    v. & all this unity, wisdom, wealth &, an ideal projection

The illusion of two canopies.

Surely there's more to this canonization lark?

Even when Mercury, our god of money,
gives the party an elevated status

among the doctors & the magi,

how to remain
    at the center
        of power

& rework
    the word
        of love?

vi. Loft & air

No brush, no chisel
lightens the soul.

To work though stone,
to find the wall of love

& the ice—
the wall of ice

now dissolves
in unison

with the industry of men,
rhetoric, theater & illusion—

to dramatize yourself
as an ideal man,

rich in trade & craft
& so to come to some fortuitous conclusion

behind the mask
of democracy

in this Pantheon of small gods,
& the desire

to impress

Minerva,
      Mercury,
           Apollo.

Unique in the world
of ever-blooming myrtle.

vii. Light through glass in the Annunciation

YHWH.

The lion, the divine love.

Spaces of unpredicted clarity;
the turbulent light
that emerges
through the darkness.

Across the altar
        in the mass
as the glory
        of angels
suffuses in light.

& in the down-glow,
dogs play
just enough

to convince us
to believe.

II.
The Infant & The Stinging Nettle

i. Counterrevolution

The seeing & adorning,
& where the mind will be
taken care of,

in the harmony
of the spaces
loved in, lived in.

From this place
the water services

the kitchens, the gardens
& the most excellent fruit.

This painting is large
& could hold

many many
figurines.

ii. The eyes that behold

in the fountain of the aristocrat's garden
among the swans & ducks,
& goldfish,
the king of the beasts
brandishes a sword—

& once again
the light resounds
divine providence

& the bees carry
the keys to the kingdom.

Is it not a time
to draw perspective?

iii. The heartbeat of a building

Transverberation.

Fragrant hymns of praise
& divine celebration—
the smoke of creation.

Journeys that do not end.

Surpassing the sweetness of pain,
the institution's divine right to rule.

What is the vocabulary of power?

You can't read the features
until you're up close to the travails,
observe the naked benevolence,

the descent from the cross
with only one hand
on the reins—

. . .

O the arcs & the swirls …

Where the eye cannot focus
as one myth assails another

& suffused with nostalgia
within the shadows
of sculpted space,

in the everyman
of everyday
departing for the Isle of Cythera.

iv. & in the microcosm of the garden,

the effects of past time,
the truth unveiled,

movements
between the hills & the dales.

• • •

The art of liberty.

The staking out of order
& that fever
of Revolution.

Was it just the failure
of the harvest?

or was it the oath
in the mausoleum?

v. A secular **pied d'état,** *a political ideal*

Now the stars of the empire

    far from the magic bean

        of enlightenment,

the *plume* poetry interviews 1

    the urban proletariat

        & the clouds of Revolution

            gathering.

The abstraction

    that prepares us

        to give our lives.

The anecdotal.

    A natural being

        with untamed appetite.

The primacy

    of the eye

        on the surface of appearances

        An imprecise definition of form.

Oh how the light

modifies matter

    & toys with grand design.

vi. Worshipping the serene Buddha

When does the disquiet
become bourgeois

& the yawning background

descend

    in celestial revelations?

v. On the Sun's consciousness

How to handle the modern?
How to find a kiss
for the whole world?

Behind a beautiful curtain
the objects of mystery & desire.

The dislocation.

& the savage made congenial through—

impromptu, flimsy,

but deadly serious
pure plastic rhythm.

• • •

Oh to follow the flight of the swallow
through the storm of the future

& to become
that bird
in space
in your own right.

vi. How to remove the object from the center of the eye?

Space & sense

      & the dream

& then, the enthusiasm

of Man as iceberg.

All those babblers, dilettantes & swindlers

opening doors

into different futures,

following the minotaur.

vii. But a shadow falls upon history

repairing the shattered cultures
& thus
backs
turn

into their own expression
followed by sand

& waste

& rubble,

O—no subject,
but content …

no document
seared
in the corners

of a lifetime
within a fixed timeline
degrading the colors—

• • •

the speed of change,

    the saturation

        of objects,

            packing,

preparing

    for a wide spread—

• • •

unheroic,

anywhere,

anything,

no more windows,
but a field, a horizon,
an assemblage,
a tremulous clutter

in the small,

the mundane,

the profane, then the real

viii. & the disposable,

A libation.
A liberation.

The transformation of the flesh,
sweeping away,
generating a vision
of what already is

with immediate
content—the dissidents
& their images of glory.

• • •

Watch closely!

• • •

Here come the corporate collectors.

Abstractions have become ordinary
& the myth of progress
grinds down to a tiretrack.

What controversy?

ix. Where's the leverage in the pluralism?

What then can we say
of the symbols of belief?

Can you hear the silence
of history breaking?

The phantoms inform
but do not transform.

. . .

Inject yourself back
into the earth
& become a sphere.

Become evidence
of former lives.

You can only predict
the probability
at odds
with experience.

x. Still, in the knot of perspective,

a voice-over says:

All roads are traveled.
Vibration determines everything.

O, if only
for a quick, tight
Hollywood
ending.

Christopher Buckley
interviewed by Nancy Mitchell

NM: Chris, I can't tell you what a kick of pleasure, as well as a kick in the gut, this boomer is getting out of "The Half-life of Revolution—Particle Physics, History, Baseball and Baby-Boomers." The upshot, so unabashedly bleak, is somehow redeemed by your unique perspective, wit and craft. Against Carl Sagan's mellifluous lullaby "We are made of star-stuff" still lava lamp-ing in our collective boomer brains, the lines "all of us lucky / leftovers, though / our particles are petering out / from the get-go …" clang like a hammer, shattering our cherished illusions that star dust was really pixie dust, keeping us "forever young," and irrefutable scientific proof of our eternal, indestructible, "heavenly connection to the starry dynamo in the machinery of night" and beyond. Yes, Joni Mitchell, we are stardust, and yes, every last bit of us came out of the same blast but we are falling, like the lines falling down the page in stanzas, falling DOWN like "soot from a Beijing sky so saturated with particulate / you cannot see / five feet in front of you / let alone / to the night stars from which we all arrived." So, sorry Joni, we and Jojo who was a man before he was a woman ain't getting back anywhere, at least not to our long-gone Edenic garden … and no disrespect intended to you, Walt Whitman, dear paterfamilias of our poet-tribe, but "every atom belonging to me as good belongs to you" is not a really such a cheery message, when every last one of those atoms is "ticking steadily away / before being / reallocated / to the circuitry of the stars."

Maybe it's the effects of too much caffeine on a sleep-deprived brain, or the evocative, generative power of this poem, but, (and coming from a boomer, this is a high praise) I'm hearing Bob Dylan's voice in these stanzas in a rhythmic variation of "It's Alright Ma (I'm Only Bleeding)." In the interstitial paragraph between stanza sections one and two, I see the wise/wry Stranger in *The Big Lebowski* at the bowling-alley bar, leaning over a beer … "Orwell wrote a book." And I can hear the Talking Heads whispering, "same as it ever was, same as it ever was" across the asterisks between sections.

CB: I couldn't hope for a better, more simpatico, overall reading of the poem than these first two paragraphs. Our baby-boomer age is certainly the perspective/filter for the poem. Yes, somewhat predictably, I over-spent my youth in the '60s listening to Joni Mitchell and Dylan. For a few years, Dylan's lyrics were hard-wired into my grey matter; and among popular singers, Mitchell was always one of the best writers in my view. But there were no conscious echoes or references when writing the poem—decades since I listened to them, but certainly the zeitgeist of the times is all there, and you never know what tracks are replaying in the subconscious and working almost to the surface.

As for "the circuitry of the stars," I started reading articles and books on cosmology, astro and theoretical physics in the early '80s. Articles in *The New Yorker* on dark matter (hence the title of a poetry book a good while back) got me started. And before I go any further I need to say that I am not trying to sound like an intellect. I barely passed high school chemistry, took no physics, dodged all the math I possibly could in college. But many scientists started to present the new information coming up in a pre-masticated and imagistic style that would be accessible to folks like myself with essentially a 7th-grade understanding of physics and the universe—7th grade in 1959–60, that is. How else could they sell books or TV programs? So thanks indeed to Carl Sagan and bless his memory, and to *NOVA* on PBS, and Stephen Hawking, and Timothy Ferris, Marcia Bartusiak, K. C. Cole, and more recently of course Neil deGrasse Tyson and many others who have popularized the understanding of cosmology and its continuing shifts. Right off, I saw that all of this new information fit right into/supported the old arguments and inquisitions re metaphysics, mortality, the temporal beauty of the world—my ongoing arm-wrestling between Faith and doubt, so of course science and religion. Political, economic, spiritual, philosophical—I've been trying to appraise our part in a cosmic roll of the dice, trying to find connections between the local, the global, and the cosmic.

NM: I, too, couldn't get enough of that stuff: I was obsessed, thrilled, and later a little resentful that what "we" had always known in our hearts and guts had finally been validated ... that wisdom spoken by poets—"every atom belonging to me as good belongs to you"—artists, prophets, collective wisdom implicit in folklore, tribal ritual—for instance, the Jewish ritual of circumcision is performed on the eighth day after birth for a reason other than tradition; it's only then a newborn has developed sufficient vitamin K to clot the blood—was now given the official imprimatur of the god Science ... but I digress.

I'm intrigued with the poem's references to events during the heyday of the boomer generation—Johnson, Nixon, the Vietnam War—as well as references to historic and contemporary events. Is each event, framed in its own stanza, an "article of evidence" of the degenerating dross we are and have always been, evidence of our continued concurrent devolution?

CB: "Only connect" as E.M. Forster has one of his characters say in *Howard's End*—so that is my project here in the specific: to be able to move from atomic dissolution through history to see/realize what a mess we are making and have made of things when we could do otherwise. One thing informs/plays into the other and the structure is intended to be symphonic—theme, variation, recapitulation/synthesis...

NM: Symphonic, yes! And how beautifully the structure is sustained throughout: "There's a line that loops back / to Wu-Han / from the 1960s and Vietnam / via *M*A*S*H*" gracefully connects us to the aforementioned historian Wu Han who obliquely criticized Mao Tse-Tung by writing about "another charismatic bandit leader, the first Ming Emperor, 1368," in the same way *M*A*S*H*, a TV show about a mobile army surgical hospital during the Korean War, criticized the Vietnam War.

Wow; it just occurred to me that this symphonic structure (and again, we see it in the section about Ai Wei Wei, who, while trying to testify to the slipshod construction of a school that collapsed in the Sichuan earthquake of 2008, killing 5,385 students, was beaten by police and required emergency surgery for a cerebral hemorrhage looping centuries back to Sima Qian, who was "convicted / of treason, / and castrated instead of being executed / for supporting the honor / and loyal record / of a defeated general" is remarkably similar to the structure of string theory itself!

Thoughts?

CB: Well, the last part first … I do not want to say that I understand string theory, especially since it is essentially MATH! As a theory, it has been around a while, but just a few years back, one scientist/math-guy re-worked the math and came up with 11 dimensions instead of the previous numbers, which—relying on my grey cells here—went from 5 initially to 10 dimensions. Everything made of infinitesimal strings, looping back into each other, we cannot see in dimensions we cannot see. You have to trust the math, they say. So it is the notion of looping back into each other, the interstices that in fact do connect that made sense to me about history.

So it seems obvious to me to say one reflects in the other. The boys who went to Vietnam …

NM: Ah … The boys who went to Vietnam—Chris, please forgive me for interrupting again, but my god, your lines in the poem about those boys … your boys, my boys, America's boys … well, those lines just broke my heart … "58,000+ died, / just on our side— / mostly boys / born after WWII, / 18-year olds/ fresh from high school, who were replacing/tires and shocks at SEARS, / driving Allis-Chalmers through corn or alfalfa fields" … and I'm going stop, right now, because I don't want to spoil our readers' pleasure of seeing these beautiful musical lines arranged, not unlike a musical score, down the page.

Those lines put me in mind of Samuel Barber's haunting *Adagio for Strings*—I immediately put it on—which, as you know, was the theme song for *Platoon* … the movie about those boys in that war.

CB: As I was saying, the boys who went to Vietnam, for example, brought that experience home with them. The politics of the '60s is the example of the immediate influence of one on the other. Moreover, and again obviously, moral and ethical concerns transcend all borders:

the neighborhoods in Santa Barbara when I grew up, or the borders in Korea, in ancient or contemporary China. People in our generation do not forget the lies of Johnson, Westmoreland, Nixon and Co., the oppressive government, conscription, all those who died for political capital and corporate profits. There was no "Tonkin Gulf Incident:" Westmoreland lied about all the numbers of the Tet Offensive to keep the war machine cranked up in Congress and the appropriations committees; Nixon was bombing Cambodia and Laos all the time he was on TV telling us he wasn't.

NM: You know, just reading the above still fills me with rage. We were duped, and would have continued to be if a constellation of events hadn't ruptured the facade and exposed things as they really were and, honest to god, had always been.

CB: I think we all know that now. But interesting for me are the connections to ancient China, to *M*A*S*H* and the Korean War, to the same type of totalitarian government working in China for the last 60 years. We do not, as a species or political bodies, seem to have learned a thing in all this time.

In the last fifteen years or so, it has seemed more important to me to engage the political when I can find a way to do so that does not involve political cant. It seems that if you are a good citizen of the world, you will be a good community member as well. We learn, of course, our larger attitudes toward the global community from what we absorb locally, growing up, and there is an obligation that we have, one person on the planet to another. Yet, at the root of it, to understand what we are doing on the planet and what hope there might be, if any, for us after our physical lives, must be hard-wired into the basics of philosophy. But no matter what we choose to believe, our common mortality and the science about us should give us pause, as they used to say.

NM: In the paragraph between stanza sections two and three (Ken Burn's voice) "'History is totally political in China, and I think it always has been.' writes Frances Wood, historian and authority on China. They pick and mix, editing and inventing facts." Do you see parallels with the recent news of middle-school history textbooks which erase, neutralize the historic horrors of the slave trade with rhetoric like "immigrant workers" to "tens of millions who died in Mao's Great Leap Forward …"?

CB: Yes, surely there is a parallel between these editings. The cliché "History is written by the winners" certainly applies. Or it is written by the government, or those with the most money. Here is a chilling thought: what would the history books read like if the Koch brothers bought up the publishing companies? We already have Murdoch and Fox "News." For years now far-right religious types in middle America and the South have been demanding school boards edit out evolution from science texts, and insert their religious mythologies. I taught in the University of California system for 20 years, and over the last 15 years especially—though I was primarily teaching writing workshops—I would have to stop and offer the background for the Spanish Civil War, WWI and/or II, Vietnam, the economic and political movements in America over the last 100 years, and often even had to gloss references to the Bible to the top students in our state. This was all due to some of the events and information being left out of history texts and sometimes it was due to students not being taught history or paying no attention when they were. Surely we are used to Putin and the Chinese consistently dissembling on the news programs and in press releases. To some extent, we have almost become inured to it.

NM: I'm wondering if the answer to the poem's question "Where did we go?" addressed to boomers now hiding under haircuts, driving Hondas and hedging their bets with hedge funds, is that our fate was always in our flawed, deteriorating stardust?

CB: Well, only in the most tangential and extrapolated sense. Though Schopenhauer wrote, "After your death you will be what you were before your birth," and that strongly points to a return to stardust, we cannot abandon an ethical mode of living simply referencing the likely absence of any life beyond this one.

NM: Absolutely! It requires the greatest courage to live, to conduct our lives with empathy, integrity in the most hopeless of times…. Do you remember the old black-and-white film about the *Titanic*, ironically entitled *A Night to Remember*? A much finer movie, in my opinion, than the bloated blockbuster made years later—I was so moved by that handful of men who didn't rush for the lifeboats reserved for women and children but stayed with the ship as it went down. Contrast that with the trampling stampede of Black Friday shoppers.

CB: In my view, the answer to "Where did we go?" is about the materialism that has replaced moral conviction, political action. Greed in America has supplanted most everything in my view.

NM: Alas, yes, materialistic greed has infected every institution, even those we thought were citadels of moral conviction: universities are now corporations, education is commodity, students are consumers. The overhead screen has replaced the lectern, and professors (not this one) are relegated to the corner computer desk projecting PowerPoints. Yet, it's not just greed for materials, but an insatiable greed for attention, for praise, evident in the relentless, unabashed self-promotion via social media. You'd recognize the face of an author sooner than you'd know what was authored! Hey, Chris, is it possible that this new generation is more evidence of our bum cosmic DNA, in another stage of the burnout?

If so, does it take the onus off of we humans, particularly we boomers? Could we, who grew up under the looming cloud of an atomic blast, who cowered under school desks in air raid drills, who lived in homes with *Life's Picture History of World War II* on coffee tables ringed by our war-scarred fathers' beers and whiskies, who watched JFK's assassination, his black blood splattering Jackie O's suit, looping our black-and-white TVs, and we who, a day later, witnessed on a live national television broadcast as Jack Ruby shot Lee Harvey Oswald dead, point-blank, at close range. Could we, raised on war and death have left any other legacy? Or as cosmic leftovers, did we, outside of a few of us, even have it in us to do better? Does the fault really lie in our stars?

CB: I don't think the onus is taken off any of us. Greed, political ambition, have always been corrupting influences, just as the desire for power and self-promotion has always been the temptation and each individual must answer for his/her actions. Many of us in the '60s took a moral and ethical political stance, many did not. And you tie in a very relevant point with your comment on unabashed self-promotion via social media! Everyone can leave a comment, write a blog. It no longer matters if you are qualified to speak on the subject, have done your research and reading, have accomplished anything in the field you are commenting on; just post a comment and you are on a level playing field.

One particular example galls me particularly. When Philip Levine was appointed Poet Laureate for 2011–2012, the articles and comments online were uniformly praiseful and celebratory, realizing what Levine had meant to contemporary poetry for the last 45 years and acknowledging his generosity and importance as a teacher. But there was one ill-willed and self-important guy writing for the Huffington Post who said Levine was a horrible choice. He equated his poetry with several other American poets he obviously did not approve of (he was writing from England) and those poets he mentioned had nothing in common with Levine. He went on to say he was sure the young writers in American would not be well served and could learn nothing from Levine. What an idiot. I had never heard of him as a poet or as a critic, never seen anything in poetry by this guy. But he found a platform and shot his mouth off. I was gratified to see that the *Chronicle of Higher Education* ran an essay by two young poet-teachers from John Jay College in Manhattan that went to specific lengths to point out how uninformed and irresponsible this writer had been.

And while the final quote here from *Julius Caesar* poses a very poetic question, that idea of "fate" is really not offered up or addressed in the poem. The rest of the catalog, ending with a legacy of war, certainly makes a trenchant point about what our generation lived through/was exposed to; my hope is that these experiences should even more strenuously have us examining our motives regarding the military-industrial complex, corporate lobbyists, military intervention around the globe and what our responses should be as ethical citizens of the globe.

NM: Well, Mr. Buckley, this poem has certainly re-awakened my political awareness, and given me a great deal of pleasure in the process. Readers, I give you:

the *plume* poetry interviews 1

The Half-life of Revolution—Particle Physics, History, Baseball, & Baby-Boomers

Half-life ... is typically used to describe a property of radioactive decay, but may be used to describe any quantity which follows an exponential decay.
 —Wikipedia

So far, the information
                          is that quarks and leptons make up matter,
photons are mass-less,
                neutrinos jump around
                              like fleas on a dog—
yet every last bit arrived here out of the same blast ...
                                    all of us then lucky
leftovers, though
                our particles are petering-out
                                  from the get-go....
Same difference no matter how
                        we record or interpret our actions,
our dissipation—
                every last atom ticking
                              steadily away before being
reallocated to the circuitry of the stars.

                         *   *   *

Three years back, radical Islamists in Egypt joined secularists to oust Mubarak, then the Muslims took over with a front man in a Western suit and tie, who promised rights for all—a democratic split—who never delivered, who legislated and strong-armed in their own theocratic favor. Now, the military is back, more blood in the streets—no change. Orwell wrote a book....

        *   *   *

Sima Qian, the first,

the *plume* poetry interviews 1

                      and some say, greatest historian,
said the purpose of history was to teach
                                     rulers how to govern well,
not to record how men die.
                         Convicted of treason, he was castrated
instead of being executed
                        for supporting the honor and loyal record
of a defeated general.

   *   *   *

"History is totally political in China, and I think it always has been" writes Frances Wood, historian and authority on China. They pick and mix, editing and inventing facts. In the Great Museum in Beijing, you hear about 1964's first nuclear test, the great reform era after Mao's death, and not one syllable about tens of millions who died in Mao's Great Leap Forward or in the Cultural Revolution.

                     *   *   *

Often compared with
                Mao Tse-Tung,
                              the first Ming Emperor, 1368,
was also a charismatic bandit leader
                              who spiraled off his rocker.
In 1950, historian and deputy mayor of Peking,
                                    Wu Han, unwisely,
wrote that early Ming history
                      as Mao was sinking into paranoia.
Wu Han died in prison in 1969
                    for criticizing the current government
by writing about the past.

                     *   *   *

the *plume* poetry interviews 1

Artist and human-rights advocate,
                            Ai Wei Wei, was tortured 81 days
for investigating the "tofu-dreg schools"
                            that collapsed in the Sichuan earthquake
of 2008.
    While trying to testify to the slipshod construction,
                                            he was beaten
by police in Chengdu
                and required emergency surgery
                                for a cerebral hemorrhage.
Nonetheless, he published a list
                of 5,385 students killed in the quake.
The great proletariat struggle
                is now dead
                        in the middle of an industrial revolution,
an expanding consumer economy
                    that ships boatloads of third-rate products
to Walmart and Home Depot.
                    With all the factories and imported cars,
the air in Beijing is so saturated with particulate
                                        you cannot see
                                                five feet
in front of you,
        let alone to the night stars
                        from which we all arrived.
The men at the top
            press the automatic window buttons
                            closing out the grainy view
as they're driven
        in their Party-provided Buick Regals.
                            They could run successfully

for Congress as Republicans
    not opposed to oil, fracking, or redevelopment.
      * * *
There's a line that loops back
    to Wu Han
      from the 1960s
        and Vietnam via *M*A*S*H*,
a TV show about a mobile army surgical hospital
        during the Korean War.
Everyone knew the subject was Vietnam,
      the war's human and political failure,
but given the hawkish mood of the nation then,
      (*Let's round up all those hippies,
drop them in the jungle with their peace pamphlets,
        and see how they do!*)
you couldn't get backing
    for a show about the Vietnam war.
        No, it had to be
dressed up in a Korean time-warp
      with movie stars and laugh tracks
to insinuate any political critique....
    Robert McNamara, prime architect of the war,
fell out
  with Johnson and the Joint Chiefs
     for advising freezing troop levels, a cessation
of bombing in the north,
    handing the ground fighting back to South Vietnam.
In '67 LBJ forced McNamara to resign,
      but in '68 Johnson bailed,
        leaving the bodies
on the ground, leaving the door open for Nixon, who,

the *plume* poetry interviews 1

                              emphasizing a good economy
     and successes in foreign affairs—(establishing relations with China)—
                                                                    won
     a landslide re-election in 1972 despite four more years of war.
                                              We were not
               bombing Cambodia,
                         he was not a crook....
                              58,000+ died, just on our side—
     mostly boys
      born after WWII, 18-year-olds fresh from high school or replacing
     tires and shocks at Sears,
                         driving tractors through corn or alfalfa fields, kids
     who went surfing
                    and dropped out of City College ...
                                   the body count announced
     each evening on the news
                    after the RBIs on the sports report.
                         *   *   *
     When it ended, we thought we'd come out on top, but it was another
     swing and a miss, the CEOs circling the bases with appreciating
     portfolios from Grumman, Boeing, General Dynamics, Standard
     Oil, McDonnell Douglas, Pratt & Whitney, Colt Manufacturing,
     Bank of America ... you name it.... Same ballgame, they just kept
     changing the pitchers.
     Now, we all have haircuts,
                         Hondas, mutual funds—
                                        those of us, that is, whose
     pensions were not scooped up by corporate raiders,
                              "private equity restructuring"
     and international takeovers.
                    No one's bothered now

the *plume* poetry interviews 1

                                      by offshore banking,
tax loopholes, the military GNP, and corporate welfare?
                                                    Where did we go?
Way past the halfway mark here,
                         the only community thought arrives
in direct-mail circulars for Assisted Living….
                                        What will there be left
to say for ourselves
               with war our only legacy
                            before we return to particles,
to the irrefutable history of dust?

the *plume* poetry interviews 1

Emmanuel Moses
translated by Marilyn Hacker
interviewed by Nancy Mitchell

NM: Good morning, Emmanuel. Your beautiful poems have emboldened me to suggest that we transcend this sensually impoverished cyberspace and meet this morning on my pond dock for a version of *My Dinner with Andre*; perhaps Coffee with Emmanuel and Nancy? The aroma of coffee—or is it espresso, for you?—hovers the dark elixir of fallen, damp leaves and fugitive wood smoke. A rowdy scatter of geese gathers itself into a flock, forms a respectable V and rises up and over the pond to outlying farm fields to scavenge corn spilled during the harvest, their cacophony of honks fading into distant traffic grinding down the highway. Little dark slips of birds flicker yellow leaves as they flit from tree to tree, their bright songs chipping away the morning. "Quick!" you might say, as you write in "Time of Color," and point to the small bush the passing light has burst into flames, or "quick! ... see how, in the water's shimmery reflection, the trees along the opposite shore are like smeared paint of an autumnal palette."

EM: Nancy, this beautiful restitution of the landscape, as you add to the colors and hues, bird voices and cars sounds ... your reverie becomes all of a sudden my reverie....

NM: Ah! Then we are indeed here, Emmanuel ... Look! how quickly the sun has dried the pond dock of dew from everything except for our shadows. So, here, together, we begin:
    For this poet, the litmus test of real poetry—which these poems certainly are—is the phenomenon that while reading it, I fall into a poetic reverie. By reverie, I don't mean the fuzzy, dreamy trance, which precedes a nap, but a poetic reverie, which Gaston Bachelard, in *The Poetics of Reverie*, distinguishes from the common daydream in that "it

situates one most fully in the present, where all the senses awaken and fall into harmony." Certainly, your poem "Time in Color" snaps us awake and calls our attention to an electric present/presence with the imperative "Quick! Colors through the window! / Colors on fields" and reminds us of the fleeting, ephemeral quality of these moments:

> Before the weather changes
> And changes everything
> Empties fields and forests of their substance
> And ponds and farms
> How fleeting the sun is!

Your imagery is so original, all "newborn poetic images," which Bachelard identifies as the undisputed "offspring of poetic reverie." Here are but a few stunning examples of such offspring: "Let life drown itself in fumes of wine / Let death flee like a pickpocket" and "Mother, you hid your tears under the pillow / Like a miser hiding gold coins" from "My Life."

And again from "Time in Color":

> The yellow of colza in nearly-black fields,
> The silver of streams
> The silt-browned green of fish-filled rivers—quick!
> Cabbage's purple in well-mannered squares—quick!

as well as the breathtaking "The black of a village chimney silent as a closed mouth—quick! / The black of a village church-bell never to be caught up in the saviors arms—quick!"

And I would be remiss not to mention these lines from "A Stolen Dream":

> But of shop window dummies
> Male and female
> White, so blindingly white under the dead leaves
> That arouse from within me and perhaps came from all the cemeteries

and from "Portrait of My Friend":

> The tobacco in the bowl of his pipe glowed too
> As dark as time
> Burning like life

Emmanuel, I'm compelled to ask: if your poems induce reverie in the reader, is my intuition correct that they were composed in reverie, as well? If so, do you access or fall into reverie via solitary contemplation the natural world, which Bachelard posits is "the transcendent vehicle to poetic reverie," or via other vehicles?

EM: When I write, or, more precisely, when the urge to write surges like a moor-bird from the weeds of this no-man's-land betwixt consciousness and unconscious, I am that person who turns his back to the world and craves for golden light, who suffers from low sinister skies, but at the same time, I am his dreamy-lazy spirit and eye wandering in the landscape framed by the window, under celestial influences, again, but also nourished by details and particulars brought to my sight by the complexity and movability of things within me, by the intimate and secret inner climate and seasons we all harbor. From the conjunction of those powers and phenomenons, the poem is born, a kind of earthly-aerial creature, half golem, half butterfly.

NM: Lovely ... so if, as Bachelard argues, "The man of reverie and the world of his reverie are as close as possible; they are touching; they interpenetrate. They are on the same plane of being," is it not possible that the reader who falls into reverie while reading what was written in reverie enters into a poetic ecology of sorts with the writer which could indeed be the fusion of two reveries?

EM: I do agree with your idea of a mutual reverie, the one of the writer and the one of the reader. The writer, in a strange process, closes himself up like a snail to enter the external world, which, of course, is HIS external world, and the reader is opening himself up to that inner-outer singular world of the writer.

Those two apparently contradictory movements create no tension but an encounter. Almost a sexual one, between the self-centered writer, yet going toward the outside, and the reader being entered by the text he reads and being changed by it.

I think there is a gap between the creative and the created and that an immense loneliness befalls both. And yet, they do touch, naturally.

NM: Yes… that gap between the creative and the creative is such "an immense loneliness" … so sorrowful … so, to continue with mutual reverie, as the reader is entered by the text, she is simultaneously entering the writer's reverie-text. Yet, alas, this very real and profound sense of connection, paradoxically via the dissolution of self, in reveries "which take us so deeply within ourselves that they rid us of our history. They liberate us from our name" is so fleeting … is it not so like sexual union, before we fall back out of reverie and via "the gap" fall back into our separate selves?

But while we are in reverie we dwell in an atemporal terrain of the immediate present, as a non-personal presence in which we are not defined by our past or are pulled by an imagined trajectory of a future. In fact, it is precisely this quality of your poems that I find so original, refreshing and enlivening. We hear in the speaker of "A Stolen Dream" a consciousness so unencumbered by time or identity it's capable of inhabiting the dream of another:

> While reciting the stolen speech
> I realized that the dream wasn't mine either
> I was in someone else's dream
> As I might be in the body of someone else's wife

I want to ask you about your poem "Prayer," which opens your manuscript. It seems to function as both an invocation: "God of drizzle and resonant earth," and as a petition: "Give us the strength to get through the bad days." I'm wondering if it might, too, be a threshold, a door into the manuscript itself; would it be a stretch to say that the speaker/poet is also the priest/shaman, the guardian of the threshold, who, via prayer, opens the door?

EM: Who is that God, Nancy? Who am I addressing in this short poem? I remember Saint Augustine's words: "God is more intimate to myself than myself." I am speaking, then, to my most secret and unknown self, to a hidden energy whose rays are filling the world, my world at least. This infinitely intricate net of time (times, actually), space, dimensions of space, of nature, which is a reflection of the boundless. I am addressing the unseen I who is both deep inside me and outside me, in eternity and infinity. This nucleus, axis, fundamental note of which I am a vibration, or a set of vibrations, is a staff, a consolation, an aspiration, it is the God of good hope and the God who pours the *Lux Perpetua* from and on the tenebrous reality, realities, in which we are all thrown, as it is our destiny of beings-towards-death, to quote Heidegger's profound words.

Prayer, as the gesture, the movement of addressing, invoking, of one's voice—as the translation of one's soul, our invisible breath—lifting itself up, rising and pointing to what is greater than myself (yet, as mentioned above deeply rooted in me), to what is higher than my daily dust; prayer, then, is the begetter of poetry. It is a Psalm and poetry is of a psalmistic essence. Therefore, Prayer. Praise, exultation, fright, hope and despair constitute the chromatic scale of prayers, Psalms and poems, its palette. Prayers, Psalms and poems are addressed both the unreachable transcendency and to the unfathomable depth in us.

NM: Emmanuel, anything I might add would be superfluous; we'll let your response lead our readers directly into your featured poems.

Prayer

God of drizzle and resonant earth
Give us the strength to get through bad days
God of exotic birds and astounding flowers
Give us the joy of the sun streaming through a tangle of branches
God of sap and fog
Give us the sensual sweetness, the melancholy sweetness
Of the seasons passing

Pisz Na Berdyczow

"*Pisz na Berdyczow!*" That means "Write to me at Berdichev!"
Since all the merchants of Poland, Lithuania and Russia
Passed through Berdichev, a main commercial and banking center
 of the region
But when commerce moved to Odessa, the city went downhill
 quickly
And "*Pisz na Berdyczow!*" became "Write to nobody!" or "Leave
 me alone!"
He writes "*Pisz na Berdyczow!*" on a piece of paper and tacks it to
 his door
But no one reads Polish here, people don't understand what he
 meant
So they knock, they ring the bell, they slide messages between the
 doorframe and the parquet
They whisper or they shout, they speak rudely or with distinction
According to the circumstances
What can you do under the circumstances?
"*Pisz na Berdyczow!*"

A Stolen Dream

In my dream I asked to speak
I went up to the platform
I gave someone else's speech
The men and the women in the audience
Were divided by an aisle
As they would be in a synagogue
While reciting the stolen speech
I realized that the dream wasn't mine either
I was in someone else's dream
As I might be in the body of someone else's wife
I thought that this other person might be dead
And that he had willed me his dream
Or that perhaps I had killed him
To steal his dream from him
I thought that perhaps I myself was dead
And that I was dreaming a living man's dream
In order to linger in life a little longer
The way vampires nourish themselves with fresh blood
So as not to die entirely
And the speech
Was in fact about death, or about the dead, more precisely
And about the continual birth of those who survive them
But as I continued my remarks
I was thinking that, on the contrary, faced with the dead,
    survivors die too
They die tirelessly
At every moment of their miserable existence
I said "There is light,"
And I was thinking "There is no light."
It seemed as if dead leaves were coming out of my mouth
That they emerged in continuous waves and fell silently all

>   around me
> It seemed as if they were falling on the silent audience
> That was not made up of living beings after all
> But of shop window dummies
> Male and female
> White, so blinding white under the dead leaves
> That arose from within me and perhaps came from all the
>   cemeteries

Time in Color

Quick! Colors through the window!
Colors on fields and forests
Before the weather changes
And changes everything
Empties fields and forests of their substance
And ponds and farms
How fleeting the sun is!
How the sky mocks our admiring gaze
Eternity is an optical illusion
Immensity a dubious abstraction
The wheatfields' gold—quick!
The pink of bricks piled on a building-site—quick!
The foliage's chilly green—quick!
The rust-color of bushes, train-tracks, roadbeds, quick!
The yellow of colza in nearly-black fields,
The silver of streams
The silt-browned green of fish-filled rivers—quick!
Cabbages' purple in well-mannered squares—quick!
The road's grey—quick!
The absolute blue of clear sun-softened autumn days—quick!
Red! Red! Red of tractors, cars, traffic-lights red—quick!
The red of a hunter's cap, his rifle wedged in his armpit—quick!
(And soon the imagined red of a slain beast's blood)
The metallic green of our roadside poplars—quick!
Blue slate roofs—quick!
The blue of distant mountains—quick!
Stone blue, horizon blue,
Blue light falling in a fine mist on the world—quick!
And white—I had almost forgotten white—the white of dusty
    roads,
The white of cows lazing in pastures—quick!

Omnipresent white, that the eye disdains
Of a wall between two cypresses, of trucks going swiftly past
White—quick!
Then black! Black! The black of fertile earth ploughed over and
    over again—quick!
The black of a horse driven mad by the trains
Who gallops in crazed circles alongside the fence—quick!
The black of a village chimney silent as a closed mouth—quick!
The black of a village church-bell never to be caught up in the
    saviour's arms—
quick!
White, black, green, pink, blue and gold—
Quick! Quick! Quick!

My Life

Mother, I'm taking my life with me
Father, I'm taking my life with me
Woman, you are taking my love, I see you on the dusty road
Where once we kissed

Let the sun dance on women's backs
Let the rain hammer men's hands
Let life drown itself in fumes of wine
Let death flee like a pickpocket

Mother, you hide your tears under the pillow
Like a miser hiding gold coins
Father, you hide your face under the earth
And your feet are planted in the clouds

Woman, I carry my shame in the depths of my pockets
I drink and I smoke what doesn't fit there
One day I will be Cain
I'll be pursued for what I did with my life

My arms will never embrace the sun
My mouth will never drink up all the rain
Life will go to the devil
I'll catch up with old death

Father, it's time to sleep
Mother, it's time to leave
Woman, dust can be a lovers' bed
Shame weighs down my steps on every road

Portrait of My Friend

He had been waiting for me for five years
Behind drawn venetian blinds
We talked right away about hatchets and revolvers
The frozen sea, the whole caboodle
He no longer wrote a word
He saw nobody
Because literature had lost all interest for him
Since you earned less with it than by selling tomatoes
And because his friends were now
Black inscriptions on white stones
Tormenting his persistent memories
He had had enough of the noise of the city
The noise of the family
The noise of the past
He hoped for a silent future
Saw himself in beloved cities, their streets deserted
Through motionless nights
In the arms of taciturn and tender women
A river would flow
Discreet as everything outsize
You could make out the wind only from the contortions of flags
And leaves rustling
On the trees of refined gardens
And still later there would be nothing but nothing
This thought transformed his face into a smile
His eyes into two suns
The tobacco in the bowl of his pipe glowed too
As dark as time
Burning like life

Cynthia Cruz
interviewed by Nancy Mitchell

NM: Hi, Cindy. I don't want to spoil our readers' pleasure in your graceful and convincing argument that Marguerite Duras was a mystic, and how the act of writing established her in the long tradition of spiritual practice, so I won't say too much about the particulars in your featured essay "Duras, the Mystic."

However, I'd like to chat about one particular point, which gave me pause. As you write, Duras has largely been described as an alcoholic. Edmund White, in his essay "In Love with Duras" posits that if one is an alcoholic, one cannot be a mystic; as if the former condition naturally precludes the latter. He writes, "She said she drank because she knew God did not exist." In your successful counter to this with textual evidence to the contrary from Duras in her book *Writing*, I was reminded of Carl Jung's letter of January 30, 1961 to Bill Wilson the founder of Alcoholics Anonymous, in which he writes of a patient "His craving for alcohol was the equivalent of the spiritual thirst of our being for wholeness, expressed in medieval language: the union with God," footnoted with "As the hart panteth after the water brooks, so panteth my soul after thee, O God" (Psalm 42:1).

CC: I agree with you: there is a strong connection between alcoholism and addiction overall, and mysticism. In fact, one can argue that drinking (as one example) is a means of protecting one's self from the closeness of God, of that intensity. One thinks of Hölderlin, for example, and his madness resulting from his connection with God. Or, even, perhaps, Simone Weil's starvation, which of course became anorexia, as another example of this attempt at self-protection.

NM: Interesting. I think White's assumption reveals a commonly held belief that as a necessary pre-requisite, the character of a mystic must be whole and sober, saintly. This ignores spiritual practices that constitute the structure of the mystic's quest in her quest for wholeness via reconciliation with self, or Thou, or God.

I take issue with this because it's precisely the kind of prevailing puritanical attitude that perpetuates misunderstandings about addiction and the addict, and keeps both in the shadow of shame and out of the light of understanding.

CC: What's interesting to me though is how labeling Duras "alcoholic" diminishes her while at the same time when we speak of masculine genius alcoholism is often closely tied with it.

NM: Yes; it seems to be a form of the same old "slut/stud" double standard.

CC: This argument parallels the confessional label that serves to silence female writers while doing nothing to weaken the strength of male writers. For example, Plath's confessional writing reduces her writing to mere juvenile journal entries while the same label does nothing to diminish the reading public's interpretation of the works of male so-called confessional poets such as Robert Lowell or John Berryman.

All of this relates to the work I have been doing in the past few years on silence and Otherness and my examinations of women writers and artists. What I have been wondering is why some are silenced using the same language (i.e. alcoholism, confessional writing, and so on), while others are not affected.

NM: I've wondered too about this....

CC: Furthermore, I am interested in ways that those who have been silenced then use this silence in their work, resisting the binary, resisting the terms of the power structure.

NM: Yet, this resistance has it own deep power and roots in literary tradition.

Duras' practice, "that of writing" like other spiritual practices, allowed her to drop into two of "the three main tenants of the spiritual exercises" silence and solitude, or, as you quote Duras from *Writing*, "This real, corporeal solitude becomes the inviolable silence of writing."

This practice resembles another spiritual practice of meditation, in that it is an "emptying out of oneself."

CC: And, as you say, the emptying of one's self that occurs when writing is, in itself, a kind of communing/communicating with God; a type of prayer. And Duras writes precisely about this in *Writing*, for example, when she explicitly states "The text of texts is the Old Testament." One can read, in fact, not just the act of her writing but also the act of drinking alcohol as a type of prayer. Prayer via the bottle; prayer via the word.

NM: Ah! Further rebuttal of White's "She said she drank because she knew God did not exist." But getting back to Duras' spiritual practice of writing: although it resembled meditation in the process, it really wasn't meditation *per se*, was it?

CC: Meditation implies a level of calmness in reflection that I don't see in Duras' writing. If I had to, I'd say her writing is more one of desperation, an aspiring toward absolute truth. Her work is passionate—she is stepping directly into the fire (as opposed to considering, reflecting). As a result, I'd say then the reader is also put directly into the fire—and the fire is impossible to bear (this is precisely why Duras needs the booze, as she says). This intensity scares some off, while others insist her work is too intense, that she is making too much of things. This intensity is too much for some readers to bear. In her final work, *No More*, as Duras moves nearer to death, her voice and the writing become more intense, more clear and honest. Again, this type of transparency, this nearness to God or truth, is often too much for people. They respond with a visceral reaction, a condemnation: Duras is hysterical, that she is making too much of things. She has no control. When, in reality, she is translating truth for us, a kind of mystic.

NM: How much of your own writing practice is a spiritual practice?

CC: My own writing is less a meditation, which I understand to mean, literally, a type of contemplation or reflection or, spiritually, a communing with God, and more a kind of word machine or quasi philosophy in that I generally use poetry as a means to move nearer to an answer or better understanding.

NM: So, your writing practice resembles Duras' in that "Duras used writing as a machine-like apparatus, as a means to drop further into the unknown," yet differs from hers in that you use this "machine" as "a means to move nearer to an answer of better understanding?"

CC: What I don't know, I write and wrestle with on the page through revisions and re-visits. What the poem is then is a kind of shell or relic of that wrestling out of/for meaning.

NM: "… a kind of shell or relic of that wrestling out of/for meaning"… fascinating. I think of a snake's skin, a chrysalis, even a placenta, all of which retain the shape, bear the history and contain the genetic information of that which grew, evolved out of it. This puts me in mind of Jung's theory of transformation: when the individual has the ability to access unexpressed psychic material via meditation and the courage express to it in a tangible, physical form outside of the body (on paper, in this case) the evolution to wholeness can begin. The incarnation of this material takes on an independent life outside of the body, and the "host" body is literally and psychically transfigured.

It's intriguing to look at "some underwear and a white feather." and "Glitter of leaves near the gutter" from your poems "Charcoal" and "Medicine and Magazines" included in this feature and see them as relics, evidence of a hard-earned struggle.… I'm reminded of the line "As if gods wrestled here" from Yusef Komunyakka's poem "Work."

CC: Essays and art reviews serve the same purpose for me. I don't write essays or art writings when I "know" something. If I thought I "knew" something, I would not need to write about it. I'd move on. All writing is, for me, this kind of moving toward.

NM: As you write of Duras' writing, you, in your essay "Duras, the Mystic" and your poems in this feature, are "following the star of the next world with blind faith." Thank you for letting us follow along with you.

Duras, the Mystic

Writing comes like the wind. It's naked, it's made of ink, it's written, and it passes like nothing else passes in life, nothing more, except life itself.

—Marguerite Duras, *Writing*

In his essay, "Spiritual Exercises," the French philosopher Pierre Hadot describes the Spiritual Exercises used by the Stoics as a means to drastically alter themselves and their lives. About askesis, another term for the practice of Spiritual Exercises, Hadot writes:

> It is a conversion which turns our entire life upside down, changing the life of the person who goes through it. It raised the individual from an inauthentic condition of life, darkened by unconsciousness and harassed by worry, to an authentic state of life, in which he attains self-consciousness, an exact vision of the world, inner peace, and freedom.

According to Hadot, the main spiritual exercises are: "Learning to Live," "Learning to Dialogue," "Learning to Die," and "Learning How to Read," Each of these exercises is meant to help the practitioner to free himself from the passions. Hadot writes:

> In the view of all philosophical schools, mankind's principal cause of suffering, disorder, and unconsciousness were the passions: that is, unregulated desires and exaggerated fears. People are prevented from truly living, it was taught, because they are dominated by worries."

The French writer Marguerite Duras has been largely described as an alcoholic. In his essay, "In Love with Duras," the writer Edmund White writes:

> There was always something preposterous about her. When she was feeling well enough she surrounded herself with courtiers, laughed very loudly, told jokes, and had opinions about everything. She was

an egomaniac and talked about herself constantly.

And, though I can't dispute either of these, I believe, also, that Duras was a mystic. That in fact it was the very act of writing that performed for Duras a spiritual exercise; it was through writing that Duras practiced asceticism and her own means toward freeing herself from the passions.

Saint Anthony was the first of the Desert Fathers, the first early Christians, to take literally the instruction of Jesus to "Go sell all that you have … and come and follow me" (Luke 18:22). Here, the desert is Egypt, the land of Moses, of Saint Catherine, and of the burning bush. The desert is the cathedral of fire, the place where all things come to life, where all things come to die. It is the place of pilgrimage, but it is also metaphor: for the silence within, the searing white light of one's spirit. Those who can, descend into the desert. Those who cannot or choose not to, descend into the silence within themselves. This retreat takes many forms. One form is the formal practice of meditation. Another similar practice is that of fasting. But for Duras the action, the spiritual practice, is that of writing. Writing necessitates silence and solitude. It is a taming of one's mind and spirit. To take what one has in one's mind and translate it into words on the page is a way to remove the thoughts and ideas, the beginnings of passions, directly out of one's mind and body.

And though White writes, "She said she drank because she knew God did not exist," I have difficulty swallowing this. Within the few pages of her short book (45 pages), *Writing*, Duras mentions Christ twice, God once, and also The Old Testament. Of Christ, she writes, "Like the love of Christ or of J.S. Bach—the two of them breathtakingly equivalent." About the Old Testament, she writes, "The Text of Texts is the Old Testament." What Duras said, specifically about God and alcohol was "Alcohol doesn't console, it doesn't fill up anyone's psychological gaps, all it replaces is the lack of God." What this says to me is not that she did not believe in God but that, rather, she felt the lack of God's presence. This lack is, of course, only noticeable by one who has belief. In the first place, one cannot notice the absence of something they do not expect to appear. The absence of God is the shadow of God.

In the chapter "The Absent One" from his book *A Lover's Discourse*, Roland Barthes gives his definition of absence:

absence / absence

> Any episode of language which stages the absence of the loved object—whatever its cause and its duration—and which tends to transform this absence into an ordeal of abandonment.

So what we see now is that the absence Duras describes when she writes about the absence of God is the absence of the Thou, of the lover. God is the Thou, is the lover and it is through the spiritual practice of writing that Duras means to reach him. Returning now to Saint Anthony and the early Desert Fathers, they fled their churches because the churches were no longer filled with silence; they were beginning to become social spheres, filled with the sound of laughter and voices. It was through leaving their lives and descending into the desert, into the unknown, that these mystics hoped to find, or at least come closer to knowing, God, the Unknown. And this is precisely what Duras is describing in *Writing*.

Hadot, in his description of the first of the Spiritual Exercises, explains that philosophy for the Stoics was not mere theory, but that it was, in fact, a way of life. It was, he writes, a means to drastically alter one's life:

> In the view of all philosophical schools, mankind's principal cause of suffering, disorder, and unconsciousness were the passions: that is, unregulated desires and exaggerated fears. People are prevented from living, it was taught, because they are dominated by worries. Philosophy, this appears, in the first place, as a therapeutic of the passions.

In other words, philosophy was seen as a set of rules of

spiritual exercises which one could use in one's life to affect change. For Duras, writing was her philosophy, was her sole spiritual exercise. For Duras, everything was writing. She writes, "Around us, everything is writing; that's what we must finally perceive. Everything is writing." This is also what many faithful believers say of God: "God is everywhere. God is in everything." She used her writing as a means of learning how to live, and it was through her writing that she was given direction. When writing, Duras was, in essence, descending into the desert of the unknown. In *Writing*, she writes:

> Finding yourself in a hole, at the bottom of a hole, in almost total solitude, and discovering that only writing can save you. to be without the slightest subject for a book, the slightest idea for a book, is to find yourself, once again, before a book. A vast emptiness. A possible book. Before nothing. Before something like living, naked writing, like something terrible, terrible to overcome. I believe that the person who writes does not have any ideas for a book, that her hands are empty, her head is empty and that all she knows of this adventure, this book, is dry, naked writing, without a future, without echo, distant, with only its elementary golden rules: spelling, meaning.

Writing, for Duras, is the decent into the desert. It is following the star of the next world with blind faith. "Writing," says Duras, "is the unknown. Before writing one knows nothing of what one is about to write." It is this act; the act of swallowing something, one can neither see, hear, or otherwise comprehend that makes Duras a believer, a descender.

"Learning to Dialogue" is Hadot's second Spiritual Exercise. By this, he means: to meditate, "Meditation," he writes, "[is] the practice of dialogue with oneself." An important part of meditation is silence or solitude, for it is only in moments of silence, away from others, that one can hear the voice of the Divine. Again, Hadot writes:

> Furthermore, in Plato's view, every dialectical exercise, precisely

because it is an exercise of pure thought, subject to the demands of the Logos, turns the soul away from the sensible world, and allows it to convert itself towards the Good. It is the spirit's itinerary towards the divine.

For Duras, this means solitude:

> The person who writes books must always be enveloped by a separation from others. That is one kind of solitude. It is the solitude of the author, of writing. To begin with, one must ask oneself what the silence surrounding one is—with practically every step one takes in a house, at every moment of the day, in every kind of light, whether light from outside or from lamps lit in daytime. This real, corporeal solitude becomes the inviolable silence of writing.

On this theme, she continues:

> When one takes everything from oneself, an entire book, one necessarily enters a particular state of solitude that cannot be shared with anyone. One cannot share anything. One must read the book one has written, alone cloistered in that book. There is obviously something religious about this....

But this also means silence, which is related to solitude, hinging upon it, and yet—the two are separate. Duras writes, "Writing also means not speaking. Keeping silent." This silence and solitude are necessary in order to meet the unknown, to descend. Like a pilgrim walking into the white-hot shock of the desert, Duras descends into the unknown of the book.

Hadot lists the third of the Spiritual Exercises as "Learning to Die." He writes, "There is a mysterious connection between language and death." In *Writing*, Duras asserts, "One can speak of writing as sickness." "Solitude also means," she writes, "either death or a book." Here, she conflates the two: writing is a kind of death; it is a leaning into one's end. In this way, Duras aligns herself, knowingly or not, with the philosophers. Hadot writes:

In the apprenticeship of death, the Stoic discovers the apprenticeship of freedom. Montaigne, in one of his best-known essays, "That Philosophizing Is Learning How to Die," plagiarizes Seneca: "He who has learned how to die, has un-learned how to serve." The thought of death transforms the tone and level of inner life: "Keep death before your eyes every day ... and then you will never have any abject thought nor any excessive desire." This philosophical theme, in turn, is connected with that of the infinite value of the present moment, which we must live as if it were, simultaneously, both the first moment and the last.

And Duras lives this way. For her, each day is a *tabula rasa*, a blank page, an empty book. "Writing is the unknown," Duras writes. "Before writing one knows nothing of what one is about to write. And in total lucidity." This terror is a variation of death, an obliterating, self-annihilating act. Hadot writes, "Training for death is training to die to one's individuality and passions...." To be made new, to be reborn, each and every day. And engaging in this, this active looking at death and the end, every day, all the time means being at risk, putting one's self at risk, always with one's writing. Doing this, writing what one must not write, becomes, then, the only salvation, the only means to stay alive. Duras writes, "first and foremost it means telling oneself every day that one mustn't kill oneself, so long as every day one could kill oneself." It is there, at all times, the specter of death. This keeps us honest. As long as we see death in everything, we will be moved to say the one thing we simply cannot.

It is in the death of the author, the loss of one's self, that the writing arrives. "Language develops," Hadot quotes Brice Parain, "only upon the death of individuals." The French philosopher Hélène Cixous writes at length about this very topic in her book *Three Steps on the Ladder of Writing*. In it she states:

> Dostoyevsky received the world through having lived it (we always come back to the experience of Abraham and Isaac), received it

because he was condemned to death, because he was in front of the firing squad and then was pardoned, in extremis. This is grace: death given, then taken back.

Similarly, Duras writes:

> To be alone with the as yet unwritten book is still to be in the primal sleep of humanity. That's it. It also means being alone with the writing that is still lying fallow. It means trying not to die.

For Duras writing was both entering the realms of death while, at the same time, using writing as a shield against it.

Duras was a survivor, of course. Born into poverty in Saigon, she lived with her mother and brother, who both beat her. Her father died when she was still young. She suffered her entire adult life with alcoholism. In other words: death was always breathing into the small corners of her life. She knew it, she beckoned it to her, she spoke to it on a regular basis. Of death, she writes:

> My presence made that death even more horrible. I knew it, and still it remained. To see, see how that death would progressively invade the fly, and also to try to see where that death had come from.

Duras was a mystic, using writing as a spiritual exercise, as a way to move out of her world and into the next. Writing as a means to enter into death, to dialogue with it, while, at the same time, using writing as a means to drop into the solitude, into silence, into the abyss of not-knowing (God's world)—these are the three main tenets of the spiritual exercises. Duras used writing as a machine-like apparatus, as a means to drop further into the unknown. Like a saint descending into the white-hot sun of the desert, Duras descended into the white-hot desert of the page—blank as death, in silence, in solitude.

CHARCOAL

In my brown leather bag:
some underwear and a white feather
I found along the pavement
on Sunset in Silverlake
when I was eleven. Sweet
Marianne playing
on the black plastic radio
in the tremendous muck and doom.
On the train to Versailles:
three girls from Basque
and the one
painting her short boy-like nails black.

MEDICINE AND MAGAZINES

Glitter of leaves near the gutter
at the Museum of Natural Tragedy.

Succulents, bougainvillea, the toilet
of our history.

California salve: the plum
like hum of death's white music.

Tess Gallagher & Lawrence Matsuda
interviewed by Nancy Mitchell

NM: I'm intrigued with the shifting and recurring perspective, tone and imagery within each of the individual poems and consistent across each of the three sections of *Boogie-Woogie Crisscross*. In Section I, "Pow Pow Shalazam"; Section II, "Wild Haired-Labyrinth Renga"; and the final Section III, "Blue Cocoon," the recurring imagery particularly seems to create a constellation of sorts, a coordinate by which this "Crisscross" might have been charted … maybe a *Boogie-Woogie Starcross* of sorts?

LM: No title change at this late date. It is too embedded in the work, and "Starcross" seems like it is something ill-fated, like star-crossed lovers.

NM: You're right, of course; and I wouldn't presume to suggest another title—my comment was a result of the feature's contagious "mischief and zaniness" Tess mentions.

TG: Each of the sections has a different tempo and central concern, although, as in the dance "boogie-woogie," we swing each other wide and wild at times, trying to challenge each other's balance and comeback. "Blue Cocoon"'s central image comes from a painting by Josie Gray, my Irish companion of 24 years now. When we carried the painting, which is named *Blue Cocoon*, to show the Irish painter Sean McSweeny, Sean commented on the fact of the blue in the painting not receding as blue is suppose to do when used correctly. In fact, what I loved was the unmannerly levitation of that blue. And some other unmannerly elements come forward, such as the Irish company, following their host, picking up their dessert dishes and licking the cream from them! So there is mischief and zaniness and the notion that rules are being broken in a jubilant way. Josie, who never went to art school, doesn't mind if his blue refuses to recede.

the *plume* poetry interviews 1

NM: Yes! I love this!

TG: Earlier sections like "Pow Pow" dipped in and out of comic book language and car lingo and the drive-in-movie era. The style is careening like on a carnival ride, veering this way and that. "Wild-Haired Labyrinth Renga" is perhaps the most political section as it deals with the death of an Indian immigrant woman by sepsis due to misconceived Irish laws, which failed to consider the life of the mother during birth. The woman did not receive correct attention after the child was allowed to die within her, and she died. Her husband recently settled with the hospital and the Irish health board for an undisclosed amount of money, and the case never came to trial.

NM: Correct me if I'm mistaken, but you began the first section in 2011, the second in 2013, and the final recently?

LM: No is the answer—The sections are purposely out of chronological order. "Pow Pow" in 2011, "Wild-Haired" in 2013–15 and "Blue Cocoon" was completed in 2015.

TG: Yes, Larry is correct here, that we placed "Blue Cocoon" between our first section and our second. We liked the feel of it there, incubating between the two snap-crackle-and-pop sections. In the book the order is "Pow Pow," "Blue," and then "Wild." "Blue," even though it was the most recent and shortest, fit best in the middle.

NM: You both gave yourself permission to respond spontaneously, directly to each other's poems, which creates a delightfully immediate and playful tone. Did you ever go back to these original responses and revise them?

LM: "Wild-Hair" was revised more than 28 times and the others were in the teens for revisions.

TG: As Larry says, there was a long process of revision since the poems were published first in *Plume* online and we proofed them for that even after we had worked exhaustively on our own with them. Although the poems were conceived in a spontaneous way, they were worked over to a close finish.

NM: Did you find yourself challenged by this process?

LM: The *process* was not a challenge because it was like sending emails. The challenge was responding to Tess in a fresh fashion so that new and interesting ground was covered that was entertaining, informative, and as real as poetry can be in terms of telling a story without becoming didactic.

TG: I think the fun and challenge was, as Larry says, to come back to each other's work with something engaging and yet that would move the exchange forward. Larry had to educate himself to the entire political event of the death I mention above, which stimulated a change in Irish law as regards childbirth wherein the mother's life receives equal concern as the unborn child's now. In "Blue Cocoon" we had to take in several developments concerning islands that came to be devoted to singular purposes like importing a population of cats to kill mice to protect the silkworms, and on another island rabbits who became feral when exposed to poison gas during war-making experiments. Islands within islands became a topic. And this section is also a kind of island within the other two sections.

NM: How do you feel the tone and perspective of these exchanges evolved/morphed/changed over time?

LM: I would say the first poems were more of me as "little brother" bothering my older sister. But very quickly I pushed forward to gain ground and occupy a more level playing field. But I never was able to maintain that position, as the next response from Tess was like a tidal wave coming in. So after each wave I gave ground and ventured out again as the tide receded. My determination was the core theme from my point of view. But I never could declare victory except that the exchange made me grow as a poet under the tutelage of the master.

TG: I love Larry's game revivals of spirit and subject matter each time he responded to a poem from me. Whatever I could bring forward he took on with vigor and audacity. He is a fighter for women's rights and against those who plunder our procreative gifts and use outdated laws to bind us into untenable bargains set by religion or laws, which in Ireland made it against the law to use contraception in 1935. I also come into his corner when he brings forward elements of his birth in Minidoka and the many losses and humiliations the Japanese American people suffered during the unlawful incarcerations of WWII.

I'd say we had a rollick in these poems, but they have their serious undertone, which is possible because the tone is of the dance and doesn't allow the reader to sidestep the business at hand.

NM: Yes, indeed; a rollick, a wild ride, a whirl, but with a serious undertone as a ballast.

TG: The beat and the avalanche speed of the poems whirl forward, sweeping all before them, scooping up a more than normal amount of material. I think one of the things the poems display is just how wide-reaching a series of poems can be. We hopefully learn a lot about Irish and American points of view and concerns, but not with too heavy a hand!

NM: Tess and Larry, thank you; "Blue Cocoon," *Plume*'s final installment of *Boogie-Woogie Crisscross*, is an amazing, unforgettable ride. Readers, fasten your seat belts!

This is the last installment of the series. The entire book (three sections) is *Boogie-Woogie Crisscross* (MadHat Press, 2016).

BLUE COCOON *(from Larry to Tess)*

In Ballindoon, lambing over
and hay baled high,
Josie wears his red shirt
as he drives to your County Sligo cottage.

After 40 years some call you *Yank* or *blow-in*,
woman with perfect eyebrows,
who attracts gold finches, coal tits, and chaffinches
to a pastoral scene overflowing with bird calls and songs.
Hedge cats skulk like Serengeti lions, nose

your milk dish in anticipation. The two Eileens up the road
brew pots of Lyons or Barry's tea, expect you at their door
before Josie's family reunion where you claim your place
among his clan: sons, daughters, grandchildren, great-
    grandchildren,
and his late wife's memory.

In Portland, Oregon I rise in my hotel room,
pillows strewn helter-skelter,
scene reminiscent of marshmallows floating
in a hell's broth. I recall our mutual friend, Alfredo,
who lands in Portland like a shanghaied sailor
unable to remember anything beyond
his Blue Moon Tavern binge in Seattle the night before.
Alfredo's adventure rivals the night he stacked

two unsecured paintings on the roof of his car,
navigated hills under the influence
and pin-balled down Ravenna Avenue.
His canvases must have sprouted Edvard Munch-like

expressionist arms and hands to grip their extraterrestrial
mosaic faces in fear as they screamed all the way home.

I discover Portland is a carnival wonderland where
bacon drapes maple bars and pretzels impale chocolate
voodoo doll donuts filled with raspberry blood.
Food-cart shantytowns sprout in downtown parking lots,

gypsy chuckwagon villages, magnet for hordes of lip-smacking,
khaki-clad office workers and itinerant street musicians.
As a visitor I search for the *Yin* and *Yang*
of Portland's vibe, only to dodge
snares where amplitude sine waves intersect
and outstretched hands release grocery baskets piled
with bursting garbage bags.
Gauntlet of medieval palms reach out to me.

To the beggars, I am a lump of protein
zigzagging a trespass across *their* sidewalk,
sidestepping invisible webs that snag coins
in a spare change geometrical world of angles.
Scrawled message dangles from a liberated Safeway cart,
The last person who stole this cart owns it.
From my ten-story hotel room,
I open curtains to a miniature crime scene below—
life-size G.I. Joe toy action figure face-down—
twisted in a camouflage sleeping bag on the lip
of a vacant storefront.
No blood trails, blue police lights,
or crime tape, just a voyeuristic sense of peering
into private corners of a lost soul,

someone who in a different reality might have
killed enemies who looked like me.

In the morning I embark on an urban fishing adventure—
bind a net and two spinning rods,
pull a red Igloo Cooler strapped to a luggage cart
past food trailers and the Chinatown Gate
to the esplanade on the Willamette River's east bank.
My cart clack-clacks, echoes
through the homeless cardboard shanties in rhythm
with tires whining on bridge grates above.
Below the Burnside Street overpass,

glowing eyes track me like prey.
My designer glasses or yellow skin mean nothing here,
only the sound of rattling wheels—passport
to polite nods of recognition as if I were
a lost brother seeking the cathedral built for myself.

Tess, when lambing is over and hay is
wrapped in plastic like giant jelly rolls
scattered across the shorn fields,
what rattles your wheels when Josie gathers
his clan around the evening hearth?

the *plume* poetry interviews 1

Cat Mountain *(response from Tess)*

Polish coal rattles into the grate, signals
the ozone layer over Ballindoon that the EU's tax
won't snuff carbon fumes here any time
soon. Poverty, the great instructor, inhibits
change. Though overnight the Irish quit smoking
in pubs, they huddle to their open coal fires and will not
easily surrender them, even against taxes. These

are a people who ate grass during The Famine
to stay alive, and the old Chinese proverb says
"*If a person can chew roots they will be able
for anything.*" I am among a people, Larry, able
for anything. I remind myself of this daily, watching
Mickey Moran head to the bog on his tractor
to haul out sticks to extend his coal fire. As for

shopping carts, it takes a 2€ piece to free one from
a locked chain of trolleys. Failing that you must shop small
with a handbasket. Make trips. Poverty puts good legs
on some. Helmeted bicyclists whizz past my windows as petrol
goes up. The moon could care less how we get around,

but I swear sleeping under the Sligo moon has swept my usual
dream-cargo free and cleared my spirit-realm of
festering. Like sleeping under cherry blossoms,
a gentleness falls through me, sifts my proclivities
for connecting to the troubles of others, and stays
temporarily my need to bind up the world's

miseries. Not to say I can't be outraged
by daily ignorance: the Sligo doctor quoted as

saying he could not tell if his East Indian patient had jaundice
"because of her color." At one report she has kidney failure,
the next she's dying: Dhara whom her husband called:
"*the light of my life.*" That light snuffed a few days after
her boy was delivered by caesarian. The inquest witnesses

her relegated to a maternity ward instead of ICU,
though she presented with "more than two organs in
failure." Bloods drawn, but not read. Doctors in attendance
but no alarms to save her. The worried husband mollified
by a nurse, told to get his wife a lemonade if he wanted to help
her. Here, Larry, skin color is more than punitive
with daily humiliations; it can cost you your life.

The headline actually read: "*We can't tell if Dhara has
jaundice due to Indian skin.*" I want to howl and crawl
into a hedge. I want to live on Cat Mountain, far from
such goings on. Though months have passed since I left
for America, Bashō-cat has magically returned, perhaps
from Cat Mountain. I swear he raised a paw in a salute
of good luck, as I put down his dish of milk and fish.

I am worse than itinerant, more like a strange comet
that not only falls out of the sky but up
out of the ground! Not even a cat should depend
on me. Especially since I fell while gathering lake stones
for the garden and broke my wrist. The Japanese warning
not to move stones by daylight
comes back to me. I hug the roadway hedge
to Eileen Frazer's only to find she's in Sligo General

with a broken hip. Ahh, we are such egg-shell manifestations,
such feverish migrations. It's a wonder birds don't
entirely desert us, we who infuse the day with spiritually illiterate
peckings and preenings. Only my great-granddaughter Jade
saves prospect. She paints a bracelet of flowers
and cats' whiskers around my cast. The world needs more
of her. She can recite poetry and draw dogs

leading people around on collars to "Obedience School."
On my cast I wear to the NY premiere
of *Birdman* she scribbles "*Mummy Teresa,*" gets the giggles,
then cartwheels into the hydrangea. Oregon,
she says, is where you get "onto The Trail." She's
not sure if she would like "The Trail" but without it, she says,
nobody in America would have arrived anywhere
West. Most of all she'd like to meet an Indian. She'd trade

two magpie feathers for an eagle shaft, or
bargain black bogwood for a string of beads,
and be happy to go fishing with you, Larry. But you'd better
have something to trade. Remember she's of the tribe
that chews roots, a mighty lot. You'll recognize each other, your
    being
from the tribe that forages mushrooms among
sword ferns. She says she would rather
go to Cat Mountain though,
than to Oregon.

CAT ISLAND AND BUNNY TOWN *(response from Larry)*

While drift-fishing for King Salmon at Point Defiance,
I spot a floater, not a plastic bottle or Coke can but
a large black feather. Feathers should sink
among crabs and mud sharks, not
bob on green waves. Since there are no flying turkeys,
it must be from the bald eagle I call Icarus.

Like World War I biplane fighters, crows
dive for Icarus's tail feathers in flight,
harass and squawk, defending their turf.
I examine the feather closely. No UPC codes,
made in Japan, China, or USA markings.
It is a magnificent quill pen, something
Jefferson would have used to sign
the Declaration of Independence.

Your great-granddaughter, Jade, would have loved it,
except it is a federal crime to possess an eagle feather
unless you're a Native American. It carries
a $10,000 fine, an amount that could free 4,000
Irish shopping carts from their 2-euro cages,
depending on the currency exchange.

So I set the feather adrift with a short prayer
of thanks and good wishes. It swirls, then holds close
for a moment, like the bottle-nose
porpoise who plays and follows me on occasion.
Gently the feather breaks free from my gravity
and floats like a happy wayfarer riding the currents
towards Vashon Island and Quartermaster Harbor
until it fades, a dot in the distance.

Tell Jade if I visit Ballindoon, I would take her
for a grocery cart ride past the pubs and stores in Boyle,
the nearest town. First I would liberate Josie's red shirt,
then don black and white war paint, tie a scarlet bandana
around her forehead and place a turkey feather in her auburn hair.
We would stop at every bakery, sweet shop, and tearoom,
feast on delicacies—not grass or roots—
then trundle towards the horizon and disappear
like a movie iris dot near Eileen's cottage where

her teapot waits, cradled in a salmon-colored cozy.
I would tell stories about Tashirojima Island,
Japan, and how cats were shipped in to chase mice
that ravaged silkworm cocoons. When the company moved,
animals outnumbered villagers.
They had cared for the cats, hoping the felines
would bring good luck to the few remaining residents.

It was a scene reminiscent of the medieval maneki-neko story—
cat who raised its paw in salute as a rich priest's palanquin passed,
a sign the holy man should stop for the evening.
The poor village prospered when travelers learned
of the priest's favor, spawning hordes of ceramic
maneki-nekos and plastic charms to clutter Japan today.
Can you imagine an island governed by wily felines,

representing different independent parties?
You and Bashō, the hedge cat, would be in heaven
and I am sure the cat citizens would be
enlightened enough not to pass a coal tax.
Laws against dogs would serve better

even though none would ever have seen one.
This village should not be confused with Okunshina, the island
of feral rabbits, which Jade would like more
than you and Basho. Offspring of those used

for poison gas experiments run free
after the plant closed. Tame and friendly they wander
the island protected. This twisted tale reminds me
of a movie call for Japanese extras
I answered last week. They asked that I shave,
bring a white shirt, and a suit, only to stand around
8–10 hours for minimum wage. I declined
when I found the movie was about Japan winning

the war and occupying America.
That falseness meant my relatives in Hiroshima
and those in Nagasaki were never incinerated alive;
that the Japanese liberated us from American concentration
camps in the desert after 3 years of confinement; that we
would have been heroes and not the vanquished foe

looking like the enemy after the war.
"Slightly jaundiced" would be the preferred national
skin color and all property lost from our unjust
incarceration would be returned. Ironically this topsy-turvy
fantasy turned me inside out and badly disrupted
my psyche, unless, of course, it was a comedy.
Alas, Tess, how many belly laughs can you
pack into a movie about America
losing the war?

the *plume* poetry interviews 1

By the Sea *(response from Tess)*

All afternoon in North Sligo lunching in the artist's studio:
tubes of paint, tubs of gesso, paintings
big enough to make your bed on. Sean McSweeney
and his wife Sheila dancing the conversation from rugby to
the Peace Rose planted early in their marriage, rose devoured
by sheep. Orna, their daughter, reads
Akhmatova in Russian, serves apple tart with full

cream, the apples picked dewy from the orchard.
I smile conspiratorially, pick up
my plate, rediscover the tongue,
that neglected snail. Cats have nothing
on us, Larry. We lick cream. Blessed freedom
to sit at table with one's grown friends in old age

and caress sweetness from a dessert plate.
The cats on Cat Island sit about all day licking only fur
while Chuang Tzu dreams he's a butterfly mistaken
for a bird. "Wake up! Wake up!"
we shout. "Wake up and be a man or
be eaten or mauled to death!" Chuang Tzu flutters open
his eyes and loses his life

as a butterfly. One less butterfly on Cat Island
makes no ripple on the indolence of cat multitudes
dreaming in sunshine. Meanwhile, the floating blue
at the center of Josie's painting has perplexed
Sean who says "blue should always recede."
But this frisky, ill-mannered blue levitates
as *Blue Cocoon*, asking us to tolerate its daring

masquerade as art plundering the rules of art, blue
successfully deluding itself it doesn't have to lie down
to the artist's brush. Your refusal, Larry, to appear
in the movie slated to undo the outcome of WWII,
has kept mountains of history books from having to be
burned on street corners. Meanwhile Alejandro's *Birdman*
pecks the indolent money-pocked eyes of the Hollywood

Buddha, trying to generate more than cookie-cutter
heroes. Josie's unruly blue raises its blue salute,
suggests we throw a party where we all lick
cream from white porcelain plates at a long table
by the sea—a blue-green sea that tosses waves
at Cat Island. When asked to offer a story, an Irish custom
at occasions, I'll tell of meeting the wizened man

near Lough Arrow who insisted I stroke
the breast feathers of his tethered hawk—after which
I quoted Wilfred Gibson:
Because I set no snare
But leave them flying free
All the birds of the air belong to me.

Those lines, committed to memory, free
a multitude, our minds floating out like music.

If we provoke the imagination of the captor, even
for a moment, Larry, he might wake up from his
power-dream to witness
a leather glove of cow's hide flying his empty hand
away, away over the blue-green fields.

ISLAND WITHIN AN ISLAND *(response from Larry)*

Chuang Tzu, dozing butterfly,
dreams of being a man.
Absent his vibrating wings,
the world spins sideways for a nanosecond.
During a harmonic convergence,
rain storms meant for parched vineyards
of the San Joaquin Valley twist through Port Angeles
and the Straits of Juan de Fuca.

Wake up, Chuang Tzu, your life is more than you think.

Like the sound of heavy cream slurped
from an apple-tart plate in Ballindoon,
smacking lips and gulping conjure squeeze-box
rhythms of an Irish ballad pulsating from Josie's brush,
spreading blue hues across the painting's heart.
I recall gazing down at Campbell Lake from

Mt. Erie on Fidalgo Island where an island sits
in the center of blue like a watercolor painting, an island
within an island. As the wind rises over the cliff, I remember
what my first wife used to say,
No man is an island, Larry, except for you.

Instead of quoting Gibson when asked to offer up a story,
I visualize a sugar-frosted Easter egg decorated with pink swirls
and clear plastic viewing port with a diorama
of a miniature bride and groom. I am the white-haired minister
in a blue aloha shirt next to the mossy waterfall
in Kubota Gardens. We stand on the edge of a cliff
under a canopy of pine trees. Anna's hummingbirds,

goldfinches and butterflies flutter in celebration. We are all
butterflies on the verge of morning.

Like an Irish sleepwalker Josie wields his brushes,
madly paints Tess's Ballindoon cottage blue instead
of the promised white as she flies like an untethered hawk
over the Atlantic from Dublin.
Flap your butterfly wings, Chuang Tzu, parched
San Jaoquin hardpan and thirsty grapes beckon. Monarchs
cluster in the park, expect your entrance as the teapot whistles
a high-pitched warning.
Stop your nodding and chase sleep from

the silkworm cocoon of your mind, wake from lazy dreams
of hammocks and mulberry leaves. No longer
a sheltered worm, know you are
more than a Moon Pie treat, silent victim
of cat-lightning.

Thomas McCarthy
interviewed by Hélène Cardona

HC: The first poem is titled "Waterford Crystal." Tell us about Cappoquin, County Waterford, where you're from, and Cork, where you now live and were librarian, and how they've influenced you. You said of Cappoquin that it's a place that breeds poets.

TMcC: My native county, Waterford, is where the famous luxury glassware is made, though in recent years this business has had difficulties. Cappoquin is a little town on the banks of the Blackwater, a beautiful river that dominates the atmosphere of the town: "Cappoquin he came from, Cappoquin on the Blackwater" is what Molly Bloom says of her Gibraltar lover in Joyce's *Ulysses*. Though it's a town of fewer than 1,000 people, it has a long tradition of poets, from Padraig Denn, the Gaelic poet, to Maurice Walsh and Michael Cavanagh, poets in the English language. Nearly forty years ago when I told the great Irish poet Maire Mhac an tSaoi where I was from, she exclaimed "Ah, Cappoquin of the Poets!" The salutation says everything of my native place.

HC: You are a poet and writer. You've written poetry books, novels and essays. I would call you the ultimate poet, as poetry informs everything else you do. Poetry has influenced your approach to fiction and non-fiction. Do you agree? Can you speak to that?

TMcC: Poetry governs everything I write, and it has from the very beginning of my writing when I was a teenager. In Ireland the "poet" as political idea, as moral leader, is still very strong. This has a lot to do with our national history and our continuous revolutions that always seem to have a Latin American flavor. Poets were often the theorists and propagandists for a ruined nation. It is a powerful idea or affirmation for a poet. But it is also dangerous because one begins with very little skill and too much public expectation. In Ireland a poet has nearly always begun by wanting to save Ireland, only to end up trying to save himself or herself. This pattern continues, even today.

HC: "What the Poor Are For" is such a powerful and poignant poem. You address "the malleability of [my] memory—." Memory is a double-edged sword. You write, "It is life that finishes / Our sentences;" and it hits the reader like a hammer. Will you share your thoughts?

TMcC: The poor are always with us. I come from a poor family myself; I understand that incredible alienation from success that poor families feel. That atmosphere of remembered failure comes back to me from my childhood, that sense of passivity, of hopelessness and displacement. To be poor is to be an inner exile in any nation. In Ireland, especially, we've had a huge element of poverty and even famine in our past. It is something that Ireland has had to deal with for at least four centuries since the earliest land confiscations from the Gaelic land owners by British settlers in the sixteenth century. The story of Ireland is the story of the re-integration of those historically dispossessed and the expulsion, by mass deportation, mass emigration or mass famine, of the surplus population. In Ireland, unlike North America, this native population refused to die. The poor of Ireland constantly reassert their right to life. This struggle fascinates and horrifies me. I want to know, genuinely, politically, why does a modern society tolerate conditions of poverty for, perhaps, one third of its population; and why is this tolerated generation after generation?

HC: You've been steeped in literature and books your whole life. You edited, at various times, *The Cork Review* and *Poetry Ireland Review*. How did your editorial work affect your writing?

TMcC: I think it's the other way round. I mean my writing affects my editing. All writing has an element of editing in it. As poets we only know how to be editors by expanding outward from our own work, by perfecting our own voice and aesthetic and by learning to read other poets through our own aesthetic. The key in editing is to arrive at a view of what constitutes a truly successful poem, even when someone else has written it. Editing calls us out of ourselves and forces us to be part of a wider community, a community of others who really struggle hard to write well. There is something deeply poignant about being an editor. Sometimes you can be almost overwhelmed by witnessing so many individual struggles to write well, but you always dream of receiving a manila envelope full of brilliant new work.

HC: You're also a historian. *The Last Geraldine Officer* features ballads, a series of poems in quatrain form, and a sequence of prose poems consisting of the campaign diary of an Irishman serving as an officer in the British army of the Second World War. It's a masterpiece. It mixes mid-century Gaelic verse and County Waterford recipes.

Can you tell us how this book came to be? And can you speak about arranging the poems in this collection and your use of form?

TMcC: This book was in my head for over twenty years. I wrote the short lyrics in Gaelic (a kind of pastiche of the Gaelic language as published in the 1920s and 1930s) in 1987, but the collection wasn't published until 2009. The material is riddled with ambiguity and it is difficult to settle on a poetic form that might embody two points of view in history. The book is narrated by a persona, Colonel Sir Gerald FitzGerald, based on the character of someone I was very close to personally for many years, an Anglo-Irish aristocrat who gave me a library and an apartment to work in when I was only seventeen years old. I had that beautiful refuge to retreat to until Brigadier Denis Henry FitzGerald, a grandson of the Duke of Leinster who'd spent his childhood at the great houses of Carton and Kilkea Castle, died after twenty years. It is not normal for an Irish poet, or any Irish citizen, to take on the uniform of a British officer, but I always found Denis's love of Ireland and Irish culture intriguing, as, socially, he would be seen by most people as English; imperial English, that is, having been educated at Eton and Sandhurst Military Academy. He led an Allied Tank Regiment through the awful battles of Normandy, Arnhem and the Rhine Bridges. He survived a Waffen SS Heavy Tank battle, several Stuka bombings and the sinking of his troop-ship off Norway in 1940, but if you met him on the street in Cappoquin you'd think he's just been a gentle gardener all his life.

I should explain that Ireland, like much of Catholic Europe

and South America, was neutral during the Second World War, but thousands of Irishmen and women went off and joined in the fight against Fascism in Europe. While I politically understand Irish Neutrality, I admire those who donned a British or American uniform to fight Hitler. There are two lines in that collection that sum up the key feeling I wanted to communicate about this Anglo-Irish viewpoint: in these lines my Colonel FitzGerald addresses his fellow-Cappoquin man, Sergeant Foley, who has gone to war with him—

> 'An naisiun priobhaideach do dheineamar
> Fe eide Ghallda: saol ionraic san Iodhbairt Dhoite'

which means

> 'The private nation we made together
> in that foreign uniform: an honest life in a Holocaust.'

No further comment is necessary, I think.

HC: *Merchant Prince: The life and passion of Nathaniel Murphy, gentleman-merchant, in Italy and Ireland* is a prose novella set in Italy and bookended by two sequences of poems, set largely in Cork, in the period from 1769 and 1831, all of which are interrelated. The writing is refined, splendid, and the novella reminds me of Henry James. This is a very original, lyrical book, with again a mixture of verse and prose. What inspired you to write it? What research did you do?

TMcC: I loved writing this large book. I completely indulged myself, and my publisher, Peter Jay of Anvil Press Poetry, also had complete faith in the project. I think Peter enjoyed Nathaniel's company as much as I did. The novella at the centre was originally planned as a mass frieze of footnotes beneath the lyrics, in the manner of an early-nineteenth-century edition of Byron with Hobhouse's great notes or an edition of Sir Walter Scott. But Peter Jay, the publisher, didn't think the "notes" worked, so I rewrote the entire prose as a novella. The Italian poets translated by my Nathaniel are not Italian at all, but Italian versions of living Gaelic poets of Ireland, so that Count Luigi da Pora is really the brilliant Irish poet Louis de Paor and Principessa Nulana Nigonelli is actually the sublime Nuala Ni Dhomhnaill and my "translations" from Italian are really translations of texts by these Irish poets; but I have exchanged Irish place names for Italian place names. You can see what I mean by being self-indulgent—it is the kind of project dreamt up by an English professor in a provincial university who hasn't been given enough work to do by his Department chairman. My created character, Nathaniel Murphy, is an 18th-century Irishman who goes to Rome to study for the Catholic priesthood, but loses his vocation after making love to the wife of a Vatican silversmith. Yet again, it's a novelistic narrative that comes out as a set of lyrics. But again, it's all about ambiguity, Nathaniel's deep faith versus his sexual needs, Nathaniel's patriotism versus his cosmopolitan viewpoint. The book was quite successful, getting terrifically respectful reviews; and I see that it is stocked in most of the great University libraries in America. I became so obsessed with the writing, I remember my wife, Catherine, used to say to me "Are you finished talking to Nathaniel for the day, now could I talk to you about the kids' school reports?" She used to say that nobody will understand this; it's too Irish, too Cork. But I think of it as my happiest book, a book that created an entirely benevolent atmosphere in my life for several years.

HC: Your writing is exquisite, so precise, concise, the work of an exacting, meticulous hand. What is your editing process like? Do you have a daily writing routine?

TMcC: When I was a teenager, and, really, until our two children were born in my early thirties, I wrote for two hours every day. These two hours were sacred; I would feel ill if I didn't have them. If I knew I was going out in the evening I'd get up at 6 a.m. and have my two hours of writing. Children change every routine; with children you must learn to catch-crop, to snatch hours. Now I am writing full-time again, having left the Library service after over thirty years. I sit and read or write for five hours every day. Reading is also a kind of writing, as day-dreaming is as good as full dreaming. I am like a young man again, indulgently writing away, hidden away like a badger and pretending not to be at home. My only task now is how to write well. I've become obsessed with this. It is the only task. NOT to write a lot, but to write WELL. I have become a much sharper reader of poems, of other people's work, as I learn to concentrate fiercely on texts and texts alone. I am not interested in what texts might mean—that is academic work—but in what texts DO on the page, the music of the thought, its weight and shape, its emotional aptness. I went back to giving poetry workshops again just two years ago. I had given up on workshops for years and years, but now I think I will do two workshops a year from now on; as long as the workshops last for six sessions or fewer. It is good to see new work and new voices, and we must learn to praise the young and push them onward. I am much more purposeful, much more ambitious, for new poets. I don't see why they shouldn't be the best, the very best, and why they shouldn't intend to be published in the very best places. The competition is fierce, yes, but that only helps standards of writing. This all comes from my own sense of a renewed purpose. Don't ask me where this new energy came from, it just did. I think I have a burst of such energy every seven years or so.

HC: I love the opening sentence of the novella *Memory*: "It is poetry that constitutes our deepest memoir; and my sojourn at Rome—kept by me when I was hardly formed as an Irishman—is best remembered as an act of translation." Would you say a few words about it?

TMcC: The words are Nathaniel Murphy's, my narrator in *Merchant Prince*. Rome to him is now like a dream, something so far away from Ireland that it is unreal. So it is as unreal as a different language, and the life lived within linguistic differences between people. Because Nathaniel is a poet as well as an ex-priest, he knows that poetry is the source of our deepest strength because through poetry we can get in touch with the deepest parts of our nature, with what is divine or immortal within us as humans. That's what he means by poetry as a deep memoir.

HC: Can you tell us about your new poetry collection, *Pandemonium*?

TMcC: Hopefully, *Pandemonium* will be published by Michael Schmidt's Carcanet Press late this year or early 2017. It was already with Anvil Press Poetry when Anvil had to shut down because of a catastrophic loss of funding. Carcanet have taken over Anvil Press Poetry lock, stock and barrel in an incredibly brave move, taking me, Martina Evans and James Harpur into the Carcanet fold. These poems were written during the dark years of Ireland's great Recession following the Banking collapse and the beginning again of mass emigration (both my children have emigrated). I spent a great deal of my free time walking the seashore of County Kerry and brooding darkly on things, from banking to the deaths of two key poets, Seamus Heaney and Dennis O'Driscoll. The seashore, water, waves, seabirds, cliffs, the Atlantic wind, all permeate the lyrics I wrote and create a peculiar atmosphere in the collection. But it is a book of individual lyrics, written when I was beginning to find a new technical energy and a renewed ambition for my poems. Hopefully, people will like the book.

HC: What are you currently working on?

TMcC: I am reading voraciously and writing steadily. I've been thrilled by encounters with American poets like Linda Norton and Jan Beatty and new books by Terrance Hayes and August Kleinzahler have really blown me away. But I write in bursts now, not hour by hour, so in the closing months of 2015 I wrote maybe fifteen new poems and in a burst of blessings in February–March this year I also wrote a bunch of sharpish lyrics. I have also been working on a play called *Barry Mulholland*, set in my home place of Cappoquin, Co. Waterford. That is a different task entirely and nothing may come of it. But it is worth trying something different, something that keeps the prose out of one's poetry.

HC: You've had an incredibly busy year with new poems published in *Poetry Review* and the *London Journal*, among others, and many readings, a filming of you reading memorial poems in the Gardens of Remembrance in Dublin, and the Listowel Writers Week in early June. What are you looking forward to most?

TMcC: I am really looking forward to the two workshop sessions, at the Molly Keane House in Ardmore, Co. Waterford, in May and September, and at the Listowel Writers' Week in June. It is nearly thirty years since I directed a workshop at Listowel, the mother of

the *plume* **poetry interviews 1**

all Irish literary festivals. I'm really looking forward to meeting old friends and remembering old friends with those who, like me, have survived so far. We have lost so many poets in Ireland in recent years: Heaney, O'Driscoll, Davitt, Michael Hartnett, Gregory O'Donoghue, Desmond O'Grady, that I feel very grateful to be here still, to be able to drink a drop of whiskey or wine and chase after strong new poems. Isn't that what life is all about? Isn't that what makes a poet get up in the morning and greet the new day?

Waterford Crystal

We were brought up in a country that loved glass crystal.
Lead crystal seemed to grow on the trees and on frosted glass
That shattered underfoot in December. The red beads
Of holly seemed to have dropped from a furnace, turned
On their wires by birds; everything as burned as my father's face
Was burned by a lifetime of picking through fire. The gorse
On the Comeraghs right now, warped and giving,
Is merely a cold liquid left by the factory's sudden firing.

The Eve of War

Amber was more than a woman's name beyond the seashore,
Though as words go she always wore a Jaeger jacket;
And she pauses awhile with other rich names on the Corso,
At a café table not far from where the Eternal City
Opens out into a reddish basin of light, as if Amber
Were no morbid secretion but four bushels of light
To cast upon the ashy stones of evening, to shine
As every Amber does at candlelit dinners on the eve of war.

Ice Cream

That time in the long ago when my father said we are what we eat

He must have meant my Venezuelan half-and-half or the triple-
Shot slim latte that you so adroitly downed in three seconds flat.
If my memory serves me correctly it was three Raspberry Ripple
Ice-cream cones I'd consumed outside Fraher's old shop, bought
With money I'd earned for myself on the early morning news
 run.
But my idle father was not ready to cede authority, or not yet
Willing to abandon the upper-hand. He was fooling no one; even
Then I had no time for advice. Like my stomach, I was basically
Idle and middle-aged at the ripe old age of ten, maybe eleven.
Worst luck for me rather than him, but my hatred of authority
Would set me breaking windows inside my own stomach. It is
 not,
Let me repeat, it is never, a good thing not to listen to your father
Even if he's drinking lukewarm whiskey from a flask Dan Fraher
Gave him: even if his voice has begun its collapse into cigarettes.

Worse than Nothing

Even then I knew that my life would be far less painless

Than my father had predicted. Cigarette poised
In a very superior gesture, a great gesture

Of idle, ill-deserved grandeur, he explained
That any effort I might make in Ireland

Would come to something worse than nothing.
It is this wet November drain I'm clearing of

Rotted leaves and cigarette-butts that puts
Him in my mind now—a beautiful cynic

For a father, a father who'd laugh at dreams,
Who only loved that one Noel Coward song

There are bad times just around the corner,
Not realizing as I did, though a boy, that Noel

Coward must have poked at many versions of
That before the sludge moved, before the song came.

BATHING IN RIMINI

Five hundred ocean-going yachts in out-of-season
Rimini, white stallions bobbing in the Adriatic trough

Here where rich Europe plunges its ravenous snout
And rises for oxygen in a gasp of folded spinnakers.

Female stragglers, in one single fountain of Italian
Breasts, play dangerously in the late waves. Connoisseurs

Of human beauty maintain their unembarrassed gaze—
It is never nearly enough to have once loved, to have

Lusted after everyone while young; but, if you own
A sixty-foot ledge of heaven, you must maintain

The hope of eternal youth, of that male eternity
Covered in fresh varnish; an eternity ravenous still

In the way hard cash is ravenous when it faces sexuality
Or the way a blob of *gelato* melts between us and the sea.

What the Poor Are for

Permit me for a moment to abandon hope
Of poetry: you must not think as you read
These words that any enjambment of thought
Or music is more important than the rhythms
Found in speaking plainly. It is life that finishes
Our sentences; and it is this perpetual thought:
That the poor must have some purpose in the end,
The abject poor, surely, must have a reason
To be constantly there, like rain in Ireland
Or the certainty of mist after a very warm day.
That I was born to a poor mother is
Undeniable; and the malleability of my memory—
I mean the memories of a childhood—
Is proof of the pudding. Or lack of pudding.
It has always struck me how adroitly
The poor amplify memory in an effort, no doubt,
To conform to some bourgeois expectations.
Of Christmas, for example, that festival of child-
Like trust in things fulfilled. Of Christmas
A poor child would prefer less said. I mean
At Christmas every poor child waits
In the foyer of life but is never called
Forward. A poor child capable of labour
Will work in frost or rain to carry Christmas
To an idle father, or to a catatonic mother.
Accept this. Nothing shall be asked for.
It is important to remember that nothing
Is asked for, still. Memory is not important:
It will pass away in a flourish of choirs
Where the comforted go, one of life's parades
Where the soul of the poor is an onlooker.

This is what it means to be poor; and when
I hear some well-meaning child
Of a bourgeois household, a child now
Grown to adulthood, a commentator
Upon the injustice of the world, a
Place-man from a long line of place-men
In Ireland, I am filled with a violent rage.
I am as violent as Hugh MacDiarmid
Or as violent as Knut Hamsun, that
Consumptive healing himself on his own,
On the roof of a fast-moving train.
I am exhausted with rage; and I am
Bitterly alone at the edge of this great cave
From which I emerged, one afternoon,
While God was busy looking after someone.
Even now I see God still shutting the cave
Doors, God in a rage that someone poor
Escaped. His Universities raising their fees,
His lists of the waiting. His hospital
Queues. There must be a purpose to this,
Don't you think? There must be a purpose:
It can't be without purpose that the best
Of our bourgeois sons, and of private schools,
Could manage four generations of public
Life only for us to end up like this—
I am thinking of all the jobs available
In the service of the Poor. I'm thinking, still,
Of the great passivity of the excluded.
Of the poor bringing purpose. Of everything.

Ira Sadoff
interviewed by Nancy Mitchell

NM: Ira Sadoff, you're one of American poetry's most distinguished senior poets, of whom the esteemed elder poet Gerald Stern has said, "Nowhere else in American poetry do I come across a passion, a cunning, and a joy greater than his. And a deadly accuracy. I see him as one of the supreme poets of his generation's culture." As well, you're a man of letters whose essays have had a great impact on the culture and conversation in contemporary poetry. You've been and continue to be a beloved teacher and mentor to generations of now-established and aspiring poets. I thought we could chat about the personal and cultural forces which have shaped the trajectory of your career and your poetry.

IS: Well, Nancy, I sure am senior. I'm 71. I was born in the Bensonhurst section of Brooklyn; my parents were second-generation lower-middle-class Jews. We moved frequently around the city, which probably contributed to my being something of a loner, often relying on my imagination for companionship. I felt the transiency of friendships, which in my adult life made authentic and loyal friendships both more precious and rare. I ended up in a suburban Long Island high school, Glen Cove, segregated almost as much by class as by race (and like most suburban schools it was motored by cliques, conformity, measuring someone by how he or she dressed or which expressions he or she used). That was probably the first time I felt like an outsider but also, since my father had abandoned our family and we became suddenly impoverished, I came to understand how much class position contributed to confidence and self-worth.

NM: Was there a galvanizing moment in your childhood when you knew you were going to be a writer?

IS: I don't remember any. As a young person I never felt I wanted to be—or was destined to be—a poet, though one of my neighbors recently reminded me that I showed her poems when I was thirteen. I used to love drawing and was headed to Music and Art when my parents moved out of the city into the suburbs. It wasn't until my junior year at Cornell when, half-consciously desperate to find a means of personal expression, I took my first poetry workshop. I had no special gifts, had not read any modern poetry (which is where many "gifts" actually come from) except Allen Ginsberg. I was deservedly given virtually no encouragement from my teacher, A. R. Ammons, who was a very good poet but had few skills in teaching the craft of poetry. But writing poems gave me my first real opportunity to feel engaged: I just loved doing it. When told I wasn't good enough to become a poet, I took fiction-writing classes and wrote stories. I then took my MFA at Oregon in fiction writing and published two stories, but in the interim had stopped writing poems.

NM: Did you find that same engagement, connection with writing fiction, or was poetry always beckoning?

IS: At the time I really just wanted to be a writer, and if I couldn't be a poet I still was overjoyed and received enormous pleasure and reward from writing fiction. I remember the precise moment fiction writing caught fire for me in grad school. I was taking a course in American Lit from Burt Sabol (who'd recently graduated from the Iowa Writers' Workshop): he generously asked to see a story of mine. In conference he went over the story line by line, not only editing but also showing me the power of timing—missed opportunities, moments where I could dig in deeper or moments when I had talked my way out of a scene. I've carried this knowledge with me my whole writing life.

I continued to write and publish fiction until I was fifty and I could see the imaginative limits of the work: my almost involuntary fidelity to autobiography, a cautiousness—based on the myth that sincerity and an allegiance to subject matter had the highest priority—proved to limit my artistry as a fiction writer. I wrote and published a novel when I was thirty and it was my transposed personal story. I kept trying and failing to write another novel but the work wasn't compelling enough to complete even a draft. I couldn't find my way out of this dilemma in stories either, so I put my prose energy into writing essays.

NM: When did you begin to write poetry seriously?

IS: During my first teaching job at Hobart and William Smith when I was twenty-two. My colleague, Jim Crenner, became my first real teacher (and virtually the first poet I'd met).

When I shyly showed him a poem I had written, he said "this work's strong because … this writing is weak because … now read these writers." He was so generous, reading many a poem of mine, and soon I was absolutely driven by passion for the art. In my own autodidact way I started reading everything, catching up. Good writing then no longer seemed like a gift from the gods but an attentive laboring. Every day I woke up at five in the the morning to write for four hours before teaching.

NM: Ah, Jim Crenner's generosity changed your life. You were so lucky!

IS: I absolutely was and I've always aspired to bring that generosity and rigor to my teaching. I know how much it means to be taken seriously. That's also why I'll never make judgments about "talent" in a young poet. There's almost no way to know.

NM: What was it about writing poems rather than fiction that made it a more fulfilling means of expression, your art of choice?

IS: The short answer: I had access to my imagination and the joy of play. Working by association I felt both a sense of freedom and discovery. I could become a better listener to the multiple suggestions of a line, of a poem. I look for density and emotional complexity in a poem: I believe this way of thinking reflects the richness and complexity of experience itself. Listening to what the page gave me—questioning preceding lines or intensifying them, qualifying or arguing with them, but always seeking out what's next rather than insisting on a narrative or a preconceived idea—opened my poems up. I began to understand writing poetry as play, the process as sculptural and flexible.

NM: Were you lucky enough to have encouragement from and influential friendships with other poets as you were starting out?

IS: I had some early encouragement from literary magazines, but other than that I was a kind of self-made poet. While at Hobart—this was in 1969, I think—Jim and I started *The Seneca Review*, and then I started corresponding with other poets, learning my craft because I had to make judgments. I began developing some poetry friendships, Charlie Simic and Phil Levine among those who became lifetime friends.

NM: How nourishing for a young poet to be in conversation, develop friendships with established poets, and be in close, daily proximity to the poetry hum, via teaching and editing *The Seneca Review*.

IS: Retrospectively I feel very fortunate to have grown up during a prosperous time (assuming you were white and middle-class). I didn't worry about making a living, just finding meaningful work. It was a time when counter-cultural values were ascendant and becoming a poet seemed like one plausible way to change consciousness.

NM: So, making art at that time was both a personal and conscious political act?

IS: Yes. The poetry I admire most questions authority and convention, attempts to integrate or wrestle with the fissures between private and public life: it's what Blake called Vision. Periodically in American poetry, you'll find the dominant aesthetic a private or transcendent poetry, mostly written by white middle-class people who have the luxury to feel insulated from the forces that shape them, their values and their art. But I started writing during a bold and exciting moment in American poetry and history: the civil rights movement, the anti-war movement, the second wave of feminism, all pressurized our views of experience and the function of poetry. The Sixties brought doubt to our unbridled belief in reason and the Enlightenment Project, in the American Dream, in universals, in the absolute wisdom of the fathers. Our philosophers were Nietzsche, early Freud and Heisenberg; those who recognized the force of subjectivity, desire and entropy.

NM: What an incredibly dynamic era to be coming of age, and into one's art; seismic shifts which artists were struggling to find forms with which to express them.

IS: The dry rhetorical academic poetry of the Fifties was dying out; we discovered what would later be called the new Internationalism—recognition of the great poetry written and translated from other languages. The most influential poets were Neruda, Lorca and Vallejo, Rilke, Ritsos, Trakl, Apollinaire, Desnos, and Eluard, Transtromer, Popa, the post-War Polish poets like Herbert and Milosz. Robert Bly's *The Sixties* and George Hitchcock's *Kayak* made many of these poets widely available for the first time.

The often willfully naïve and transcendent view that politics belonged to sociology and not our daily experience was exploded by poets like Neruda and Bly, James Wright, Adrienne Rich, Charles Simic, W.S. Merwin, James Tate, and many others—after all, we had an immoral war to face; the destruction of our cities; the more visible oppression of minorities; the oppression of women in the workplace, the kitchen, and the bedroom. These poets modeled for my generation of writers a new and necessary way of speaking.

NM: And to think that those revolutionary poets are now established in the canon of contemporary poetry! We owe so much to your generation for radically enlarging the frame of reference, the consciousness, and aesthetics of poetry.

IS: Their poems were mostly characterized by a faith in the image (sometimes called the deep image) and surprising metaphors and juxtapositions, in embodiment, in the irrational and the dream life (hence the neo-surrealist movement), a return to the "direct treatment" of the thing, to poems that didn't gloss their own meaning. I wouldn't personally take credit for this change, but I was happy to participate in the shifts: they were enormously important to my development as poet and person.

NM: How were your poems using the deep image?

IS: Perhaps "Disease of the Eye" from my first book, *Settling Down*, was the earliest example of the kind of neo-surrealist influence I can think of:

Disease of the Eye

Sometimes I wake up in the middle of the night,
in the middle of my own house, to discover
some woman has had her clothes in my closet
for years. She has even slept in my bed.
I feel like a child in an old movie,
asking myself where have I been. A film
covers the eye, and I can only recount events
out of sequence, in a haze. This is not clear
enough. It is as though I were a doctor
looking into my eyes with a strange
light, chasing the pupil into an endless tunnel
which is not endless. The pupil shrinks
like a schoolchild who does not know
the answer. I demand to know everything
below the skin. Who's the stranger sleeping
in my hands? What does a wife mean at night?
Something strange is going on
in my bed. I ask my wife, "Who is this man
you married?" She answers, "He has eyes that run
behind the lid." For this ailment
the doctor recommends the following:
cover the eyes with a cold compress of hands.
The stranger will disappear. The lights
will dim, but you'll know where you have been.

NM: Surreal indeed—it's a conversation between the selves, the layers of consciousness via mediating the image, isn't it? Do you agree that this consciousness of the selves within the self has been a consistent characteristic in your poetry?

IS: Absolutely. I'm really interested, and suppose I've always been more interested, in asking more questions of a poem and its competing feelings than dispensing wisdom or solving problems. To think of poems with an arrival point is to reduce experience. What a revelation to know that we have many feelings at once. That poem knew more about me then—I was twenty-three, I think—than I did. Which is, I guess, how it should be in poems. For me these imagistic poems helped me mediate a controlling intellect. The aspiration of those influential poets was to embody, to acknowledge feeling precedes knowing, and to incorporate what we called the "darkness" (a shortcut for mystery, the irrational, and the unknown).

NM: Yes … in the same way imagery in surrealistic paintings disables the mind by refusing a reference or representation on the conscious level. How did this exploration change the shape of the poem on the page?

IS: Formally this verse solidified the trend toward free verse and away from received forms; it often moved away from traditional punctuation, toward fracturing the line through line break, and suggesting more open-ended closures. We were critical of the ideology of new criticism's faith in paradox and transcendence (which we saw as serving the soul over the body, "organic" unity over complication).

NM: Yes, there was a longing for a Whitmanian wholeness, an organic connection, to "the starry dynamo."

IS: Right. The "truth of experience," and finding a language and form that would reflect the breaking of artifice and boundaries. Further, there was a movement toward more direct speech using more fissures in syntax, extending the line. Also we refused the strategy of emphasizing the more obvious, clangy surfaces of alliteration and onomatopoeia, the ornate diction that had made poetry seem decorative or "pretty." In subject matter we saw a turn toward the erotic, toward acknowledging an untamed interior life, but paradoxically also a turn toward the social.

NM: Maybe there was a sense of a shared interior life … a shared consciousness? How did your own poems track these changes?

IS: Again retrospectively I can see the first stylistic changes in my work came with the second book, *Palm Reading in Winter* (just reissued by Carnegie-Mellon as part of their American Classics Series). Jon Anderson's *In Sepia* literally changed my life. I was so moved by the intelligence of the poems, the austerity and music, I wrote a long review for *Seneca*. I was teaching at Antioch College at the time and Jon thought I'd so captured his aspirations that he decided he and his wife and child and dog would come visit me for a week. It was a wonderful, eye-opening week, and it served as one of my first deep friendships with another poet. It allowed me to put more conviction in my poetry. That's when I wrote more direct poems like "My Father's Leaving," and "Depression Beginning in 1956."

MY FATHER'S LEAVING

When I came back, he was gone.
My mother was in the bathroom
crying, my sister in her crib
restless but asleep. The sun
was shining in the bay window,
the grass had not been cut.
No one mentioned the other woman,
nights he spent in that stranger's house.

I sat at my desk and wrote him a note.
When my mother saw his name on the sheet
of paper, she asked me to leave the house.
When she spoke, her voice was like a whisper
to someone else, her hand a weight
on my arm I could not feel.

In the evening, though, I opened the door
and saw a thousand houses just like ours.
I thought I was the one who was leaving,
and behind me I heard my mother's voice
asking me to stay. But I was thirteen,

> and wishing I were a man, I listened
> to no one, and no words from a woman
> I loved were strong enough to make me stop.

NM: I've loved this poem for a long time … the static images, frozen in memory "The sun / was shining in the bay window, / the grass had not been cut" … the precision with which the mind etches, documents shock to distance from it. It seems out of this moment is a burgeoning awareness of the selves within the self which I mentioned as a characteristic of your work. "But I was thirteen, / and wishing I were a man, I listened" … so beautifully vulnerable.

IS: Thank you, Nancy.

NM: Would you go so far as to say that this poem was a "threshold" poem—"I opened the door"—which led to other changes?

IS: For a while, yes. Actually I'd written many poems about my father's leaving before then, and Greg Orr suggested why don't I just let the camera roll on the event without commentary? That helped me really live inside that moment. In the closure I coupled that strategy with a conviction based on what dramatic evidence the poem had provided me.

I'd say the next most dramatic change in my poems came during the time I was writing *Grazing*. I consider the poems in that volume the most adventurous I've written, breaking the fourth wall, using collage, interrupting sentences, fragmenting narrative, using more fissures in syntax. Also extending the range of emotions I could use within a poem, which I would call a kind of wildness. At the time I was reading the language poets and though it may be difficult to see the influence in the work, I was challenged and nourished by poets like Lyn Hejinian in her *My Life*. I began thinking more about the urgency of associative thinking in poetry, and realized my feelings grew out of a lifetime love and appreciation of jazz: the syntactical response to what's already in the air or on the page, and then following it both through improvisation and the memory of what you've heard. I've written, for the American Poetry Blog, a blog entry about it: blog.

bestamericanpoetry.com/the_best_american_poetry/2012/09/mr-pc-imagination-and-improvisation.html

NM: Can you give an example of how this works in jazz?

IS: Yes; David Murray's "Deep River" riffs off a John Coltrane tune, "Mr. PC" (PC is for Paul Chambers). If you listen to the Coltrane first, youtube.com/watch?v=Jv5j_Lx2R4g, you'll hear the improvision on Murray's "Deep River": song365.name/track/david-murray-mr.-p.c.-268584.htm

NM: Whoa! I can hear those connections!

IS: Murray didn't exactly make this adventurous Coltrane cut sound tame, but Murray took the changes and created endless melodic invention from them, varying speed and rhythm with an almost manic propulsiveness. While writing poems during this period I not only began to trust the language in the poems but I was able, in the best of them anyway, to write more associatively, a little more wildly, and to forefront the medium the way a painter would make use of paint. After all, an audience is moved—that is to say changed—by the words we use, how they're arranged on the page.

WHEN I COME HOME

after the Xenia tornado of 1974

In Cincinnati the river is the color of nausea,
and in Xenia the tops of houses
have been taken off and rest in the river.

When I come home and she's not home,
the worry thickens, I think she must be sick
not to want me. I still have a picture

of that naked girl on fire in My Lai,
her arms high in the air, her hands
screaming, and behind her, her mother

waving a handkerchief on a stick. And behind them
the whole village running from their village,
napalm scorching their thatched huts to slag.

Xenia means friendship. Xenia means flower.
See what a name means.
To be afraid of Xenia is to be afraid of the other.

The sky is mud and thunder. The air is green,
thick with pollen, my wife and I swing on a porch swing,
listening to the frogs and crickets, thinking,

The elm tree is a thing of beauty. The elm tree's actually an oak,
but we can hear the stream unfurling.
We enjoy the wetness of it. The essence of it, dripping.

We are only twenty-one and twenty-two, singing.
I still have a picture of her, her arm
wrapped around my arm, her lips on my neck, pursed.

When I come home and she's not home,
the story of the world is not of interest. I am
speechless, going back there, to the four room cabin

in the dense Ohio wood, still further back,
waiting to disappoint, failing to predict how to soothe.
The sick are nothing but plasma, whereas the healthy

play the saxophone and saturate the river.
The world is not as heavy as the door to my room, open.
She lost her wedding ring in the crack beneath the buckled floor,

so she's free. I think about fire dropped on a child,
the funnel spinning, coming closer, the sky white as knuckles,
a snow of splinters, how I'm behind the couch, waiting.

I can feel the blood rush in and my skin on fire.
To listen to my heart, you'd think we'd seized it, the music,
the state called rapture. Where the river runs in summer,

nothing but a few flies and stones to disturb it. The two of us
sitting and listening, unprepared for what comes next.
This is only a story, so I can say what I want. I can hold back

the ending for a moment, when I come home from school,
when we call out, when the bloody soldier burns away
attention span, when a helicopter wheels him off to heaven.

NM: Yes; I can see how jazz influenced the leaps, empathetic connections via imagery between the self and others and the parallels of the private and larger worlds blown to bits:

> ... I think about fire dropped on a child,
> the funnel spinning, coming closer, the sky white as knuckles,
> a snow of splinters, how I'm behind the couch, waiting.
>
> I can feel the blood rush in and my skin on fire.

This must have been a thrilling, liberating poem to write.

IS: It took a long time to take out ritualized writing and responses, to let the leaps stand, but yes, I knew after I'd written it that the poem had advanced my work. At this time I also became impatient with poems dictated by subject or narrative poems dictated by chronology:

most of them seemed willful and predictable. You knew as much at the beginning of the poem as you did at the end. I began to feel, and still feel though I rarely execute it, that if you're writing poems you're using a very particular medium and that part of your job as an artist is to advance the medium beyond a priori conventions. It just makes sense that when you think of Pound's "make it new" he's embracing the way the Modernists changed poetry, the way we write and think about it. In my view we should still be doing that.

NM: Wasn't it about this time that the neo-formalist backlash to this kind artistic adventuring reared its head? A backlash that you so boldly challenged in your essay, "Neo-Formalism: A Dangerous Nostalgia" which essentially split the American poetry scene into two camps … a civil war of sorts, a glorious ruckus, a huge, passionate controversy.

IS: Yes, though I think that poem was written a couple of years before the essay. Sometimes I'm a little too passionate about the art for my own good. I remember reading Foucault and Derrida in the late eighties: their work reinforced my understanding of the contexts of poetry. The art's never written in a vacuum: it's no accident that the Romantics' obsession with the self and subjectivity occurred during the beginnings of the industrial revolution: institutions, church and state, failed to reflect the needs and values of the culture. So here we were during the Reagan administration, the AIDS crisis, a time of terrible entropy; it's in this context that Conservatives fought on so many fronts to try to retrieve concepts of universality, patriarchy, and the nuclear family. You saw the ideology reflected in Christopher Lasch's attempt to rescue patriarchy in *The Culture of Narcissism*, in films, the neo-classical movement in painting, and of course in poetry.

Someone then sent me a review copy of Robert Richman's *The Direction in Poetry*. Of course the poems were terrible, nostalgic in subject matter and almost fascistic in the editor's insistence on singsong meter. It was the artistic equivalent of suggesting that we compose music as Bach did, with the same harmonic limitations. Or that we compose in sonata form. But music's everywhere in our speech, it's multi-cultural in every sense: our meters are variable, not anarchic, but in varying meters the music does grow out of our improvisations and associations. If you can't hear different musics in John Ashbery's poems, for example (he uses various rhythm structures and levels of diction to create those cadences and competing stances), you're not listening carefully enough. And my own opinion is that we'd have a lot of difficulty naming many great poems written now in fixed forms. The last great formal poet was Elizabeth Bishop, and with the exception of "One Art," her greatest poems are the late ones written in free verse. I think the pre-modernist cliché (perpetuated by Frost) that writing in fixed form liberates content is mostly nonsense, one that's perpetuated by exercises in writing workshops to this day. Or, okay, maybe not complete nonsense but rather it's true in a limited and pretty desiccated way: that counterpoint worked for Mozart, where the steady left hand created tension with the freedom of the right hand. But it was an Enlightenment idea and doesn't really apply to the multiplicities of rhythms we experience in our music and speech today.

Anyway when I sent the essay to *APR* (a magazine that's been very generous over the years in giving me a platform for my views) I knew it would be provocative and I expected it to be met by some challenges. I didn't expect it to have the lasting effect it apparently has—both negatively and positively—but the essay, substantively re-written in *History Matters*, still basically reflects my views, not only about poetry but the oblique but inescapable relationship between poetry and culture.

On principle I've tried not to be political (with a small p) in anything I write, which is to say worrying about whether people would be angered or approve of what I say. I've made a lot of enemies and I'm not proud of that, though most of my critical work sings the praises of poets I love. We know that in private most poets are much more free and authentic about what they feel about other poets, but people worry about how saying x and y might affect their "careers" or, more honorably, affect their friendships. So we get reviews of friends reviewing friends, writers inviting readers to their campuses as a commodity exchange.

NM: You bring up a good point. I wonder to what extent "career" considerations have impacted poetry itself, especially as creative writing programs have been assimilated into academia. Most university teaching positions require publication, an MFA plus a PhD, and the track to tenure can be slippery if one doesn't mind one's political manners. Maybe "making it new" and being authentic is too risky?

IS: The whole MFA question has been batted around a lot. I think because writing, like painting, is a mentoring art (a good writer/critic can save a writer time and put some important questions in a student's head), graduate programs can help one become a better, more ambitious artist. The dangers of these programs are pretty well known: consensus workshopping and the desire to please authority can certainly dampen adventurousness in the writing process. It's also true that when teaching steers toward mechanics, separating the craft from the art, the result is an empty well-made exercise. The larger issue for me is the kind of careerism some programs engender, encouraging students to send out their poems, publish books, establish their own presses before the students learn the art. Beyond the economics of the academy, encouraging that kind of worldly ambition is all about a hunger for fame and recognition. That's a cultural problem and speaks to the emptiness of American life, its self-absorption and celebrity culture.

NM: Ah, sadly, yes. Do you address this emptiness in any of your recent poems?

IS: Yes, not intentionally, but the subject comes up. Sometimes you'll see it in the desire for community, sometimes feeling melancholy or envy for those who belong, sometimes receiving real pleasure from the solitude. "I Never Needed Things," a poem I recently published in *The New Yorker*, reflects all of those feelings: newyorker.com/magazine/2016/02/29/i-never-needed-things (readers can also hear Ira read the poem aloud on the *New Yorker* website.)

NM: That's a terrific poem. Ira, you've been so generous to share some of your newer poems with *Plume*; again, thank you. I love these poems, and in them I see the characteristic "energetic syntax and the astonishing range of idiom and tone," which Alan Shapiro has praised, as well the "unpredictable weaving together of individual and collective life, the insightful, almost seamless integration of personal experience in all its unredemptive anguish with the heterogeneous realities of American culture." What do you perceive as the most significant shifts in these new poems?

IS: In my most recent poems, though they seem to be more representational, I still try my best to follow the language: I begin with a line or an image and then ask what's next. I try to ask as many questions of a poem as I can, not to close it off before the most difficult and urgent questions posed have been advanced. I look for opportunities for disruptions. They often serve as metaphorical episodes that I hope intensify the poem's progress. And ultimately that's what I'm after in poems—intensification. To feel fully, to inhabit, to move beyond the narrow confines of the self, but not to solve or advise, and certainly not to re-write what I've already written. In the present tense, though you might not know it from the above comments, I try not to be too self-conscious about what I'm doing. Though I'd like the poems to continue to be adventurous I'm obliged to follow the poems where they authentically take me. I always want to honor authenticity, which includes the shifting and partial selves we inhabit, so that the poems display some inner necessity, poems that really need to be written.

NM: You know, these new poems are intriguing, paradoxical; although they're maybe more representational/narrative than your earlier poems, they lead us into darker terrain. And because you try to "ask as many questions of a poem as I can, not to close it off before the most difficult and urgent questions posed have been advanced" the poems reveal their mysteries. For instance, in "Wilderness" (below) we follow the speaker into

> this great wilderness, a snow-patched meadow
> above the tree line— the air so thin
> hiking left me out of breath
> in this green, unkempt site just off the map

which is linear enough until "just off the map" alerts us that we have left the beaten narrative path and find ourselves observing a "fangle"(fantasy + tangle) of almost mythic/primordial beasts. Here, in a reversal of the Darwinian sequence of reptilian-to-mammalian evolution, it's the surfacing reptiles which scare off the warm-bloods. (Why do I see Bly's face here?) It seems that in the speaker's immersion in the moment references to the self-in-context begin to blur.

> I couldn't tell you where I was
> or how I landed somewhere glorious: I can't describe
> the jumble of sensations, the dizzying changes
> in the light, clouds appearing, passing, and shading
> the muffled ball of sun.

For a moment the speaker is suspended on the precarious brink of transcendental dissolution, pulls back in a flash of self-awareness: "I didn't think I could take this in, / how it all just came to me, slid into my horizon." The speaker struggles to believe that grace is given, not earned by personal suffering: "Was this scene more precious because / of what I'd brought with me, years of wanting, striving— / for what—all those years with holes in them?" Even if he could accept an unconditional "amazing grace," he cannot, because to do so would leave the "others" behind:

> my friends from Bensonhurst: strap marks on their flanks,
> knife fights on the buses, break-ins, little balls of white bread
> they considered breakfast, the whispers
> behind their backs: What imbeciles you are. Where's their gift?

Whether the "I can't forget" is the self-admonishment of "you musn't forget," or the speaker's inability to forget is moot; he cannot forget. And the speaker, in a stunning acceptance and integration of "the shifting and partial selves we inhabit," surrenders to the knowledge that grace and its attendant bliss, whether given or earned, will never absolve him of the responsibility incumbent upon him witness for those who are "still waiting for it." A modern-day Moses, he returns from the mountaintop to "drive back home to a more familiar wilderness: / my cluttered desk, street noise, all those voices calling."

IS: Thank you Nancy. You've taught me something about that poem and its ambitions and the function of memory in my work as bringing me back to community. Memory can serve to connect us with other humans by making us more empathetic, or it can paralyze us and make us feel overwhelmed. I think in that poem both those feelings surface.

NM: In the poems "Between Shifts" and "SHHH!" the speaker's tone is that of an understanding, wiser self, who, if not ready to forgive the younger self for fuck-ups, then will make allowances. The speaker acknowledges that these blind missteps were committed in innocence, under the barometric pressures of personal history, under the cloud of "before the fall" which looms darkly in the future. I don't want to spoil our readers' pleasure by the same degree of analysis with which I indulged myself with in "Wilderness," but would you say that this is a relatively new tone, one that has been developing over the past years?

IS: Oh, Nancy, I'm not so sure. I know it comes up more often these days. I suspect these changes in the work reflect changes in the life: growing older, looking back, seeing that younger self wrestle somewhat blindly, or at least incompletely, with some of life's struggles. Now that I think about it, I seem to almost want to guide that self through the labyrinth of difficulties, navigate with, as you say, generosity and honesty. To be as honest as one can be with oneself.

NM: The penultimate poem in this sequence, the exquisitely haunted "Chambermaid" inhabits and moves "beyond the narrow confines of the self." The intention of the final poem "A Moment's Calm" is announced by the epigraph by Primo Levi, and posits a tentative acceptance of a self in which the "fangle" of selves tangle. Yet, maybe at the same time there is a ruefulness that this grace, which has been hard earned by living squarely in this life, comes a little belatedly?

IS: Maybe more "rhomboidly" than squarely, but thanks. I wish I'd seen more, known more, on some occasions acted on desires, on others made a few different choices. I don't see how anyone lives a long life without some moments of regret. So yes, rueful, but that's only one part of the story. I know I've had many opportunities, have been blessed to have this work, to be granted the teaching life (I've had so many wonderful students, poets and non-poets, who've become life-long friends), to have loved and been deeply loved, and to have been given the gift of resilience, which has allowed me to bounce back—or sometimes limp—from adversity. I think what I've gained from a lifelong commitment to poetry is a kind of attentiveness, a capacity to listen better, to hear suggestion in someone's voice, to continue to be, imperfectly, open-hearted. To match the words with the life, that's one of the great things writing poetry can do.

NM: Ira, it has been an incredible pleasure. Readers, go get your headphones, and enjoy this rare treat.

Wilderness

Just yesterday, when I came upon
this great wilderness, a snow-patched meadow
above the tree line—the air so thin
hiking left me out of breath
in this green, unkempt site just off the map
I was reading—I saw a pond
with moose, cows and bulls in a fangle
slurping at its edge until some sound stirred them,
and how clumsy and rushed their exit
before some reptiles surfaced from the water.
I couldn't tell you where I was
or how I landed somewhere glorious: I can't describe
the jumble of sensations, the dizzying changes
in the light, clouds appearing, passing, and shading
the muffled ball of sun. I didn't think I could take this in,
how it all just came to me, slid into my horizon.
Was this scene more precious because
of what I'd brought with me, years of wanting, striving—
for what?—all those years with holes in them? I can't forget
my friends from Bensonhurst: strap marks on their flanks,
knife fights on the buses, break-ins, little balls of white bread
they considered breakfast, the whispers
behind their backs: What imbeciles you are. Where's their gift?
They're still waiting for it. And what does it all add up to,
my being here, sitting on some granite as the sky darkens?
It's night, noiseless, the moon shines on the snow patches,
there's a nudge of wind. I wish the pond were a sea, I wish
my friend John were still here, I wish I could keep this day
in parenthesis, but I can't, so I hike to my car
and drive back home to a more familiar wilderness:
my cluttered desk, street noise, all those voices calling.

BETWEEN SHIFTS

Jesus and I were flipping channels,
mocking TV preachers' mania for money
and sin: we were high on something,
but when it came to the aura
around the set—and there was light—
we saw things differently. This before
the ruined motels of the Catskills
littered the hillsides of upstate New York.
I hadn't been there for the Robeson concert
but uncle Max had come back to the city
bandaged up in his bashed-in Chevy wagon.
I remember too when Jews were barred
from hotels elsewhere, how we paraded
around the Catskills, playing cards
but mostly trying to act like Christians.
I suppose we drank gin and wore ties and jackets.
We didn't really know any Christians. Which is why
it was so funny hanging out with this Jesus
who was half Puerto Rican, a hundred percent Catholic.
This Jesus had come back from the War scarred:
my ancestors, he'd said, had murdered him.
Otherwise what were the nails for, the needles?
I don't know who swung first,
and maybe there was light on the floor
where we wrestled for some purpose kept from us,
but when we surfaced, bloodied and dazed
there was our boss at the door, calling us back
to bus our tables, and beyond him
early morning light seemed to pry open
the fingers of the branches: for a little while more
we could retreat to our separate Gods.

SHHHH!

We walked in the woods, like Dimmesdale and Hester,
only back then I didn't give a shit about literature:
there was this woman who adored me:
probably she didn't know me, she confused me
with some antidote to her self-absorbed boyfriend.
Maybe she saw the two of us as the same person.
Later she'd join some sexless sect that wore white robes
and burned incense—she was rightfully earnest about it all,
because we were both lost: I had a shitty marriage
I couldn't mention or think about.
Everybody I knew was careless or reckless as I was,
from the drugs we took to the curves we took
in the dark, and short of being saved
sex gave us the kind of oblivion we deserved.
And I should never say this, I remember her breasts exactly,
and her round face and her curly hair
and her conversation, some exact phrases: we told secrets here,
we groused, we knew no one cared about us,
we had nothing to offer, so let me open up the world
a little more because this is getting claustrophobic:
we'd invaded another tiny country:
who could bear enemies so close? The Clintons
were locking up the poor, and in spite of all her humiliation,
Hillary stood up for the Defense of Marriage Act.
That's all I knew and I could get agitated about it, but the point is
we were sitting on a log by a stream, no one saw us,
we could have kept on going to a deeper and darker place –
but I suppressed the urge to tell my wife
I wanted to start over before it was too late,
because it was already too late to describe
the disdain we felt for each other, how we found more

and more irritating every sentence the other spoke,
so I shut my mouth as I almost always did
back then, cooked a meal I can't remember and slept
in the marriage bed a few years more.

Chambermaid

As a child I was a chambermaid,
bent over, picking up after, doubling as a cook—
better the kitchen than the bedroom—stirring the caldron
so volcanoes bubbled up and sprayed the kitchen walls
with the graffiti of green pea soup.

Sent to my quarters
I fumed like an orphan in literature, or more
like an infant, irritable and colic. But while in lockdown,
labial forces were set in motion: not the usual
shame and silence, but plots to set the palace ablaze.

Being a man then
would be like being a particle of soot
from an old incinerator, circa 1955. But this hasn't happened yet,
so we cocks-of-the-walk can rest easy now, light up
at a café on the left bank and discuss
our favorite subjects, from Spinoza to sacred texts
like the Odyssey, where fathers pack a suitcase
and disappear when children must be fed.
I waved goodbye to one from the harbor.
And searched for him with my lantern
in neighborhoods where no one would want to be seen.
But since I spent my childhood as a chambermaid,
I know that place where you knock on doors
and no one answers.

And what comes next: cleaning up
their rooms, emptying out the wish bin
or something more fulsome I'm crossing out, trying to imagine.

A Moment's Calm

I live in my house as I live inside my skin: I know more beautiful, more ample, more sturdy and more picturesque skins: but it would seem to me unnatural to exchange them for mine.
    —Primo Levi

Now for a moment's calm. Maybe it will go on
and on, like a Strindberg play,
or it could be brief, shockingly brief, like a life.

Maybe I've been waiting my whole life for this.
What I call waiting is settling into a barn
with a ceiling fan to circulate the heated air,

wood beams from another century. In this stillness
I'm not disposed to making corrections.
I'm at peace with your happiness even if you're gone,

invisible, even if we fought over the fate of the universe.

Jean Valentine
interviewed by Nancy Mitchell
Saturday morning, June 4, 2016, Schumaker Pond, Salisbury, Maryland

Our conversation began the last morning of Jean's four-day visit to our house in Maryland. Because we spent most of our time in the company of water, canoeing or walking forest paths along the river, our clear, cool, blue-skied days had the dreamy quality of reverie, and our conversation ebbed and flowed with memories. We sat on the sun porch overlooking the pond, all windows and doors open to bird song and sweet breezes, and recalled our dinner conversation of the night before, in which Jean, my husband, another guest and I were relating childhood experiences which seemed to forge a primal connection to what eventually would be our life's work, a connection which led us down a path beyond childhood and sustained us through more challenging adult years. Jean and I marveled that although the circumstance and context of each of our childhoods varied, they shared the lucky happenstance of providing us with guides along the way who validated our efforts, and encouraged us to go on. It was in the spirit of gratitude toward these good, encouraging souls, so many of them now gone, that we began our lovely, three-hour conversation.

NM: What experiences in your childhood got you started on your path to poetry?

JV: Mother Goose nursery rhymes! Our family had babysitters, nurses, so our only close time with our mother was when she read to us—she loved reading to us—my sister and me, close in age; our brother came five years younger. It was a peaceful time, very comforting, sometimes by the fire.

NM: Ah, that constellation of pleasant sensory experiences makes an indelible impression at an early age … just ask Proust!

JV: Yes. Getting the sound of poetry in your body at that early age, right in your heart from the beginning in a loving way.

NM: Poetry is for you a deep connection to the family, to your mother?

JV: Yes, it was. In later years my sister was interested in and read poetry. She was older and I worshipped her and wanted so much to be in her world. I remember looking up at all the books of poetry lined up on her shelf and I said "I love Yeets!" meaning Yeats … and she corrected me in an imperious way—not really imperious, but loving—with "It's Yeats!" She was a wonderful big sister to me.

NM: Do you remember the very first poem you wrote?

JV: Yes I do: "I think I am a mole / sniffing and sniffing / in his hole."

NM: Wonderful! Bravo!

JV: You like it?

NM: Yes! Do you know how old you were then?

JV: I don't; I hope I was very young! I don't think I was in my thirties.… I think I was maybe ten or eight or something like that. I mean I really wanted to do that. I really wanted it.

NM: Was it always poetry?

JV: I think it was art, or the idea of it. I liked piano too, but I never thought I had a calling for it—I never thought I had a calling for poetry either. I had a wonderful piano teacher who just loved music. Yes, music was so important—it was so helpful to hear it—as you know sound is so important in poetry.

NM: Did your parents support your interest in art?

JV: Well, I think time and history and money may have supported our interest in it. We got to go to schools where it could be encouraged by certain teachers. I think we had a kind of leisure for higher things that they hadn't had when they were growing up. My mother and father were of another generation, they were hard workers—they weren't poor at all, they were well off, but they were hard workers—and didn't have the leisure for art. We were given the privilege of thinking of art as something we might do. A part of our minds and souls could be freed up in a way that theirs might not have been able to be inwardly or outwardly. I'm very grateful for that.

NM: Did teachers encourage your interest in poetry, in writing?

JV: Yes. By 5th or 6th grade I had teachers who really loved literature and encouraged me to write.

NM: Did you start out writing poetry?

JV: I tried to write prose, fiction when I was in high school and in college, but it was no good at all. My family had a writer friend, John O'Hara, a very good fiction writer, famous at the time. This would have been in the '40s and '50s and it was exciting for me to meet a writer. In fact, I met two with my parents; John Hersey, who you know was a very good non-fiction writer, and he wrote a novel too. John O'Hara—I worshiped him because he encouraged me. My father told him that I was writing, when I was very young, around fifteen. So John got a very special kind of interest—he was a very sweet man, and got an interest in encouraging his friends' children if they wanted to write—and he was very kind to me. I wrote what I called a novel when I was sixteen; it was like a story and it had no length to it, and it had no talent! But I worked hard on it and it probably helped me. I showed it to John O'Hara because he was so kind to me. And he read it and he wrote me a letter: "It's not good. You know why, but keep punching." Punching or some expression like that. Of course I was terribly wounded that it wasn't a great novel; only 15 pages long, or something like that! But, it was very important to me that he had answered me. It gave me some, however frail, connection with the world, you know. And then later when I was in college—probably in high school—I shifted over to poetry. I remember meeting him again with my parents, and he asked if I was still writing and I said "Yes." And he said, "What are you writing?" And I said "Poetry!" And he looked at me just like this [incredulous expression] and said "Why?"

I had no idea what to say. But it was very much like him, he was kind of brusque, he was warm, but kind of like "Why? Why would anyone do that?"

NM: What a great story! You went to boarding school, right?

JV: Yes, Milton Academy, up in Milton, Massachussetts. My father and his brother had gone there so it was in the family, sort of.

NM: Did you like it?

JV: I loved it. Loved getting away from home, and I love the school! You know, at fifteen, it was a very stable, safe, boring place; it was comforting and I had a couple of wonderful teachers who encouraged my work, you know, my writing. Miss Wood, who came from the war in London was still shell-shocked when she came to us. She was wonderful. When I say shell-shocked, I mean she was nervous, a sensitive person; she had been through the Blitz in London. She was the first person I'd known outside of my father who had been in the war. She was very brilliant, a Latin and Greek scholar, and she let me translate Latin into English. Latin poetry. She encouraged me.

You know, Nance, when people talk about teaching writing, I think the one best thing that you can give a student, like giving them a candle, is encouragement.

NM: That's lovely.

JV: It's true, though. I think, looking back on my life—I mean all these things I've been talking to you about were so encouraging to my writing.

NM: All those people holding up candles along the way, lighting your path.

JV: Early on in my life I got encouragement, and later on a lot towards anywhere I wanted to go. I think encouragement is more precious than anything we can give as teachers.

NM: It's true, and so easy to forget when we get so caught up ...

JV: We wouldn't worry so much about if we were good teachers if we could remember that. It's a way of seeing someone. A way of saying, "Be you. Don't be me."

NM: Ah, yes. After boarding school you went to …

JV: Radcliffe.

NM: Was that a big change?

JV: Yes, huge. Radcliffe was another world. I'd never been in the company of so many bright people in my life, faculty, and students. Radcliffe itself was maybe a thousand or so young women and Harvard was ten thousand young men. The whole world of that area in Cambridge, it was awesome to me. I was very glad to be there, but also very shy. It was the biggest place I'd ever been in, the biggest world I'd ever been in by far. I was extremely shy; I had a couple of friends I'd gone to school with and I'd see them occasionally, but I had no real close friends there. It was a lonely time in some ways but on the other hand it may have been all right because that is life. I was fascinated with everything, all the courses I took—astronomy, Spanish … a whole new world had opened up for me. I was finding a world of the mind that I didn't know existed except from reading the classics.

NM: Did you meet Adrienne Rich when you were at Radcliffe?

JV: No, I didn't meet her until much later. She graduated the year before I went to Radcliffe; she was five years older than me. This is a nice story: I was walking down the sidewalk in Cambridge one day in my freshman year and this older gentleman was walking along and fell into conversation with me—in Cambridge they do that—and asked me if I was going to college and what I was interested in, and I said "Poetry." He asked "in reading or in writing it?' And I said both. Then he said, "Well, we had a very interesting young poet here, who graduated a year ago. I wonder if you've read her, Adrienne Rich." I'd never heard her name before! "Oh yes," he said, "we're very proud of her around here." Of course, I went right to the library and got her book out and started reading it. Her first book, *A Change of World*.

NM: She was published before she graduated from Radcliffe?

JV: Yes, she got the Yale Series of Younger Poets Prize in 1950 while she was at Radcliffe, and it was given to her by W. H. Auden. And he praised her—I don't have the exact words here, but he praised her "for being so well behaved." Later, after I got to know Adrienne, we thought that was so wonderful! Well behaved! Oh, yeah, Mr. Auden!

Anyway, so I went and found her book and that was very exciting to know that someone so close to my age was writing poetry and was published, and that her poetry was so good. Her poetry was so alive, because before that there had been like, Wordsworth, you know. It was very exciting.

NM: How interesting that Adrienne was mentoring you from afar years before she became a steady mentor and support, and a close friend.

JV: Yes, as fate would have it, I won the Yale Series of Younger Poets award when I was thirty. Adrienne looked me up and got in touch. I was so lucky with her and with so many others. You know, there was this dean of women at Radcliffe, Dean Kirby Miller, who would have us come by her office to get to know us, and when she learned I was interested in poetry she said, "I tell our people who are interested in poetry to take an Honors in General Studies. I think poets should read, study at will."

I'll never forget how it felt to be included, to be in the company of "our people who are interested in poetry!" She understood, and made a path for me. Again, such encouragement!

NM: Were there other professors or students at Radcliff that you felt were guides?

JV: Well, I had heard about this professor, Bill Alfred, who had a reputation for being a great poet and teacher, and I took his writing class in my sophomore or junior year. He was a huge turning point for me. Bill was very central at Harvard, brilliant, admired—he had translated *Agamemnon*! He was a grad student, studying under Archibald MacLeish, and later became a very respected playwright. His greatest gift to me was that he gave me encouragement that went deeper than any I'd had up until that point. His encouragement was crucial. I'd go to see him during office hours and show him my writing and he'd encourage me, encouraged me tremendously.

NM: What writers did he turn you to?

JV: Well, we didn't always agree! He asked what I was reading, and when I said, "Virginia Woolf," he said, "She's so sad." Well, I didn't think she was sad, I just thought she was telling the truth! But in terms of poetry, we read Anglo-Saxon poetry in his class, and, well, Chaucer of course, but most importantly he told me about Bishop, Elizabeth Bishop, about *North and South*. He said something like, "You know Bishop has a new book" and I said to myself, "Who is Bishop?" But I went right out to the bookstore and bought it. There my life changed. Bishop was more important to me at that time because she was a woman—oh, I'd read Elizabeth Barrett Browning, but she didn't speak to me—and Bishop was a living poet, was older, still working. I didn't know you could make a real career out of writing poetry, that it could be a life! Bishop was living the life and that was so important to me.

NM: Another light! Did you meet other writers around your age while you were at Radcliffe?

JV: Well, I met James Chase, who was a writer, and I later married him. I met Barry Cooke who was an artist and Andre Gregory who was an actor. At the time writers, artists were more on the fringe of things at Harvard. Artists were there, but were rare. Harvard attracted more scholarly students.

NM: What did you do after you graduated from Radcliffe?

JV: My father gave me this incredible gift of a trip to Europe. I started out with some other friends and we had a wonderful time and went all over the place, France, Spain, in a tiny car, called a Citroën Deux Chevaux.

They went back in September and I stayed—on the boat over I had met a man I fell in love with who lived in London, so I thought I'd go there and stay for a while.

NM: How long were you there?

JV: From September to January. It was an important time for me. I had a job and a bed-sit, and for the first time was independent.

NM: An independent young woman, in love, far from home and finding her way in the world—what a time.

JV: So, yes. I was certainly getting interested in men, but also I was getting interested in what to do with all this freedom I suddenly had.

NM: After London, did you go back to Cambridge?

JV: No, I moved to New York, and got a job right away so I could support myself. Later I met James Chase again and so forth. We were married quite a long time. I immediately got pregnant and had babies, you know, and I was pretty much alone with poetry for that whole time. I didn't even know poets, and hadn't met Adrienne at that time, but I was writing away, writing away. And James was writing away too. He was a fiction writer.

But I was lonely. I had working-at-home jobs like typing manuscripts, editing theses, while the children took naps. I didn't make much; it was sketchy, but it was something and made me feel like I could hold my head up about bringing something into the household. That went on, and I was writing away, and I would send things out, and nobody took anything. In fact, when Dudley Fitts gave me the Yale Prize, he wrote to me, "I've looked for your poems in magazines and I don't find them anywhere. Are you a recluse?" He had a wonderful sense of humor. I wrote back, "I haven't sent much out, but when I did, it came back." So that's how things were for those years. I married James at twenty-three or twenty-four, and at thirty I won the prize. Funny, it was only eight years from college until I won the prize, but it seemed like eighty!

NM: Those years, alone with the kids, writing in a kind of vacuum … it must have seemed like you were in the desert?

JV: Yes, it was the poetry desert, for sure. I didn't know another poet.

NM: So, tell me about when you heard you'd won the Yale Prize for *Dream Barker*.

JV: I couldn't believe it! I came home from the park with the kids and got the mail, ho-hum, and there was a letter from Dudley Fitts saying "I hope this makes you as happy as it makes me."

NM: What a moment! Did everything in your life change from that point on?

JV: Everything changed. It shifted the earth. I got a job—Jane Cooper read the book and called and asked me to teach at Sarah Lawrence. Adrienne read the book and called and wanted to be friends. She was living in Cambridge then, but later she moved to New York, just three blocks away.

NM: You and Adrienne became lifelong friends in life and in poetry! Did she become an important reader of your work from then on?

JV: Oh, yeah. She would be still if she was still alive. I mean, she would generously be. She was one of the most generous people I've ever known with her time and her heart. Yeah, we became very close friends, thank God. That was the first close friendship, except for Bill Alfred, with a writer, the first woman writer I'd ever met, actually.

NM: And you had so much in common, as writers, wives, mothers....

JV: And what it was like to be a woman with children and to write poetry seriously. She was really going into that whole subject as a feminist, you know. I was in the sidelines watching—oh, I was living it—but I was watching her thought like everyone else when she was writing those books about what it was to be a woman in those poems. She was much more intellectual. Confident. She was a real presence.

NM: You met Robert Lowell through Adrienne, right?

JV: I think so. He was keeping track of younger poets at the time and wanted to meet me, or maybe Adrienne wanted me to meet him and his wife, Elizabeth Hardwick.

NM: The poet Eleanor Ross Taylor was also very important in your life and to your poetry. You two enjoyed a long friendship, and fairly recently you edited *The Lighthouse Keeper*, a collection of essays on her poetry. How did you come to know her?

JV: I met her through Robert Lowell. He grew up with her husband, the writer Peter Taylor, and Peter married Eleanor Ross. And I think it was Lowell who first introduced me to Eleanor's poetry. He didn't see it, particularly, but he knew she was writing it and he thought I'd like her, maybe because he was thinking she was another woman poet—we weren't so thick on the ground then as we are now, in this particular part of the world. She was kind of a quieter poet, shy and that might have been what he thought as part of a kinship between us. I went to it, her poetry, of course and found it absolutely wonderful. And then, I don't remember the steps to this, but I met her. It would have have been a matter of my going there—she never, hardly ever came to New York. Peter traveled around more than she did, but he was a famous writer and got jobs to come and read and teach. She was very much a recluse. She was very similar to Dickinson, a real recluse. She had been discovered through Peter, to do him justice, the dear man, who showed her poetry to Randall Jarrell. Well, Jarrell took one look at her work and said, "This is a real poet!" She was very shy and reticent—into the world as a poet wasn't her idea. I said to her, "So Randall really sort of found you and showed you to the world?" She said, "Yes." And then I asked, "Did you fall in love with him?" And she said something like, "Well, it's obligatory, don't you think?" It was all very funny and sort of light, but I think she had a deep bond with this man who saw her, and heard her. I think they had a deep friendship and I honor Peter for that so much because he and Randall were friends since boyhood, and Lowell too—they were all at college together, at Kenyon. What Peter did for her was so large and great. He told me this anecdote later: "You know what Randall says about us"—and Peter honored Randall above all people, so it was like God saying it—"we're two people walking along the bottom of the ocean and I've got a diver's mask, and Eleanor is walking along without the diver's mask."

NM: That's so great!!

JV: You know when people ask, "What are you going for?" Well, that's what I'm going for in poetry; I want to take off the diver's mask.

NM: Do you see a big difference between your earliest poems and later work and what you're writing now?

JV: I think I started out more formal and have gotten less and less formal as I've gone along in the sense of the old forms; that definitely is true. I'm less constrained, I hope. I haven't ever been very experimental in formal terms at all. I think, I hope I've become less "outer" directed, as they say than I was—I think it would be natural for a young poet to be more concerned about what people think than an older poet, I think that's accurate. I still care very much what my dearest people think, like I'd care very much what you think. But I think in the old days it was very important for me to find somebody to publish my work. That has become easier, frankly. It's not that I'm maybe less concerned, but I get things published easily.

NM: If we can backtrack a bit. You say you were never very experimental with form. When I first read your poems, from *Dream Barker* on, it felt to me that your poems were radically different—but maybe it was less about form …

JV: I think I was following form when I started writing, as I was learning. As I got more confident, I got more interested in sound, in how to put it on the page so someone else could hear it in the same way I heard it. I think it comes from the piano lessons in my childhood, honestly, from musical notations.

What I'm trying to do now when I'm writing is to put it down as I hear it, more like natural speech, more spoken.

NM: Hear it?

JV: I'm trying to translate emotions into words.

NM: Ah! And this confidence grew from encouragement, yes?

JV: Yes. I got encouragement from being more of myself in poems, being more open, vulnerable. Again and again I've had so much encouragement to be myself, to stay open.

For Tomas Tranströmer & Max Ritvo

I looked,
and there he was, my older brother,
my guide to the underworld.
His eyes were kind. He said,
"Here, take my hand, we cross here …"

It was the little blue restaurant.

He was the Swedish poet
He jumped up over the back of the chair
and sat down right next to Max.
And Max said, "Come, lonesome one,
to the lonesome."

"Come lonesome one, to the lonesome": St. Symeon, the New Theologian, addressing his God (949–10??).

In China

We are seated on a wide stage. In the bright-lit
auditorium, a PA pronounces the directions in English:
"You are poets. Take off your masks."

A young man stands up & says, in English,
"I come from a small mountain village.
I am studying art. I want to ask,
What is beauty? What to pursue?"

I take off my mask.
What is my love?
with its old hard-beating erotic lungs—
What is my soul,
if it has lost its words?
But it never had its words.
Maybe another look, or step,
or water step or air—

In a Diner

I sit across from him—

That I know him.
That I am beginning to know him.

I—half-open:
He sees—what does a half-open
half-palomino see?

To see that.
A voice? A hand?

Not make any sudden movements.

Not lie.
Not leave.

The "thou" is holding up lit snow.

In Ireland

You wanted to see Achill Island
so I drove you there
in the rickety car
slow over the Achill roads.

Later, you called to say you dreamed
I was driving you in that car
up to the passage graves, Carrowkeel,
"the narrow quarter," and you felt safe.

"Safe"—did we not both remember then
the country road we were both once driven over
dangerously by a soul in danger
—You had cried "Stop."

At the last
the soul couldn't stop.

Final Parting

The air felt like frost
to drive through.
Dust made out of frost.
We said nothing for a while.

When you parked at the limestone house
my granddaughter stayed still, waiting
in the back seat. You held my hand
a long time to your chest. Out the window,
beech branches to the ground.

Dear Merton's God

We stand here like trees in the night,
I know you for your words
in the loud silence, your words listen,
they make room for a stranger,
for the dead & the living, the child

We stand here like trees in the night, dear Merton's God,
you throw yourself at us, I know you
for your words in body, in sign language,
I throw myself at you, God, God
you run after people, talking,

people on bicycles, pushing wheelbarrows,
baby carriages, hospital cards, you make room
—with me, you were quiet, you sent it,
or I couldn't have heard it,
sent the warmth deep around my head
like a Native American headband, only inside.

Max Ritvo (1990-2016)
interviewed by Nancy Mitchell

Before I became acquainted with the late Max Ritvo's poetry, which, poet Louise Glück writes, is "marked by intellectual bravado and verbal extravagance," I first heard of this gifted young poet from a mutual friend, beloved by both Max and me. Our friend would light up as she spoke of Max's prodigious talent, contagious joy, humor and playfulness, his wide-open-arms-to-the-world inclusiveness, despite his ongoing struggle with a rare cancer. I remember ruefully recalling the other "gifted" young male poets I had known, and, intrigued with this refreshing departure from those latter-day Werthers, promptly turned to Max Ritvo's poetry. I was spellbound by what Glück called his "dazzling suppleness of mind" which "manifests itself in electric transitions and unexpected juxtapositions, in wide-ranging reference and baroque allusion." Yes; absolutely, wow, and in spades! Yet, equally stunning, especially in these featured poems, is how Max Ritvo uses enchantment to seriously, fearlessly investigate the vicissitudes of his illness and the nuances of his relationship to it and with it. His poetry is humorous and witty, but never facetious, or coy—in poems relating to his illness, it was as if he were gently beguiling us out of our fears, inviting us, privileging us to join him in the intimate space he shares with his illness. Our mutual friend told me "Oh, you have to meet him—I hope you do meet him!" And I too hoped I might.

When *Plume* suggested a Special Feature interview with Max Ritvo, I was thrilled. In an answer to the pre-interview question if his health issues might be discussed as they related to the featured poems, Max wrote: "Can we limit cancer to two questions, tops? I assure you, Nancy, that my mind is a Rococo doodad shop, and we'll stumble on something strange that appears useless and ends up being a keystone in the way I think and feel and write."

the *plume* poetry interviews 1

On August 1, 2016, I sent an initial-salvo question to Max to which he quickly responded, "Wonderful question Nancy, and I'm working on my reply. I am recovering from pneumonia, and it's stacked with another virus, so I'm sleeping a lot. But I'm excited to spend my fresher hours working with you. I can tell we're gonna make great dance partners. My body might be a twig right now, but my brain loves lindy-hop, and I sense yours does too!"

And we were great partners, but only because Max, terrific, agile dancer, smoothly and chivalrously covered my clumsy missteps with spins and dips through several e-mail exchanges. In the following interview there are no direct questions regarding his illness, but not because we ran out of time, or because it was the "elephant" in the room. Rather, because it was the room, the ballroom, in the Rococo Doodad Shop where Max and I lindy-hopped until, after a few day's pause, I received his assurance that "I've been hard at work flowing with you and making our magnetic dots go north to south."

On August 23, 2016, our mutual friend called with the news—Max had passed on, passed beyond. Since then, I've been reluctant to wrap up this Special Feature; as long as I work on it, I'm lindy-hopping with Max Ritvo in the Rococo Doodad shop.

NM: Hi Max! In an e-mail interview, you describe your mind as a "Rococo Doodad Shop." Ah, mine is too, but I never said it so well! So, a rococo doodad shop ... like Joseph Cornell's studio, full of seemingly random objects collected on his walks that/who called to be picked up—to be used later? You know, I always had the sense that Cornell, rather than choosing objects for compositions, was listening to the objects choose each other ... all via some dot-to-dot implicit, magnetic energy.

Your poems seem informed by this same magnetism, and I sense a similar willing suspension of intention in "He yearns for a silence that will last him / through a thread of thought / so that the thoughts listen to each other" ("The Conqueror").

Am I on the right track about how your poems become?

MR: You're hitting on something deep in my mind's eye. It's unclear to me how much of my poem, at any given moment, is writing itself inside of me trying to write it. (I'm reminded of a dippy Harold Bloom book, *Hamlet, Poem Unlimited*, which is about Hamlet at some point as his play is being written turning into a real human being and fighting Shakespeare to snatch away the pen and complete the text himself. I haven't read the book but a friend described it to me thusly and it really stuck.)

I hope my image or metaphor ends up being extremely clear by the time it's fully come into being. Certainly by the time I've edited it with my rational hat on. This love of logic (perverted logic counts!) is a kind of inescapable intention in the finished poem. But I don't think you can write an original metaphor without much suspension of intention as you write.

NM: Maybe we should/could call it "suspicion" of intention, instead?

MR: I like to liken something to another thing without quite knowing why I feel that way. Or even if I do feel that way. "My love for you is like a fountain," I might write. At this point, I intend to write about my love. But the fountain lands there from a murkier part of me. The fountain-like thing in the poem, this part that finds itself in my poem beyond any particular intention, is often what you, Nancy, might call a doodad. Something that as yesterday or today progressed, seemed to glow out from the rest of time's passage.

NM: "Glowing out of the rest of time's passage"—lit from within with its own inherent energy ... again, Max, so well said. I'm thinking more kindly now of my mind's clutter as a warehouse of doodads—a strain of music, the particular slant of light against a peach bed sheet or on a peach in a blue bowl, a rocking chair, some particular aspect of a painting, an ear, images from books, all of which comprise my "personal collection" of doodads.

I'm wondering if you find odd, as I do, that while the context from which the doodad was collected may fade, the luminous doodads themselves remain "inevitable and permanent" as you write in "My Chair," vibrating with resonance until I (or they) find context in another life, maybe their real life, or Pasternak's "sister life" of my (their) making?

MR: It could be a concrete physical object that wouldn't be evocative at all to anyone else. Perhaps I spent twenty minutes enraptured by a very boring fountain in a park because it smelled funny, and I wondered if it was full of something other than water. And it wasn't. The doodad might also be something more sublime, like a Benin bronze mask or a storm. The doodad could be a pretty—but impersonal, and thus not yet poetic—scrap of thought from a conversation or meditation. Whatever it is oozes mystery like charisma.

NM: And maybe the mystery, the charisma is calling only, exclusively to you, waiting for you to notice, like Rilke's "star waiting for you to espy it?" In my more connected, (or, perhaps, more disconnected) moments I do believe that things, objects draw us toward them with a magnetic energy—they are resonating, pulsating in some dusty corner waiting for us to claim them, to give them a true context, a life. When I'm this particular "believing," I instantly feel an affinity, connection to/with a mystery that is beyond me, but at the same time a part of me.

MR: When I find a doodad out there in the world, I never know exactly what I will do with it. (I should ask my dad what to do with it, perhaps.) But I know it'll make it into the poems somehow. Sometimes I try a doodad in one intended moment of a poem and it fails miserably. But without fail, it fits somewhere—which is to say, it finds a way to help me express my feelings, my all-too intentional heart.

NM: Hmmm. Do you think the heart is indeed intentional? I somehow ascribe that quality to the brain ... maybe, again, it's my "suspicion" of intention....

MR: If you want to know why doodads create original metaphors, you must know that doodads are all porous. "My love is like a fountain" begs so many questions of the fountain. As you answer those questions, you describe my love in a way that is idiosyncratic and complex, and usually very weird. Fountains have many parts—there's the fluid and medium and noise that can all become different parts of my love. So even working with this porous image in the rough, we could cook something up. But the doodad fountain from the park, the one with the perplexing odor, leads to even more exciting questions. What fluid gushes from the fountain? What is the best rock or plastic to make a fountain that spews acid? What fish could live in acid?

NM: Ah, I'm reminded of Mary Rose O'Reilly's "Whatever your eye falls on—for it will fall on what you love—will lead you to the questions of your life, the questions that are incumbent upon you to answer, because that is how the mind works in concert with the eye. The things of this world draw us where we need to go." I'm recalling one question-evoking image-doodad from my "personal" collection—"ghost ships," floating, after years at sea, into their home harbor with nary a living soul upon them. That image—I think I first encountered it in Conrad's *Lord Jim*—has haunted me for decades. Who/what piloted that ship homeward? Do we live in oblivion to natural laws, mystery among them? Do mysteries draw us, with questions, along our life's trajectory? Maybe Rilke speaks the truth when he writes, "What seems most far from you is most your own?" Ah, questions …

MR: These questions emerge spontaneously, with no intention of mine making them, just curiosity. And then my intention gets to play along; to confess and describe my love, it must leap over many chasms, and fall into some, and build bridges over others. The doodad has introduced into the metaphor many lovely layers of entropy. As it settles into beauty, the doodad and my intention are sealed together.

NM: Sealed, but still an alchemical dynamic? In ecological terms, a "closed" system?

MR: In a way it's as if I've taken this foreign entity into my body and soul. Since what's more my essence than my poems? Although, as I write this, I'm doing some reflecting. I think this last little bit I've said about sealing the doodad into me, is really the reason I write. Even if that magic comes at the expense of my original intentions for the poem. Perhaps by putting my intention in the driver's seat, my heart in the driver's seat, I get it all wrong. Because if a doodad's spell is powerful enough—

NM: Spell! Now you're talking!

MR: … because if a doodads' spell is powerful enough—if it starts to braid itself into a series of questions that don't answer "My love is" so well as they do "My hate is," then I'll abandon my intention to write about what "My love is" very happily. (I throw out a caveat here: that if I'm an extremely emotional state, I'm less likely to notice how a failing "My love is doodad" could make a great "My hate is doodad.") The poem is still a confession and self-expression because it still must be "My hate"—I could never fill a metaphor with someone else. I don't know them well enough to do that. But perhaps I'm just willing to let out the scarves of my soul to drape over the mantelpiece where I display the doodad. I think, Nancy, my intentions may exist to serve my abundant love of doodads. Oh dear.

NM: How can we tell the Doodader from the Doodad? Hello, Mr. Yeats! and a sideways hello to Key West! Now, Mr. Ritvo, I do believe you are working some voodoo-doo-dad-ing on me with these poems, via a mesmerizing lindy-hop between the doodad and the Doodader! For example in "My Chair," the first line, a sentence, declares, "Somewhere a man gives birth to his daughter's rocking chair," which is immediately contradicted and qualified by the next couple of tercets:

> But he remembers he has no daughter.
> The man wishes his state
> was like the chair—
>
> The chair really rocks. It is rocking,
> inevitable and permanent,
> from the moment it tapped the floor.

The poem continues to move away from the first bold declaration with more facts, restrictions as to why this connection between the daughter and the rocking cannot exist until it's redeemed by the imaginary leap of naming the daughter:

> Nina, he names her, and it gives the man the cough
> He gets when he gazes at sky patches

> In amateurish landscapes he paints—

And here—I'm so excited, so please, bear with me—the imaginative leap of naming the imaginary daughter "Nina" triggers "the cough," a signs that the speaker is, via the magic connection of daughter and chair, in that terrain of the "confusing air beyond the forest," the same confusing air where the song of Keats' nightingale sings eternally. And what is so amazing is that, although the coughs, the "missives," are "from that confusing air" that are also "to himself,"

> He realizes that his coughs are missives to himself
> from that confusing air beyond the forest
> And that the missives, his art,
>
> Amount to the void in the art and beyond the forest.
> That in the future, he would not experience anything,
> he would be experience.

And abracadabra: here is the moment of beauty "he would not experience anything, / he would be experience" when the doodad and the intention—the daughter and the chair—as they settle into beauty, are sealed together.

Dear Lucky Readers, you are about to witness the magic of Max Ritvo in the following poems. But first, you must say "Please." Why? Because

> It takes pleases to get the magic
> and magic to get the love."

First Act of Self-Adoration

I've always been a people person,
but now people are failing me so

I'm going to be a personal person
and take everything personally.

You all have one death scene.
You're squandering them.

My pals hoot at an ad they keep calling art,
my wife makes me squish a spider
with the last bit of gas in my tank.

Now You I like, I'd like to be able to say
to anything, even myself.

But I'm not easy to be nice to.
I say thank you plenty—but that's all
once the favors are done.

It takes pleases to get the magic,
and magic to get the love.

FUNERAL BARGE FOR THE SUPERVISING ENGINEER

Several miles downstream of the accident a young man
lay spread on a piece of metal. The sky was of an intermediate
   darkness
—a few stars made their light, standing in for a mass
bruised out by our bright work: the glowing, healthy factories,

parties, and cars and even, in its small way,
the fire the man came from. The young man's
nice symmetrical head dripped brains onto the metal.
He couldn't get over, as he died, how the dark

smells in the breath, and the sour breading on the meat
of his memories were so remarkably familiar.
He put his hand over his heart as he remembered
the women he had abandoned, the poodle

he killed by neglect, sodas he'd let
go flat—how many deaths have I lived through?
Who is it dying? he asked himself,
and wondered why he loved the self he carried—

the self, an assembly manual for chairs
his factory ceased to build years ago,
and now, to boot, the factory was blown up.
His body, sweet even now in its filth,

takes over. It puts hands on his grief
and makes it gurgle and honk. The grief
makes the man's body like a duck's,
and this calms him. From the benign distance

of a white tree on the bank of the river,
he sees what a beautiful machine he made.
This is no different than kissing his wife:
he counts his heart beats, and there are three pillows

on the floor, two on the bed. There's no escaping math,
and who would want to escape it? In order
to look forward to anything, you have to
look forward, you have to look, you have to.

The Conqueror

Pooping makes me feel valiant—

my body is full of unconquerable knots
but these ones I can conquer.

With my health as it is, the me who poos is
the most ambitious me on earth.

He yearns for a silence that will last him
through a thread of thought
so the thoughts listen to each other.

He seeks a perfect peace—

But, Max who poos, what you're looking for
is not yours to give yourself.

Such a moment could unfold here,
right here—it's all done

and you just get to notice. In your case
you don't notice, you get reborn.
Perpetually, unbearably:

an uncozy cloth lumping into a head,
the last snap of light,
drops of water made priceless by sad salt.

My Chair

Somewhere a man gives birth to his daughter's rocking chair.

But he remembers he has no daughter.
The man wishes his state
was like the chair—

The chair really rocks. Its rocking,
inevitable and permanent,
from the moment it tapped the floor.

But he can't sit in the chair. The man's body
since he first laid eyes on himself
seemed headed in one direction only, down.

Nina, he names her, and it gives the man the cough
he gets when he gazes at sky-patches
in the amateurish landscapes he paints—

He realizes these coughs are missives to himself
from that confusing air beyond the forest
and that the missives, his art,

amount to the void in the art and beyond the forest.
That in the future, he would not experience anything,
he would be experience.

Centaur Music

for Elizabeth Metzger

All their words
have been spoken before
by human mouths.

They have to put music to the words
to make them mean anything
other than what someone has already felt.

If you said I've got the world on a string,
they would dance against our fences,
grating themselves bald as cheese.

Their lives are full of admissions
you'd rather not make.

Each Centaur's music is different according
to where they are joined.

You are the only one for me,
sings my Centaur,
horse up to the lips,
singing almost all-horse music.

Even her lady nose is shaped
like a horse cantering,
or an alien ship whining exhaust,

and I am a single gold ring,
snug round the azure planet of her words—
which in her space ship, she is fleeing from.

Contributor Biographies

Nin Andrews is the author of seven full-length poetry collections, and seven chapbooks. Her most recent chapbook, *Our Lady of the Orgasm*, was published by Plume Editions in October, 2016.

Charlee Brodsky, a fine-art documentary photographer and a professor of photography at Carnegie Mellon, describes her work as dealing with social issues and beauty. In 2012 she was Pittsburgh's Artist of the Year chosen by Pittsburgh Center for the Arts and was the 2014 Honored Educator given by the Society for Photographic Education, Mid-Atlantic Region.

Christopher Buckley's *Star Journal: Selected Poems* is published by the University of Pittsburgh Press, fall 2016. His twentieth book of poetry, *Back Room at the Philosophers' Club*, won the 2015 Lascaux Prize in Poetry from the *Lascaux Review*. Among several critical collections and anthologies of contemporary poetry, he has edited *Bear Flag Republic: Prose Poems and Poetics from California*, 2008, and *One for the Money: The Sentence as a Poetic Form* (Lynx House Press, 2012), both with Gary Young. He has also edited *On the Poetry of Philip Levine: Stranger to Nothing* (University of Michigan Press, 1991), and *Messenger to the Stars: a Luis Omar Salinas New Selected Poems & Reader* for Tebot Bach's Ash Tree Poetry Series. *Chaos Theory* is forthcoming from Plume Editions/Mad Hat Press in 2017.

Hélène Cardona is a poet, literary translator and actor, whose most recent books include *Life in Suspension* and *Dreaming My Animal Selves* (both from Salmon Poetry), and the translations *Beyond Elsewhere* (Gabriel Arnou-Laujeac, White Pine Press), winner of a Hemingway Grant; *Ce que nous portons* (Dorianne Laux, Éditions du Cygne), and *Walt Whitman's Civil War Writings* for WhitmanWeb.

A Romanian translation of *Dreaming My Animal Selves* was published by Junimea Editions in 2016. Her work has been translated into thirteen languages.

She contributes essays to *The London Magazine*, is co-international editor of *Plume* and managing editor of *Fulcrum*. She holds a master's in American Literature from the Sorbonne, received fellowships from the Goethe-Institut and Universidad Internacional de Andalucía, worked as a translator for the Canadian Embassy in Paris, and taught at Hamilton College and Loyola Marymount University.

Publications include *Washington Square Review, World Literature Today, Poetry International, Dublin Review of Books, Asymptote, The Brooklyn Rail, Hayden's Ferry Review, The Warwick Review*, and elsewhere.

David Clewell is the author of ten collections of poems—most recently, *Almost Nothing To Be Scared Of* (University of Wisconsin Press, 2016)—and two book-length poems. His work has appeared regularly in a wide variety of national magazines and journals—including *Harper's, Poetry, The Georgia Review, Kenyon Review*, and *New Letters*—and is represented in more than fifty anthologies. Among his honors are several book awards: two Four Lakes Poetry Prizes (for *Taken Somehow By Surprise* and *Almost Nothing To Be Scared Of*), the Felix Pollak Poetry Prize (for *Now We're Getting Somewhere*), and a National Poetry Series selection (*Blessings in Disguise*). He served as Poet Laureate of Missouri from 2010 to 2012.

Clewell has worked as a professional wrestler, circus laborer, and boardwalk weight-guesser. He currently labors as a professor of English and director of the creative writing program at Webster University in St. Louis. His collection of Charlie the Tuna iconography is the largest in private curatorship.

Cynthia Cruz is the author of four collections of poetry, including three with Four Way Books: *The Glimmering Room* (2012), *Wunderkammer* (2014), and *How the End Begins* (2016). Cruz has received fellowships from Yaddo and the MacDowell Colony as well as a Hodder Fellowship from Princeton University. She has an MFA from Sarah Lawrence College in writing and an MFA in Art Criticism & Writing from the School of Visual Arts. Cruz is currently pursuing a PhD in German Studies at Rutgers University. She teaches at Sarah Lawrence College.

the *plume* poetry interviews 1

Jim Daniels' next two books of poems, *Rowing Inland* (Wayne State University Press) and *Street Calligraphy* (Steel Toe Books), will both be published in 2017. His previous book, *Birth Marks*, received the Milton Kessler Award and was a Michigan Notable Book. His poems have been featured on *Prairie Home Companion*, Garrison Keillor's *Writer's Almanac*, in Billy Collins' *Poetry 180* anthologies, and Ted Kooser's "American Life in Poetry" series. A native of Detroit, he is the Thomas Stockham University Professor of English at Carnegie Mellon University in Pittsburgh.

Tess Gallagher's book *IS, IS NOT* is forthcoming from Graywolf Press in Fall 2019. *Boogie-Woogie Crisscross*, her collaboration with Lawrence Matsuda, was recently published by Plume Editions, an imprint of MadHat Press. Her ninth volume of poetry is *Midnight Lantern: New and Selected Poems*, from Graywolf Press and Bloodaxe Press in England. Other poetry includes *Dear Ghosts, Moon Crossing Bridge,* and Amplitude. Gallagher's *The Man from Kinvara: Selected Stories* was published in 2009. Her *A Path to the Sea*, translations of Liliana Ursu's by Adam Sorkin, Ms. Gallagher and Ms. Ursu came out in 2011. *Barnacle Soup—Stories from the West of Ireland*, a collaboration with the Sligo storyteller Josie Gray, is available in the U.S. from Carnegie Mellon. She spearheaded the publication of Raymond Carver's *Beginners* in Library of America's complete collection of his stories published in 2009 and as a stand-alone volume in 2015. Most recently she shepherded the use of Raymond Carver's poem and story in the film *Birdman*, directed by Alejandro Inarritu. She spends time in a cottage on Lough Arrow in County Sligo in the West of Ireland where many of her new poems are set, and also lives and writes in her hometown of Port Angeles, Washington.

Ani Gjika, author of *Bread on Running Waters* (2013), is a Robert Pinsky Global Fellow and NEA fellow for her translation of Luljeta Lleshanaku's work from the Albanian language. Gjika's poems and translations appear at *AGNI Online, Salamander, Seneca Review, World Literature Today, Ploughshares*, and elsewhere.

Marilyn Hacker is the recipient of the National Book Award, the PEN Award for Poetry in Translation, the Robert Fagles Translation Prize, and the PEN/Voelcker Award for Poetry. Her collection *Winter Numbers* received a Lambda Literary Award and the Lenore Marshall Award of the Academy of American Poets. She lives in Paris, France.

Hank Lazer has published twenty-four books of poetry, including *Poems Hidden in Plain View* (2016, in English and in French), *Brush Mind: At Hand* (2016), *N24* (2014) and *N18* (2012), *Portions* (2009), *The New Spirit* (2005), *Elegies & Vacations* (2004), and *Days* (2002). *Selected Poems and Essays of Hank Lazer,* completed by a group of translators, was published by Central China Normal University Press in 2015. Lazer's *Selected Poems* have also been published in Italy and will be appearing shortly in Cuba (including 11 tracks for jazz-poetry improvisations with soprano saxophonist Andrew Raffo Dewar). Readings and interviews can be accessed through PennSound: http://writing.upenn.edu/pennsound/x/Lazer.html, as well as in special issues of *Plume* 34 and *Talisman* 42. In 2015, Lazer was selected to receive Alabama's most prestigious literary prize, the Harper Lee Award, for lifetime achievement in literature. His books of criticism include *Opposing Poetries* (two volumes, 1996) and *Lyric & Spirit: Selected Essays 1996–2008* (2008). With Charles Bernstein, he edits the Modern and Contemporary Poetics Series for the University of Alabama Press. Lazer retired in 2014 from his University of Alabama positions as Associate Provost for Academic Affairs, Executive Director of Creative Campus, and Professor of English.

Luljeta Lleshanaku is internationally known as Albania's most important and inventive poet of her generation. A winner of International Kristal Vilenica Prize in 2009, she is the author of seven books of poetry in Albanian and six poetry collections in other languages. *Negative Space* won 2013 Author of the Year Award by the Publishers Association at the Tirana Book Fair, Albania. Her American collection *Child of Nature* (New Directions, 2010) was one of 2011 Best Translated Book Award poetry finalists and her British collection *Haywire: New & Selected Poems* was nominated for the 2013 Popescu Prize by the Poetry Society, UK.

the *plume* poetry interviews 1

Amit Majmudar is a novelist, essayist, diagnostic nuclear radiologist, and the first Poet Laureate of Ohio. His latest collection is *Dothead* (Knopf, 2016). His forthcoming book is a verse translation of the Bhagavad-Gita, *Godsong* (Knopf, 2018).

Lawrence Matsuda was born in the Minidoka, Idaho Concentration Camp during World War II. He and his family were among the approximately 120,000 Japanese Americans and Japanese held without due process for approximately three years or more. Matsuda has a Ph.D. in education from the University of Washington.

In July of 2010, his book of poetry *A Cold Wind from Idaho* was published by Black Lawrence Press in New York. In 2014, *Glimpses of a Forever Foreigner* was released; a collaboration between Matsuda and artist Roger Shimomura, who contributed 17 original sketches. In 2015, Matsuda collaborated with artist Matt Sasaki and produced two graphic novels: *An American Hero—Shiro Kashino,* and *Fighting for America: Nisei Soldiers,* funded by the National Park Service and available through the Nisei Veterans Committee Foundation or the Wing Luke Museum. The Shiro Kashino video won a 2016 regional Emmy. In 2016, he and Tess Gallagher collaborated on *Boogie-Woogie CrissCross*, a book of poetry developed from e-mails they exchanged over a period of three years where she was in Ireland and he was in Seattle, published by MadHat Press.

Thomas McCarthy is an Irish poet, novelist, and critic, born in Cappoquin, County Waterford, and educated at University College, Cork. He has published eight poetry collections, seven of them with Anvil Press Poetry, including *The Sorrow Garden, The Lost Province, Mr Dineen's Careful Parade, The Last Geraldine Officer* ("a major achievement," in the view of academic and poet Maurice Harmon) and *Merchant Prince*, a combination of poems and a novella recounting the story of a Cork merchant, described as "an ambitious and substantive book" in *Poetry Ireland Review*. His new book, *Pandemonium*, will be published by Carcanet.

McCarthy won the Patrick Kavanagh Award for his first book when he was 24. Two years later he was selected for the International Writers

Program in Iowa. His many awards include the Alice Hunt Bartlett Prize (1981); the American-Irish Foundation's Literary Award (1984); and the O'Shaughnessy Poetry Award, Irish-American Cultural Institute (1991). His fiction includes two novels, *Without Power* and *Asya and Christine*. He has also published a memoir, *The Garden of Remembrance*.

The main themes of his poetry are Southern Irish politics, love and memory, family, past, and place. McCarthy's work has been widely translated and has appeared in over thirty anthologies. He has worked for Cork City Library and lives in Cork. He is a member of Aosdána.

Nancy Mitchell, a Pushcart Prize 2012 recipient, is the author of two volumes of poetry, *The Near Surround* (Four Way Books, 2002) and *Grief Hut* (Cervena Barva Press, 2009). Her recent poems appear, or will soon appear, in *Poetry Daily, Agni, Washington Square Review, Green Mountains Review, Tar River Poetry, Columbia College Literary Review*, and *Thrush*, among others. Mitchell teaches at Salisbury University and serves as the Associate Editor of Special Features for *Plume*.

Emmanuel Moses was born in 1959 in Casablanca, Morocco. After a childhood in Cachan (Val-de-Marne), and then in Paris, he moved to Jerusalem in 1969 with his family. In 1986 he left Israel and settled in Paris where he lived from different jobs (part-time journalist, organizer of cultural events, publisher). He presently shares his time between writing and translating.

Glenn Mott is co-founder and partner in New Narrative NA, a press and publications agency based in New York. A poet and journalist he has been a Fulbright Scholar at Tsinghua University in Beijing, a Katheryn Davis Fellow for Peace at Middlebury College, and has taught at universities in Shanghai and Hong Kong. He is author of the book *Analects on a Chinese Screen*, with reporting, poetry and translations in newspapers and periodicals including *Corriere della Sera, Poetiche, The Miami Herald, The Atlantic, The Missouri Review*, and *Nieman Reports*.

D. Nurkse recently completed a book of verse re-thinking the Tristan and Iseult legend; it will be published by Knopf in 2017. His most recent book of poems, *A Night in Brooklyn*, appeared in paperback in 2016.

Ira Sadoff is the author of seven collections of poetry, most recently *True Faith* (BOA Editions, 2012) and the re-issued *Palm Reading in Winter* (Carnegie-Mellon). He's published a novel, *Uncoupling*, *The Ira Sadoff Reader*, and *History Matters* (University of Iowa Press) a critical book on poetry and culture. He's been widely anthologized and awarded grants from the Guggenheim Fellowship and the NEA. He has new work appearing in *The New Yorker*, *APR*, and the Academy of American Poets' Poem a Day Series. He lives in a converted barn in upstate New York.

Adam Tavel is the author of *Plash & Levitation* (University of Alaska Press, 2015), winner of the Permafrost Book Prize in Poetry, and *The Fawn Abyss* (Salmon Poetry, 2017). You can find him online at adamtavel.com.

Jean Valentine was born in Chicago, Illinois in 1934. She received a BA from Radcliffe College in 1956 and has lived most of her life in New York City. In 1964, Valentine's first book *Dream Barker* (Yale University Press, 1965) was chosen for the Yale Series of Younger Poets. She is the author of several poetry collections, including *Shirt in Heaven* (Copper Canyon Press, 2015); *Door in the Mountain: New and Collected Poems* (Wesleyan University Press, 2004), which won the National Book Award; and *Home Deep Blue: New and Selected Poems* (Alice James Books, 1989). She is also the editor of *The Lighthouse Keeper: Essays on the Poetry of Eleanor Ross Taylor* (Seneca Review, 2001).

Valentine has been awarded grants and fellowships from the Rockefeller Foundation, the National Endowment for the Arts, the New York State Council on the Arts, the Guggenheim Foundation, and the Bunting Institute. In 2000, she received the Shelley Memorial Prize from the Poetry Society of America. She is the recipient of the 2009 Wallace Stevens Award from the Academy of American Poets.

the *plume* poetry interviews 1

Marc Vincenz is British-Swiss and the author of nine poetry books. *New Pages* called his collection *Becoming the Sound of Bees* (Ampersand Books, 2015), "… a book where doors can fly off in 'butterflies of rust,' where poems can stretch themselves sideways across the page, and worlds can build upon themselves in dizzying descriptions. This is a collection for those who enjoy digging their claws into strange landscapes and getting pulled forth by a culmination of sounds." His book-length poem *Sibylline* has just been released by Ampersand Books.

Vincenz is also the translator of many Romanian and German-language poets, including Herman Hesse Prize winner Klaus Merz, Werner Lutz, Erika Burkart, Alexander Xaver Gwerder, Ion Monoran, Robert Walser and Jürg Amman. His translation of Klaus Merz's collection *Unexpected Development* was a finalist for the 2015 Cliff Becker Book Translation Prize and will be published by White Pine Press in 2018. His most recently released translation is *Secret Letter* by Erica Burkart (Cervena Barva Press, 2016).

He has received many grants from the Swiss Arts Council and a fellowship from the Literarisches Colloquium Berlin. His own work has been translated into German, Russian, Romanian, French, Icelandic, Georgian and Chinese; Bucharest's Tractus Arte Press released a Romanian translation of his collection *The Propaganda Factory* at the 2015 Bucharest Book Fair.

Although he has lived and traveled all over the word, Marc Vincenz now resides, writes, translates and edits in western Massachusetts.

www.ingramcontent.com/pod-product-compliance
Lightning Source LLC
Chambersburg PA
CBHW041953180426
43200CB00033B/2964